Teaching, Loving,
and
Self-directed Learning

GOODYEAR EDUCATION SERIES
Theodore W. Hipple, Editor
University of Florida

Elementary School Teaching:
Problems and Methods
Margaret Kelly Giblin

Popular Media and the Teaching of English
Thomas R. Giblin

School Counseling: Problems and Methods
Robert Myrick and Joe Wittmer

Secondary School Teaching:
Problems and Methods
Theodore W. Hipple

Will the Real Teacher Please Stand Up?
A Primer in Humanistic Education
Mary Greer and Bonnie Rubinstein

Crucial Issues in Contemporary Education
Theodore W. Hipple

Teaching, Loving, and Self-directed Learning
David A. Thatcher

Change for Children:
Ideas and Activities for Individualizing Learning
Sandra N. Kaplan, JoAnn B. Kaplan,
Sheila K. Madsen, Bette K. Taylor

Solving Teaching Problems:
A Guide for the Elementary School Teacher
Mildred Bluming and Myron H. Dembo

TEACHING, LOVING, AND SELF-DIRECTED LEARNING

David A. Thatcher
California State College, Sonoma
Photographs by Sarah C. Toughill,
by Said, and by David Thatcher

GOODYEAR PUBLISHING COMPANY, INC.
Pacific Palisades, California

Current printing (last digit):
10 9 8 7 6 5 4 3 2 1

Library of Congress Catalog Card Number: 72-97276
ISBN: 0-87620-877–1
Y-8871-9

Printed in the United States of America

Grateful appreciation is extended to the following for permission to quote from
their copyrighted materials:

On page 15, material from *Knots* by R. D. Laing. © 1970 by the R. D. Laing
Trust. Reprinted by permission of Pantheon Books, a division of Random House.

On page 66, material from page 167 of *Black Rage* by William H. Grier and Price
M. Cobbs, Basic Books, Inc., Publishers. © 1968 by William H. Grier. Reprinted
by permission of the Basic Books, Inc., Publishers, New York.

On page 84, material from page 82 of *The Me Nobody Knows* by Steven M.
Joseph, Avon Books. © 1969 by Steven M. Joseph. Reprinted by arrangement
with Avon Books.

On page 84, material from page 41 of *Born to Win* by Muriel James and Dorthy
Jongeward, Addison-Wesley, 1971. Reprinted by permission of Addison-Wesley.

On page 155, material from page 15 of *Freedom to Learn* by Edith E. Biggs and
James R. MacLean, Addison-Wesley (Canada) Ltd., 1969. Reprinted by permission of Addison-Wesley.

On page 156, material from page 197 of *Individualized Teaching in Elementary
Schools* by Dona Kofod Stahl and Patricia Anzalone, Parker Book Publishing
Company, 1970. Reprinted by permission of the publisher.

FOREWORD

A book with a title like *Teaching, Loving, and Self-directed Learning* is certain to arouse some curiosity among those who see it. Yet the titles of few other books so aptly describe their contents as this title suggests what this volume is about. It is about teaching, about loving, about self-directed learning. Moreover, all of these critical aspects of education have been given a special coloration, an added dimension that is peculiarly the result of a rare and almost mystical blending of perception and sensitivity embodied in a truly gifted teacher, Mr. David Thatcher.

For David, teaching is not merely a vocation, a means to earning a living, a way of life. Teaching is life itself. Seldom does one encounter such total commitment, such complete dedication to the noblest ideals of education, to the nurture of self-directed, fully actualized boys and girls, men & women. Yet David is no plastic saint, no paragon of pedagogical virtue claiming to be above his fellow teachers. Rather, as these pages attest, he is a sincere teacher striving daily to do better what is one of man's most responsible and demanding jobs, the educating of a nation's youth. Filled with the self-doubts that beset us all, plagued by the inevitable failures every teacher occasionally encounters, made joyful by the successes both great and small, David Thatcher serves, through this book, as an inspiring model for prospective and practicing teachers, as a human example of what they can and should be, indeed of what they must become.

Loving, as presented in this book, is a way of looking at and responding to each person, at what makes him uniquely him. It is a friendly smile for Kathy, a gentle reminder for Bruce, a lively discussion with Betsy. It is finding and bringing out of Richard his fullest potential. It is, above all, a spiritual feeling, a kinship with all creatures, but especially with one's students that makes of this permeating theme of the book such a viable philosophy for teachers at all levels of education to emulate and embody.

Self-directed Learning is a cluster of methods, which are means to the achievement of goals set by student and teacher working singly & jointly so that, very soon, the former relies less on the latter and more on his own introspection and perception. In short, the student becomes his own educator. It is a strategy for teaching useful in kindergarten and in graduate school, successful with rich kids and poor kids, black and white, bright and dull. Most important of all, it is neither so esoteric nor so bound to the charisma of a rare teacher that it is beyond the competence of the average teacher, either novice or seasoned professional.

One final plus of this sensitive book: it contains what is possibly the most exciting bibliographical references I have ever seen in one source. Throughout, Thatcher demonstrates not only that he owns books, but that he has made them his own. His encouragement to go beyond this volume to the authors who shaped his thinking and becoming should inspire all readers to examine the messages of these other books and, by so doing, to enlarge and enrich the philosophies that strengthen their teaching.

In sum, then, this is a marvelous book, warm, friendly, low key, always intensely personal and exciting, always richly rewarding to its readers. I am pleased and proud that it is a part of the Goodyear Education Series. Indeed, one might best describe this book by mentioning another popular volume in the Goodyear Series: *Will the Real Teacher Please Stand Up? In Teaching, Loving, and Self-Directed Learning* David Thatcher, a real teacher, has stood up.

Theodore W. Hipple, *Editor*
Goodyear Education Series

ACKNOWLEDGMENTS

I owe a great deal to many individuals who helped to bring this book from a collection of ideas to a unified whole. I thank them for their help.

Shirley Thatcher was my partner in the writing of the book. She contributed ideas and content, criticized my ideas, and assisted in the improvement of the English. Writing a book involves, for me, encroaching on the lives of other people. I encroached on Shirley's life much more than on any other. I thank her for her help, her patience, and her love. Ellen, Maris, and Todd Thatcher, our children, have kept me in touch with the thinking and feeling of youth, and they have challenged me to do better.

I wish to thank these friends for their help:

Stu Jones has read the whole manuscript several times over, commenting perceptively, suggesting many additions and judicious deletions. To a remarkable extent he has lived the making of the book.

Mary Edwards Goulding read an early draft of the book and offered support which has proven again the bond of friendship. Both she and Stu exemplify the loving which enriches the lives of so many other people.

Barbara Deicke, Rose Scott, Bernice Goldmark, and Frank Carson have all read parts of the book and offered suggestions.

Joanne Gerber has read more of the draft versions than anyone else. Often, she and I and Shirley would read aloud, stopping whenever something didn't sound right. Joanne has also contributed valuable material to the book. She has given me more help than anyone else.

Sally Toughill took most of the photographs used in the book and helped to place them for maximum impact. She also read the manuscript and made suggestions for its improvement.

George White suggested that I write notes to each chapter instead of the lengthy bibliographies I had done before.

I used the libraries of the University of California at Berkeley, California State College at Sonoma, and the Richmond, California Public Library. In all cases, I was given assistance as well as unfailing good humor.

I want to thank also Lymona Lee Castleberry, Kay McKenzie, Averil Anderson, Don Kline, and Carol and Rich Ponzio, who served as demonstration teachers in the two summer workshops that explored the whole range of student-teacher relationships in a self-directed learning program.

I want to thank my students in on-campus and extension classes who demanded that I explore with them the truly significant questions of our time. I learned a great deal from these many encounters.

Ellen Thatcher, Bernestine Holmes, Caron Christiansen, and Barbara Corso typed various drafts and their help is appreciated. But the greatest amount of typing was done by Shirley Thatcher. I thank all of them for their help.

I also thank Mary Greer, Ted Hipple, David Grady, Carol Talpers, Ann Harris, and the staff at Goodyear Publishing for their assistance in transforming a manuscript into a finished book.

I am entirely responsible for the book, and I am comfortable with that responsibility.

CONTENTS

INTRODUCTION

Human potentials are much greater than we have thought. Among them is the potential to enjoy what we do. Teaching, like many other occupations, can be a series of joyous experiences. This book relates the twin means—learning and loving—to the realization of human possibilities for teachers and students together. Through loving and learning we can live positively in a series of overlapping environments, natural and man-made, in which each living thing can have a place in a total environment dedicated to the continuance of all species, mankind among them. The educational program I suggest is *self-directed learning*. It starts with the learner, as any viable educational plan must.

But each of us starts as a lone individual. Jones (1969) wrote:

There is only me—and the rest of you. No one else looks out through these twin turrets—only me. All of you out there share this in common, you are out there and I alone am in here observing. Mother, teacher, headhunter, whaler, daughter, lover, tramp, musician, all of you have this in common. You are not me. I alone. I lonely. I entirely. I exist within these walls. This is the one truth, the great and stark and magnificent truth of the matter. The matter is that I matter. Beyond this there is no need. Beyond this all is trivial. Because, indeed, if I matter then all else matters too.

I start with me. Because I like me, I can like you. Because I like teaching, I can invest my emotional and intellectual energy in it.

Emotional and physical stamina help me survive and enjoy it. Teaching is a tough job, measured by any criterion. The self-deprecating remarks so often made by teachers about their profession are quite revealing. No one respects a time server who puts in time at a school from 8 A.M. to 4 P.M. five days a week. We all recognize that such a person makes little contribution to himself or to others. He is not a teacher. (I use the male pronouns to refer to persons of either sex except when a female pronoun is definitely indicated.) A teacher is an everlasting learner, a lover of learning, constantly considering what he does and how others react to it, and constantly seeking humane ways to improve what he does. The teacher recognizes that his own salvation lies in encouraging the best from every student, and he seldom pauses for lengthy self-congratulation. Success with one student gives him evidence on which to go, ideas of ways to work toward a breakthrough for other students who are not yet self-directed, not yet sufficiently appreciative of their powers to achieve and to enjoy the pleasures of loving friendships. A teacher can let go. He knows that students need acceptance as individuals, support, and concrete assistance in accomplishing school tasks, but he also knows that students need release from the bonds of relationships that are too tight. Each student, as he becomes more and more his own man, needs to be able to walk away from his mentor. The teacher, instead of being hurt by the walking away, understands it as a sign of growth by the student and encourages it.

I enjoy learning and loving, the fundamentals on which teaching is built. Learning involves so much more than the books, the teacher education classes, the practice teaching. I learn as I use my senses—all of them—in the everlasting search for bits of meaningful data I can use in the many contexts of which I am aware. I say "bits" because that's the way I usually get data—rather than in great big beautiful chunks. As a dedicated learner, I make use of the bits I get. I learn as I construct and reconstruct my view of a relationship between two students in my class. Because I care about them, I think lovingly of them. I learn as I plan educational experiences for the individuals and the groups of individuals who are my students, including myself among them. Because I am partly responsible for the learning, I give generous thought and study and preparation to my teaching. At the same time I don't feel compelled to fill in all the gaps; my gaps are entry points for other minds and spirits to venture, to contribute of themselves, to find meaning which can turn them on to further learning and loving.

I learn as I communicate based on my growing knowledge of myself and my growing knowledge of each student. Because I love myself and each student, I seek to share my feelings with each student. This does not mean sentimentality, but it means, as often as possible, the clear and unambiguous expression of those good feelings which some of us hoard for special occasions. The spontaneous expression of my good feelings—"I like that dress," "Thank you for the lovely poem," "You did it!", "Gee, that's a perfect math paper!", "I dig you"—prove to the student that I care and invite him to think well of himself.

As a person and as a teacher, I risk: I try things to see if they will work for me. I approach a person as a potential friend. Perhaps we become friends, perhaps not, perhaps later. In some of my ventures I experience failure. I plan a lesson which I anticipate will excite and involve my students. Occasionally, or perhaps frequently, I am disappointed at the way it turns out. This is one fundamental reason for encouraging self-directed independent learning—the student then takes his own risks, experiences his own defeats as well as successes, and learns from both. In my living and my teaching, I encounter failure and I encounter tragedy. There's no hiding place from the realities of the world. At the same time I can learn from experience and can find ways to deal with problems and situations more effectively in the future.

Some experiences are painful but provoke learning about one's self. You remember such experiences. If you are willing, write about one of them here.

The teacher is an observer, a listener, a gatherer of data, a diagnostician, a sympathetic friend, a shoulder to cry on, a suggester of ways and means to complete tasks, a dispenser of information, a staunch colleague to other teachers, a seeker of cooperative relationships with parents and sometimes with social service agencies, an adviser, a reminder, an evaluator, and a let-goer. A tall order, you say? I'd never settle for less. The teacher performs all of these vital tasks as parts of his way of life. There are other demanding jobs in western civilization, including those of priests and ministers, probation officers, and social workers. Like teaching, these professions seldom pay as well as the prestige jobs in advertising, business administration, law, dentistry, medicine, and veterinary medicine. But they share some of the satisfactions of teaching—the opportunity to work with people in ways not directly related to production of goods, the possibility for sharing of human concerns, and the discovery of solutions to human problems. The teacher, like the worker in these other helping professions, has the daily experience of reaching out and being reached out to, in the endless exploration of ways to enhance human existence through enriching human experience. In so many ways, this involves love.

Love is a four letter word which has been used in many ways for many purposes. I talk about several types and aspects of love in this book. I will explain the several usages of love as I come to them. Essentially, love means a feeling which I have about myself and about other people which causes me to act on my own behalf and in ways which offer friendship and possibly other qualities of relationship. Frank Barron (Burkhart, 1962) calls this "the act of wholehearted spontaneous attention in which you bring yourself into intimate spiritual relationship to the object of your attention, and know the object in part by knowing and sensing yourself in relationship to it." By giving my attention to *us/now*, I enhance my own perceptions and feelings and am more receptive to you, the other half of the *us/now*. And I can love you better as I know you better.

How does the word *love* make you feel? Write down as much as you can think of about it.

Ideas about love in its many forms contribute to my main theme: How can I, as a teacher, function effectively in my work with students? I can do so by expressing my love for them, and by using loving, supporting, facilitating techniques to aid my students to become capable, productive, responsive, and loving.

A classroom or a pupil–teacher conference is an interactive situation. Each individual perceives the situation in his own way. Each approaches the situation with his own expectations. Each has a readiness or a willingness to commit himself to the situation to some extent, however slight. The teacher has the responsibility for leadership in the situation and should show interest in and concern for pupils. By his manner and by his words he should invite their participation. In this sense the teacher should be an initiator and also a risk-taker, for each situation is unique—there'll never be another like it.

Bryan and Sam stood in line waiting for the door to open. Bryan was new in the neighborhood.

Bryan:	What's she like, our teacher?
Sam:	It's a he—Mr. Redford.
Bryan:	Oh boy, I never had a man teacher before. What's he like?

Sam:	He's OK, he blows his whistle a lot in the yard, but my sister had him last year—she liked him. Course, she likes all teachers.
Bryan:	I don't ever like my teacher—they're always so strict, always yelling at me—do this, do that—I never get to do what I want.
Sam:	Yeah, school's mostly for girls. They like to do what they're told. My sister, she says she's going to be a teacher.
Bryan:	I'm going to be a racing car driver. I can't wait til I'm old enough to quit school. I don't have to know a lot of this junk to be a driver. My father never finished high school and he. . . .

(At that moment the door opened and a smiling man invited the students to come in.)

Sam:	See what I mean? There's the whistle around his neck.
Bryan:	Yeah, he won't be much fun. But I've never had a man before.
Mr. Redford:	Allright, boys and girls, come in quietly and take the seat which has your name on it. My name is Robert Redford, just like the movie star, only I don't make as much money as he does. I want to get to know each of you as soon as I can. . . .

In this book I recount anecdotes from my own experience, some told to me by friends, and some reported by teachers in other books. Some are made up. My desire is to give a variety of examples of pupil behavior and of teacher behavior. In some cases the identity of the real people has been used, but usually I have substituted fictional names. Sometimes I have changed the grade level, but in cases borrowed from other books I have retained the names and other forms of identification used in those books. I use these anecdotes to illustrate ways teachers can work to help students learn.

I have written this book to give teachers a background for self-directed learning (SDL) and to present a comprehensive report of classroom practices which can free teachers and students for loving and learning. Learning means active problem-solving by individuals in line with their contemporary needs. I define loving as enjoying close personal relationships that prove to be enriching in different ways to all participants. Various learning and loving behaviors work to help free individuals from the repressive injunctions inferred by children from their parents' actions or words early in the children's lives. Such injunctions inhibit problem-solving and efforts by the individual to serve himself. Loving and learning give the individual a more comprehensive repertoire of skills to use in his varied interactions with others. Both loving and learning begin with the individual; in various ways, he increases his abilities to function successfully in relationships with others. Loving and learning contribute greatly to SDL. Self-directed learning is a collection of tested classroom techniques which let teachers and students deal with ideas and also with human feelings. Education generally fails because it risks so little rather than because it bites off more than it can chew. Self-directed learners prove with great frequency their abilities to succeed at jobs, as parents, and as citizens in the complex society which bewilders so many.

As a citizen I face the problems of pollution, racial conflict, the threat of serious over-population, badly ordered priorities, and wars that threaten to destroy us all. As individuals and as a collection of citizens, we need to change our behavior in order to effect needed turnarounds in the United States and elsewhere. If we can solve some of our critical problems by preventing a nuclear war and by making it possible for a higher percentage of a stabilized world population to live to a reasonable age in good health, then we can spend a greater proportion of our ingenuity and our energy on creating a more interesting and aesthetic environment for human beings to live in.

More than you bargained for, you say? "I'm just a third grade teacher," someone will say, or "Why does it always have to be me?" It always has to be me and you and you and you—because we are the people alive today and we want our grandchildren and their grandchildren to be able to live on this abused planet. My responsibility is to myself and also to others, to do the best I can to promote life activities and to avoid death activities.

I live as one whole person. My out-of-school life is related to my in-school life. My friendships, my hobbies, and my recreation refresh my spirit and enrich my knowledge and my ability to be an effective living and loving resource to students. I behave in accord with one united set of values which puts human beings and humanistic values above property rights and the demands of a mechanized culture. I enjoy wholeness as a person who chooses to teach.

This book is for teachers and teachers-to-be. Whatever your age or sex, wherever you live, you want to teach well, to make teaching a way of life rather than just an occupation. I know this is true because you are reading this book. You believe in the possibility that education can be a means to a better life for most humans on the beleaguered planet we inhabit. Each of us has our own definition of that better life.

Education is a succession of opportunities. My purpose is to broaden and deepen those opportunities for the individual human being, teacher as well as pupil. In the last analysis, our concern must be for the individual. The individual in a free society has opportunities to become many things, and to contribute to the well-being of himself and others. Any society is a collection of individuals. The whole can be much greater than the sum of its parts, and enlightened support by aware individuals is important in helping each individual to bring his potential into being. I have faith in the individual who learns to utilize freedom, to grow, to learn, and to build. I have faith in the free society whose primary purpose is to afford each individual real and continuing opportunities to grow, to learn, and to build, so that he *will* choose to give of himself to others through learning and loving.

I start with I. You start with you. Together, we can begin.

NOTES TO INTRODUCTION

In launching this book I found both ideas and inspiration in Rollo May's book, *Love and Will* (1969). May encourages each of us to look within himself for the available resources to make life enjoyable and meaningful. Another valuable book is J. F. T. Bugental's *The Search for Authenticity* (1965). Both Bugental and May say that the individual has greater freedom of action than he usually realizes and hence can do many things on his own behalf. No one can do it to me or for me—I can do it for myself.

Theodore Roszak's *The Making of a Counter Culture* (1969) describes the thinking and the acting of many Americans who seek a life more wholesome than the mechanically oriented existence of the sixties and early seventies.

While browsing in the library, I found Robert C. Burkhart's *Spontaneous and Deliberate Ways of Learning* (1962), a provocative book for anyone interested in human learning. Burkhart, an artist and teacher, suggests many ways of thinking about the processes of learning. Frank Barron's words which I quoted earlier come from the preface to that book.

It would be difficult to do justice to Lewis Mumford's *The Pentagon of Power* (1970), which I didn't see until I had finished many drafts of this manuscript. That book is a glorious expression of American humanism. Mumford continues his exploration of human interactions with machines and the culture that has evolved in the industrial nations, and he concludes (on p. 435) that "for those of us who have thrown off the myth of the machine, the next move is ours: for the rusty gates of the technocratic prison will open automatically . . . as soon as we choose to walk out."

A book that has deeply influenced me is *The Way Things Are* by P. W. Bridgman (1959). Bridgman, physicist, philosopher, and psychologist, establishes the central fact of egocentricity which Jones expresses in the quote at the beginning of this chapter. I can never wholly escape the trap of me-ness, yet I desire fiercely to join up with others of my kind in those adventures which are part of human potentiality. That potentiality has virtually no limits, according to Gardner Murphy in *Human Potentialities* (1958), a book filled with wisdom and hope.

Alan Watts helped me to recognize my own wholeness as a person. My wholeness depends on my giving and receiving in relationships with others. As Watts says in *The Book* (1967), "The separate person is without content, in both senses of the word."

John O. Stevens, writer, publisher, and Gestalt leader, in his book *Awareness: Exploring, Experimenting, Experiencing* (1971), has distilled a collection of techniques for getting in touch with one's self and with others as human beings.

The Marin Social Studies Project (1969–1971) resulted in a number of valuable publications, foremost of which is *If It Ain't Survival—It's Catastrophe* by Gary A. Knox (1971). A social studies curriculum, says Knox, must aim for human survival. I'd broaden that statement: *all* of our curriculum must aim at survival.

Two books which have helped me understand myself and my opportunities to function as a free person are *The Teacher as a Person* by Luiz F. S. Natalicio and Carl F. Hereford (1971) and *Expanding the Self—Personal Growth for Teachers* by Angelo V. Boy and Gerald J. Pine (1971).

Which books and magazine articles have you really enjoyed in the past year?

I believe that American education faces crises of gigantic proportions. If you do not agree, I suggest you read *The Little Red Schoolbook* by Soren Hansen and Jesper Jensen (1971) and Charles Silberman's *Crisis in the Classroom* (1970). *Red Schoolbook* may appear to be a book solely for students, but I learned much from it. For example, on page 25 the authors remind us that "To learn anything demands an effort from you —and some encouragement to make the effort. School should give each individual student as many opportunities of learning as possible." Silberman's book is based on a lengthy study of American schools. The study focuses on the many needs for improvement, especially improvement aimed at making our schools meet human needs rather than acting as a vast baby-sitting program and as a means of separating students according to their expected futures. The assumption has been and still is that most females, regardless of their preferences or talents, will be wives and mothers. Male students are divided into two groups—those destined for managerial or technical types of jobs and those destined to do manual labor. A system that operated on these assumptions does not address itself to the problems we face. Education must indeed be an individual affair. Schools can only be a part of an education for any individual. What we need are schools that can be a helping and liberating force. They can be, as you will see from many examples in this book.

Books on education have changed a great deal in the past ten years —in the direction of dealing with classroom realities. Mary Greer and Bonnie Rubinstein (1972) wrote and collected a very delightful and varied group of materials entitled *Will the Real Teacher Please Stand Up?* Many more, I think, are now standing up as a result of this book.

Teaching, Loving,
and
Self-directed Learning

We have met the enemy and they is us.

Pogo

One

TEACHING IS LIVING
AND LOVING

I started teaching with the naive notions that I could raise up a new generation by telling students the truth, that the power of the teacher's position and the power of the spoken and written word together would result in significant learning by most students. It took me quite a while to learn better: that the conventional behavior of the teacher as teller and tester hinders pupil learning, that the real teacher is the one who can encourage students to ask and seek answers to questions they see as interesting or important. Like John Holt (1970, p. 11), I now see learning "as a ... growing, a moving and expanding of the person into the world around him."

The teacher sitting in my office displayed her distress. She had invited her young male student teacher to dinner at her home. Her husband had been unfriendly and almost discourteous, and later he had told her never to bring the student teacher home again because he was "unconventional, he wore a beard, he'd be a bad influence" on their own children. In the past I had supervised student teachers in her classes, and I was familiar with her pattern of supportive behavior and of extending her friendship beyond the classroom. We had good communication, and I felt comfortable with her and accepted her need to talk with me. She and I agreed that her husband's attitude was parental, divorced from consideration of a person's character. When I asked her how long she was prepared to wait for her husband to change, she got red in the face and accused me of being hostile to her, in fact, she became parental, lecturing me on my responsibilities to her. A few minutes later she changed mood and became reflective. "I wonder," she said, "if my friendship with Steve, innocent as it is, is a threat to John." In the ensuing conversation, Mary revealed her ability to look at various aspects of a problem relatively dispassionately. In this part of our talk she seemed adult, sensible, thoughtful. But when it came time for her to leave she became tearful and ended up by begging me to help her to intercede with John, "to make something in my life come out right," as she phrased it. And in this mood she sounded like a desperate child, crying out for reassurance. Although this woman was one single unified person, she revealed herself as having three distinct personality modes.

Each human personality has three aspects, three manifest ways of displaying and expressing itself to others. In their work with clients, therapists who use *transactional analysis* (TA) find that each individual behaves in each of these three ego states:

Figure 1. Ego States Identified in Transactional Analysis

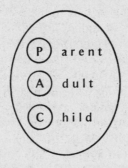

Eric Berne reports therapy sessions with a lawyer who at times acted toward other members of his family like a hostile Parent and at times like a Child bent only on enjoying forbidden pleasures through drugs and sex games. Yet at other times Berne saw him as the intelligent Adult capable of advising other people on the law. Was he then three people? Not at all. Berne realized he was one person with three noticeable sets of characteristics or three ways of dealing with the reality he observed. They are diagrammed above (Berne, 1961).

As Parent, I may say, "Don't ever do that again!" or "Let me help you with that." The former is the forbidding or injunctive Parent. The latter is exemplified by the nurturing Parent who helps the young child learn to dress himself or the teacher-Parent who helps the student with his work.

The Adult part of me deals with data relatively objectively. It makes possible calm discussions leading to decisions and action which I can support over a period of time. The Adult part of me is like a computer, capable of taking in and storing and also providing effective retrieval service for information I need: a phone number I need to call, where I put my sweater, and (hopefully) the date of my wife's birthday. Adult-to-Adult transactions or conversations are those which are least distorted by doubt, worry, or fear. My Child is the part of me which wants to have fun, to relax in joyful ways, to join others for pleasurable companionship and good times. Each of us has a friendly Child, though he may be reluctant to venture out today.

Obviously, such an outline of human personality is a simplification of reality. However, it can be tested by each of us, and I've yet to find a situation in which I could not get some insight through applying TA. For example, as Parent I might say either, "Don't ever . . ." or "Let me help. . . ." The "Don't ever . . ." exemplifies the compulsive need to dominate and control others, while the "Let me help . . ." may express the need to nurture. Both are needs we all have at different times. The Child aspect of my personality may express itself in varied ways also. The hurt Child may say, "I never get to be first," while the happy Child will say, "Come on to the store, it's my treat!" or "Let's dance!"

Another obvious point is that each of us is a whole person, even though a particular aspect or ego state may be dominant at a given moment. The oval line which encompasses P and A and C in the diagram reminds us of this wholeness. As a teacher, I think of the oval as a permeable boundary which each individual can go beyond as he learns to combine inner and outer resources in his own unique exploration of human potentialities. This happens when each of us utilizes his Adult to meet the Child's needs and still avoids getting into a jam, and when the Parent aspect can treat the Child partner with love and respect.

If I am a combination of Parent, Adult, and Child, how did I get that way?

The human baby arrives in the world with great potentials for love. If adults and children in his life-space accept him and encourage him to develop as the unique individual he's born to be, the child finds a number of ways of relating lovingly. He gives, receives, and shares love as an autonomous person, becoming more and more able to participate in complex love relationships. If not, he may develop few of his capacities, he may feel unsure of himself and wallow in uncertainty. Studies have shown the catastrophic damage suffered by orphans who get adequate physical care but very little touching and stroking in recognition of their unique and powerful needs as young children. Such children get injunctions from parents or parenting ones: "Don't be" or "Don't grow up" or "Don't make it." See Figures 2 and 3 for diagrams of such messages and the way they affect the recipient.

Figure 2. Diagram of an Injunction

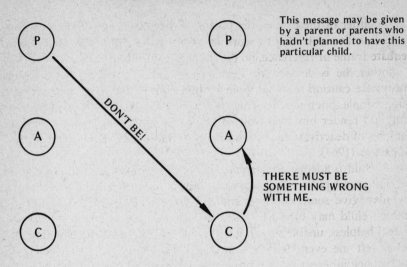

This message may be given by a parent or parents who hadn't planned to have this particular child.

DON'T BE!

THERE MUST BE SOMETHING WRONG WITH ME.

Figure 3. An Injunction and the Child's Internal Turmoil

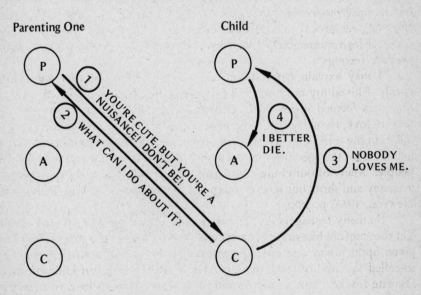

Parenting One

Child

1 YOU'RE CUTE, BUT YOU'RE A NUISANCE! DON'T BE!

2 WHAT CAN I DO ABOUT IT?

4 I BETTER DIE.

3 NOBODY LOVES ME.

6

In either of these cases, the parent or the parenting person is expressing his hostility at having to work to care for the child. The child has no adequate frame of reference, no defense against such messages. In one way or another, he is devastated. Teachers as well as parents need to exert appropriate caution to avoid giving injunctions of this or similar types to young people. Such messages may virtually deactivate the young person's Adult and render him incapable of any but the most primitive behaviors. Examples of deactivation of the adult are found in Erik Erikson's *Childhood and Society* (1963).

A child is adequately parented when his parents (or parenting ones) give him many positive affirmations of their liking for him, even though they may give some negative injunctions as well. Even the adequately parented child may have many self-doubts that inhibit friendly behavior. If I feel helpless, unable to act, it's like the feeling I had the first time my mother left me even though I wanted her to hold me, "the feeling of nonexistence inherent in discontinuity with mother" (Pearce and Newton, 1963, p. 388). That may be the initial alienation and may well appear to be the final alienation of the individual. My becoming starts with my awareness of my own existential independence, my own ability to act on my own behalf. Through this self-affirmation I can realize that my initial alienation from my mother need not be final.

Individuals feel themselves to be apart from others. Even if all his physical needs were provided for, an individual would experience aloneness as what Fromm (1963, pp. 8–9) calls a prison from which he had to break out in order to retain his sanity. So we all strive for meaningful, self-fulfilling, reciprocal relationships with others. To achieve them we overcome, at least momentarily, our parsimony, our stinginess about expressing positive feelings.

I may explain parsimony by the individual's evolution within the family. I loved my mother, yet I feared her disapproval. Habits of relating to others formed in my early years made it difficult for me to give and receive love, though clearly the choice was more and more mine as I got older. In the teen years, many of us substitute a "diffuse nonintimate 'friendliness' . . . for the specificity of deep one-to-one relationships with particular people." Many of our chum relationships and steady romances approximate intimacy and show our intense yearnings for intimacy and love (Pearce and Newton, 1963, p. 108).

So many teenagers behave parsimoniously, or seem to, toward adults. Yet they unfold like origami creations, open up like giant sunflowers, when given opportunity and encouragement. At the end of a school year, 150 so-called low ability tenth graders gave a party for Aaron Hillman, their favorite teacher. Not a stiff, formal party, but one with loud rock music, a light show, wild dancing, and lots of food. There was also lots of warm talk and touching, because the kids sensed Aaron would enjoy such a party as much as they did. Generation gap? Not when teachers like Aaron open their hearts to students, listen to what is being said, inspire students to communicate their real feelings. Many feelings emerge, but after a while, in an atmosphere of hope, of possibility, love emerges as a dominant feeling.

Each human being needs strokes. A *stroke* is a form of recognition by another that you are "there," and may be positive—a smile, a gesture, listening, or negative—teasing, ridicule, harsh criticism. Without strokes, the individual's physical as well as emotional development is impaired, at least temporarily. If a child does not get positive strokes, he'll tend to settle for negative ones and will behave in ways to provoke such strokes. He is prone to carry this pattern of behavior to adulthood. Each of us has opportunities to stroke others many times a day. If we give strokes for *doing* and few for *being*, we give the recipient the message that doing is more important than being. This happens in many conventional classrooms where the stress is on academic achievement. If we give strokes for being, as when I say "You're fun to be with," or "I like to hear you talk," or simply "I like you" or a warm smile, we give unqualified liking. To the student who feels deprived of love from his parents or others, an arm around the shoulder can be more reassuring than words. Each student and each teacher learns to relate to others in ways that elicit strokes. One way is by giving strokes, especially strokes for being.

Discouraging as it may be, most of us received injunctions of one kind or another from those who parented us. The injunctions as described by Robert Goulding (1972) are:

(1) DON'T BE. The parents who don't want a child, at least when the child arrives, convey to him by word or attitude the injunction "Don't be." This may come from the scared Child of the parent: "I don't know how to care for you—can't you see I have enough trouble taking care of me?" A teacher may imply to a student: "I wish you weren't in my class," which may have a similar effect.

(2) DON'T GROW UP. The children of doting parents may get the message "Don't grow up." An example of this is the remark "You're so cute just as you are," which is a stroke with an injunction attached. Alternatively, the parent or the teacher may say "You can't do it" or "That's too hard for you now."

(3) DON'T BE A CHILD. The young person always recognizes that he will be evolving toward adulthood, though the process seems to take forever. His Child, seeking fun, may get him into trouble with a parent, as when he hears: "Don't be a little kid—act your age." Here he is in a bind: his Child wants to have fun and realizes the opportunities for fun all around him, yet he wants the approval of his parent. Teachers, like parents, have opportunities to squelch students by saying "Act your age!" I recognize such statements as a reinforcement of an injunction many students have heard from their parents. Perhaps you have an awareness of an injunction you have given to a student recently. Does it seem possible that, by giving this injunction, you are obeying an injunction you received as a child?

(4) DON'T BE YOU. Suppose Mr. and Mrs. Leach want a girl baby,

but get a boy. He will perceive their disappointment, in effect hearing them say "Don't be you." We all know people who desperately sought to follow this injunction and others who are seriously in conflict over their own sex role. In both high school and elementary classrooms, the dominant values tend to be conventional (in the traditional sense): sit quietly, write neatly, cooperate with the teacher, don't make waves. I now see this conformist standard as a reinforcement of injunctions received by many students in earlier years, especially "Don't be a child," "Don't have fun," and sometimes "Don't be you."

In a family partnership with conflicts between the father and mother, "Don't be you" may take the spoken form, "I hope you don't grow up to be like your mother/father." I talked with a young teacher whose father had given him the injunction "Don't be like me." The father, although fairly successful as a rancher, felt that education was the way to true status and constantly reminded his son to get an education so he could be a success. The son taught for a year, didn't like it, and during the ensuing summer became self-directed and sought another occupation. He decided he no longer had to obey his father's orders.

(5) DON'T MAKE IT. If the father is a successful businessman, he may give his son this message in which he expresses his fear of competing with his son. The beautiful woman may in effect say to her daughter, "Don't be attractive to men, because that means I'm aging." Such injunctions may be frequent contributing factors to the generation gap. Both parents and teachers can become aware of the messages they give members of the younger generation. When teachers put students in "low" ability groups in elementary school or in C or Z track classes in high school, they are saying, "Don't make it—you haven't got it," a very destructive injunction. Studies show that students tend to live up (or down) to expectations. I've taught in C track classes, and the students tend to fulfill this low expectation we give them. There are many forms of segregation, all of them destructive of high morale. I know one school district where the "ability" grouping plan serves to keep most of the Chicano children in the so-called low groups. Needless to say, many of the children thus discriminated against have poor attendance records as well as poor achievement. They accept the injunction given by the school district but seek to have satisfactory lives outside of school. By contrast, in a learning environment guided by caring behavior, both teachers and students are busy achieving personal satisfaction in school as well as outside.

(6) DON'T BE CLOSE. This injunction may be given by deed as well as word. Parents who seldom touch each other give this message. A close friend of mine got it from his mother's relationship to many people, including relatives. The message he got was "Be careful about being close —it's very dangerous—others may betray you." Listening to this type of message, a person may become distrustful and suspicious, may doubt the intentions or even the sincerity of others who try to get close to him.

(7) DON'T ..., or DON'T EVER. This is an injunction from a phobic parent, as in "Don't pick up things off the ground," "Don't climb trees," "Don't appear in public without your makeup." Mary Ann felt that the most important necessity for her was to stay clean and protect her clothes. The message such a child got from her mother was "Don't get dirty!" In order to avoid violating this message, she avoided contact with other children. This excluded many of the options that would permit her to learn through interaction with them. Only when she was helped to put the message from her mother in a larger context did she unbend and begin to learn from and with her friends. As a teacher, I am always aware of the possible inhibitions which restrict pupils in the choices they see as open to them. Some teachers tend to sprinkle "don'ts" throughout their conversations with students. Restraint is obviously in order because repetition of a message tends to dilute its meaning. I believe our central message should be "Do" or "Be."

(8) DON'T BE IMPORTANT, a variation of DON'T MAKE IT. An example is the parent who gives the child no stroke or only a mild stroke when he announces an achievement, such as "I got two merit badges today!"

(9) DON'T BE WELL (OR SANE) is the message given to the child who gets attention largely when he is hurt or ill. This crazy injunction says "Be sick—we'll love you then." A classroom variant is the teacher who is only attentive or loving to the child with the skinned knee or the bruised ego: "Oh, I'm sorry you got only a C+ in Chemistry—you should have tried harder."

Dibs, whose classic story is told by Virginia Axline, came to the therapist as a desperate little boy whose response to destructive messages was the creation of his own private world. His parents, both professionals, convinced him, by their ways of stroking and their ways of ignoring him, that there must be something wrong with him, that he had arrived only to interfere with their busy lives. At one point he verbally and symbolically expressed the view that a truck was okay but humans were not to be trusted. The therapist showed great skill in letting Dibs take the lead in unlocking the doors in front of him, in encouraging him by her confidence in him. He grew to accept himself and his feelings about others, and increasingly to accept others. Through love he came to appreciate the possibilities that love offered. He gradually moved to the point where he could listen to healthy messages from others and from within himself and could enjoy living.

(10) DON'T FEEL X, where X represents a feeling the parent has a hang-up about. This may be expressed as "Boys don't cry," or teachers may be told by other teachers "Don't smile till Christmas if you want to keep control of your class."

There are many ways of dealing with the injunctions we generally obeyed as children. Bringing them out into the light of day helps. Loving friendships of teacher to teacher and teacher to student helps. Satisfying family relationships assist the teacher to keep his perspective and his balance.

What injunctions did you get as a child? Writing them down or tape recording them may help you as a person and as a teacher to liberate yourself from messages which interfere with your own contemporary living and that of the individuals you are teaching.

I have written about the injunctions for very practical reasons. Most people have gotten them in early months and years of life, and they are a powerful determinant of later behavior. The third grader or eleventh grader who still hears and listens to the message "Don't make it" is unlikely to achieve in school. It helps very little to say, "He's not motivated"—that's too general and vague. If I can say "He got the injunction 'Don't Make It' " I have some useful clues as to how I can behave toward him to help him help himself. For example, I can make it clear by word and deed that I see him as competent: By giving him responsibility, by giving him many opportunities to make choices, by praising his achievements (which may indeed be minimal at first but will increase as he increases as a person) I can help him build a more honest self-image. The odds are good that he can do better, whether his IQ is 79 or 149, because few humans are able to function at their optimal level with any consistency.

You can find out in several ways which injunctions a child was given: by observing his characteristic behavior, posture, and speech, by using other sources of data (such as other teachers, the nurse, and parent conferences), and by conferences with the student. All of these will be described later in the book.

A teacher I once knew, whom I will call Ms. Mallory, had for years obeyed the injunctions of her parents, her students, other teachers, and school administrators. But one day she began to question those rules and to explore new ways of teaching. Ms. Mallory remembered several of the ideas suggested in a summer course she'd taken and decided to try them. She had a seventh grade core group for social studies and language arts for two periods every morning. The group seemed to be going nowhere; interest was at a low ebb, morale was low, and the students sniped at each other. Ms. Mallory felt there was nowhere to go but up. So after careful planning of what she would say and what she would be willing to permit the students to decide, she discussed the possibility of a new program with the students.

She began with a *problem census*. Question: "If you had your druthers, what would we do in this class?" Responses varied from the expected "go out to recess" or "nothing" to "study about teenagers and adults—how to get along," "find out about the new countries in Africa," and "each one study something he's interested in." Because the state social studies program called for study of the eastern hemisphere in seventh grade, Ms. Mallory said the work should focus on that half of the world. In that respect, she was not ready to grant the students unconditional freedom. Three days of discussion, much of it lively as children grasped the possibility of new ways of working, resulted in an agreement to study the emerging nations of Africa. Some pupils argued that they wanted to find out first about the older, more established nations of Africa, and this was accepted as a project for those who chose it.

How would the class work? And how would the language arts be included? Further discussion ended in agreements that:

1. Those who wished to would work individually on projects they selected in conference with the teacher.
2. Several pairs of pupils would work on projects together.
3. Seven class members preferred studying more conventionally under teacher direction, and Ms. Mallory agreed to meet with them as a group for at least twenty-five minutes each day.
4. Spelling would be handled individually. Each pupil would be responsible for entering in his notebook words he encountered which he could not spell. The teacher would ask each pupil once every two weeks to show his spelling notebook and be ready to spell any word in it. Vocabulary building would be combined with spelling, with each pupil responsible for his own new words.
5. Because reading is reading is reading, the pupils decided that assigned reading in the literature book was unnecessary. Rather, each pupil would read what he needed for his social studies project, and his reading might well include fiction. One boy's father had told him of Alan Paton's novels, and one girl had seen several of Nadine Gordimer's short stories. Several pupils wrote to consulates or embassies of African nations asking for information and materials.
6. Because of the demands from teachers in succeeding grades for better performance in English usage, both written and spoken, Ms. Mallory set aside three one-half hour periods per week—out of the almost ten hours available—for text study and oral and written English practice.

She listened to injunctions from other educators that usage is important, yet she allowed opportunities for freedom in other areas. Students comprehend the necessities for compromise and appreciate honest acknowledgment of them. Ms. Mallory learned she could be honest with her students.

Three weeks later, Ms. Mallory found that she could make up a box score as shown in Table 1. She found that the noise level in the room had risen a bit, though it was leveling off. Some children showed an inability to choose a reasonable project or to stick to the one they chose. Some in this group did less well in her SDL program than in the previous conventional one. Some restlessly asked to go to the library, soon returning to complain they couldn't find anything. But several were grappling with topics they found enjoyable. And the peer pressure was slowly being felt by some of the more erratic students; they were wasting less time now. Those enjoying their work ignored most of the noisy distractions.

Table 1
Working Patterns of Class Members

Core class N = 32; Boys = 16; Girls = 16

Working Previously (before new program)	Now Working (repeats from left hand col. in ( ))	Not Working	Uncertain
Boys 7	11 (6)	4	1
Girls 9	12 (9)	3	1

On a different level, Ms. Mallory noticed that her conversations with the students had changed. Instead of assigning/directing/ordering/disciplining, she was now more often talking about individual interests and individual feelings. Several students, including Carl, whom she would have despaired of reaching three weeks ago, were able to talk with her about their real learning difficulties and were working on mutually agreeable remedial programs. Carl was studying teenagers in Egypt, and while he was having a hard time finding materials, he was keen about the project and determined to carry it through.

Ms. Mallory found that she now *felt* better about the class, not only about how the children were working but about what they were studying. It was amazing how much positive feeling they could put into their work when they felt like it. Several students had shown remarkable flexibility in modifying plans to accommodate others—for example, in sharing materials or dividing up topics so that others could participate with them. Several had helped other students on specific academic problems, purely on a voluntary basis, and seemed to enjoy it. And the ones who were helped showed their appreciation by reciprocating in appropriate ways.

Ms. Mallory saw the possibilities of a new program for her students; without this perception, she might have seen no direction to go, and she might well have floundered through an entire school year with bored students. In addition to perceiving possibilites, she mustered courage to accompany her faith. For something must be ventured if there is to be any gain. She had faith in herself and her ability to translate plans into action, she found courage, she took risks, and she achieved a considerable degree of success, as well as some failures. This brings us full circle, back to feeling again. Faith and courage are feelings which every human being needs. Parents and teachers must provide validation. The peer group can reinforce validation so that the adult can have faith and exercise courage. This is a way to OK-ness, to self-actualization, to authenticity, to wholeness as a person. And this is, as Ms. Mallory found, one way to make possible loving relationships with others. Yes, Ms. Mallory concluded, love was an active force in this classroom. Almost everyone felt it, not least of all Ms. Mallory. And she felt more in touch with herself and her teaching than ever before.

There is a great gulf between existing and becoming. Many individuals exist, go through the motions of eating, working, and the like. The word *becoming* implies going ahead, going beyond what I now am. The person becoming can always see something beyond the routines of daily life, something he wishes to reach, to know, to experience. As a teacher, I want my students to become such seekers, and I hope they will be seekers of many different things, for our civilization needs potters and painters and poets and politicians in addition to scientists and inventors.

The way to becoming is through learning and loving. I am becoming through finding out things which interest me and through expressing outgoing love. My students in teacher training recognize their own self-interest and see possibilities for self-fulfillment toward which they are working. These students are a new generation of adults with the faith and courage to contribute to the evolution of our civilization. Thus learning and loving power the evolution toward a better world. Love has the power for our salvation as human beings and we are learning to use it. That's what this book is about.

NOTES TO CHAPTER 1

In seventeen years in public school teaching, I never got away from the literature of psychology. Among the books which helped me were Arthur Combs and Donald Snygg's *Individual Behavior* (1959), and George A. Kelly's *A Theory of Personality* (1963). Combs and Snygg focus on the individual as he strives to lead a meaningful life among his peers, behaving according to his perceptions of the world around him. Kelly shows how each person creates for himself *constructs* which provide ways of living within a predictable universe of events. The ideas of Combs and Snygg and of Kelly are compatible with Transactional Analysis.

My understanding of Transactional Analysis (TA) comes from personal experiences as well as reading. I have belonged to a TA group for one year and have attended three weekend workshops. In addition, I have read *Games People Play* (1964) and *Transactional Analysis in Psychotherapy* (1961) by Eric Berne, *I'm OK—You're OK* by Thomas A. Harris (1969), and *Introduce Yourself to Transactional Analysis* by Paul McCormick and Leonard Campos (1969). Specific material regarding injunctions comes from an article by Robert Goulding, "New Directions in Transactional Analysis: Creating an Environment for Redecision and Change" (1972).

A fascinating author I became acquainted with in my reading is Ronald Laing. Try his *The Divided Self* (1965) or *The Politics of Experience* (1968). Here's an example of Laing's effort to express some of the complexities of human experience:

> *It is our duty to bring up our children to love,*
> *honour and obey us.*
> *If they don't, they must be punished,*
> *otherwise we would not be doing our duty.*
> *If they grow up to love, honour and obey us*
> *we have been blessed for bringing them up properly.*
> *if they grow up not to love, honour and obey us*
> *either we have brought them up properly*
> *or we have not:*
> *if we have*
> *there must be something the matter with them:*
> *if we have not*
> *there is something the matter with us.*

In *Knots* (1970), from which the above was taken, Laing shows many of the paradoxes of our feelings toward ourselves and toward others, especially the feelings of mothers and fathers and marriage partners.

One of my favorite fiction writers is Doris Lessing, whose *Golden Notebook* (1962) and *The Four-Gated City* (1970) delight and intrigue me. Her ability to communicate some of the constant uncertainties of personal feeling is quite extraordinary.

During my years of public school teaching, I became fascinated with futurism—the effort to project present trends into the future and to make predictions as to the nature of human experience in a given era. *Technological Man* by Victor Ferkiss (1969) is one of the useful books I read. Don Fabun, editor of *Kaiser Aluminum News*, presents ideas and information from many sources in his magazine. The *Futurist Magazine*, published by the World Future Society, also provides monthly input on the subject.

A very useful book about classroom management and discipline is *Maintaining Sanity in the Classroom* (Dreikurs, 1971).

Pygmalion in the Classroom started a controversy that will continue for years. In it Rosenthal and Jacobson (1967) report their finding that if teachers expect children to succeed, the children do succeed. Other investigators have replicated the study but with different results. Rosenthal gives a thoughtful review of relevant research in his chapter in *Psychology and Educational Practice* (1971) edited by Gerald S. Lesser. Whichever way you feel about this issue, I encourage you to do some reading and perhaps an experiment. What would happen if you made a private prediction of success for all your students?

I owe a big debt to Carl Rogers, especially for *Freedom to Learn* (1969). Whether you teach primary children, high school students, or college students, this book contains ideas that can lead to enjoyable experiences in your classroom.

If you can, see the film done for Canadian Broadcasting Corporation (CBC-TV) called "Chariots of the Gods."

To be creative means to experience life in one's own way, to perceive from one's own person, to draw upon one's own resources, capacities, roots. It means facing life directly and honestly; courageously searching for and discovering grief, joy, suffering, pain, struggle, conflict, and finally inner solitude.

Clark Moustakas (1967)

Two

I SEEK, THROUGHOUT MY LIFE, LOVING AND LEARNING

Arctic explorer Raold Amundsen (Allport, 1955) spent his life in persistent seeking. His seeking involved him in raising funds, in complex plans and preparations, and in long and arduous trips, the last of which cost him his life. This is an extreme example of "propriate striving," a sustained effort made to reach those goals the individual sees as vital to him. Relatively few of us exhibit the type of striving that Amundsen did. Yet all of us strive in the light of our images of ourselves and of our place in the world. I seek goals, reachable as well as unattainable, by means which may be efficient or inefficient, appropriate or inappropriate. A fourth grader works to master long division because he knows adults consider arithmetic important and will reward him for doing it. A teacher practices the guitar so she can accompany the children's singing. Both seek to satisfy a need to achieve and to have their achievement recognized by others they feel to be important people.

What am I striving for, really? I want to learn for my own sake and I want to love and be loved in return. Both the fourth grader studying long division and the teacher learning the guitar strive for satisfying relationships with others. Later, both the fourth grader and the teacher may come to like what they are doing for its own sake. A number system and music are both examples of human creations with intrinsic interest and beauty entirely aside from any utility.

The desire to actively love others and to receive the warmth of their responding love is, I think, a universal. I will discuss love in several ways in several contexts. Similarly, I'll give you a point of view about learning and many examples. I will also show the close relationship between loving and learning. Raold Amundsen learned in order to explore successfully, and he explored in order to learn more about the Arctic. He loved the learning and the exploring.

Why is it so difficult for many of us to love and to learn steadily and joyfully into adulthood and beyond? Many students encounter manmade difficulties when they come to school or when they change schools. Jose could read Spanish when he arrived at age seven in New York, yet public school failed to help him learn to read English. In five years in public school Jose "failed" everything, and in the process he developed seemingly physiological symptoms which made school learning impossible. He blinked, gasped, and writhed when faced with a printed page. Thus he showed that he had listened to injunctions from public school teachers—"Don't make it." Jose began to attend the First Street School, an experimental school open especially to children who were seen as "impossible" in other schools. Jose's teacher, George Dennison, accumulated a great deal of knowledge about Jose, including knowledge of how Jose *did* succeed in learning. Dennison found that it was necessary to give Jose a lot of freedom, to let him choose his own time for a lesson, to let him avoid any appearance of wanting to learn and especially any appearance of giving in to adult demands. George's carefully gathered knowledge of Jose served the boy well for a while. Such knowledgeable love can help to work miracles with children. When I love, I use my knowledge for my benefit and the benefit of others. With Jose and with students who have similar problems, love involves recognition and acceptance of the value of the language the student brings to school, using that knowledge as a springboard to learn more language or an additional language.

Each healthy baby starts life with an enormous capacity for loving and learning. Much evidence has been gathered to show how quickly a baby begins to make simple discriminations about events in his world. An infant on the first day of life "learned that the sound of a bell meant there was a bottle on his right, whereas the sound of a buzzer meant the bottle was on his left" (Roe, 1971, p. 109). The biological heritage a child brings into the world, the culture he interacts with, his experiences with others, and any given situation he faces will all be determinants of his perceptions and his behavior. I believe that experience with others is the most important of these determinants.

Each parent learns how to parent a child. There are ways to prepare for parenthood, but a very few of us avail ourselves of them. I know I didn't. I learned by parenting, trying to see what worked. Our first child arrived six weeks early, stayed in the hospital for two weeks, and was in a hurry to make up for lost time when she got home, always demanding to be fed. My patience was not always equal to the demands. I cite this as a series of occasions when I very likely gave her injunctions which later were not easy for her to live with.

H. Papousek (Roe, 1971, p. 120) "found that infants of six months will master quite complex learning tasks, such as making a head turn twice to the right, three times to the left, and once to the right again, purely for the joy of solving the problem." Such behavior is much to be desired. Yet a number of children in kindergarten show a reluctance to deal with problems. I believe many children receive injunctions in their early months and years of life, messages they strive to obey. A study by Sears, Maccoby, and Levin (Tanner and Lindgren, 1971, pp. 88–89) reports that 62 percent of mothers they asked were delighted at being pregnant for the first time, but only 34 percent were delighted at being pregnant with a second or later child. Another 34 percent were of mixed feelings or displeased at the prospect of having subsequent children. There is considerable evidence that such "unwilling" parents unintentionally hand down a number of injunctions which interfere with the healthy evolution of their children (Tanner and Lindgren, 1971, pp. 90–103). Each teacher may reinforce parental injunctions, or he may help each child to make decisions and redecisions for himself.

Many parents give injunctions. Many parents fill their days with activities that interfere with learning and loving and in so doing provide an example for their children. These injunctions and activities start the children toward a repetition of their parents' lives. Many teachers add the weight of their authority to the stifling of spontaneity in the student's search for meaningful experiences. Thus many people at age one, two, three, or four adopt one of the three negative "positions" that Thomas A. Harris tells about in *"I'm OK—You're OK."* The individual who says, for example, "I'm not OK—You're OK" tells others that he feels inferior and possibly defective. This posture may be his response to the injunctions "Don't be" or "Don't make it." Another individual reflects his feeling "I'm not OK—You're not OK" either, a pessimistic conviction of futility: the world is a lousy place and none of us can do much about it. Possibly this may be his way of living with such injunctions as "Don't grow up" or "Don't be you." By contrast, a few adopt the position "I'm OK—You're not OK" and thus express their determination to hold on to their identity. Thus, a child may recognize the stupidity of the messages "Don't grow up", or "Don't be you" or "Don't be close" by saying "I'll hang on to being me, and you must be crazy to expect me to do otherwise." Ronald Laing talks of this problem in *The Divided Self* (1965).

None of the three postures just mentioned is healthy. A person who feels inferior, depressed about life, or defensive (occasionally to the point of paranoia) makes others feel uncomfortable in his presence. He keeps others at a distance, reluctant to establish a friendly relationship with him. Thus many business and government organizations and schools limp along at less than their potential efficiency because most of the staff don't have a conviction of individual and mutual OK-ness. I know that I'm OK and you're OK too. I also realize that merely repeating the statement won't bring about the reality I seek for all of us. In every aspect of my life I listen to my wishes and express my will in outgoing behavior toward others. I live optimistically and invite others to do likewise. Loving and learning occur in large part through the taking of risks in interactions with people in the overlapping environments in which each of us lives.

Larry came into this world with a substantial number of abilities which he inherited. They include interrelated physical, mental, and emotional abilities and potentialities. All of these together add up to a collection of interrelated possibilities for emerging behavior, for becoming a whole human adult. At any given moment Larry is a total unique being-becoming.

Larry takes in data, stores it, relates it to other data he already has, and uses the data in interacting with his environment. Each of us is unique in our interaction with environment. Larry does not behave according to the facts as others see them. He behaves according to the facts as he sees them. "What governs behavior from the point of view of the individual himself are his unique perceptions of himself and the world in which he lives, the meanings things have for him" (Combs and Snygg, 1959, p. 14). Larry's perceptual field expands and changes as he grows and changes. He seeks to have fun by "letting his Child out to play." This is easier if he reads the data accurately with his Adult and turns off the injunctions from his nagging Parent. He builds long-standing explanations of behavior that serve him as he encounters people and situations. Bruner describes the manner in which children change in their ways of sorting common objects (tools, food, and so on). Younger children use such perceptual features as color and size very heavily, while older ones use the functional properties, such as the way a magnet attracts ferrous metal, much more often. At a later stage in evolution toward adulthood, teenagers look at peers of the opposite sex as possible sexual objects, as potential mates, or as those with whom they may enjoy intimate friendship.

Sara dropped out of high school after grade ten. Just a few months short of sixteen, she wasn't on drugs, she didn't have a cause to fight for. Simple lack of interest in the courses and the teachers. She listened to her father's injunction, "Don't make it." She's not trained for a job, now sits at home watching TV. She helps around the house, occasionally baby-sits or substitutes for a girl who is a regular carhop at a hot dog stand. We will never keep all the Saras in school. Some of those who drop out exercise a choice which may make good sense to them: school really has little to offer them. So we must give love as well as thought to them now by offering them more choices within a school program and by respecting their choices, including the option of leaving school and the further option of returning to school at a later time. Each of them has the potential to become a free and loving person capable of serving himself and of contributing to the lives of others. With wider choices and greater adult respect for their freedom, most young people will elect to continue their education as human beings, whether in school or out. What do you feel like saying to the Sara among your acquaintances?

Each individual sees only certain people as parts of his life, sees only certain ways of behaving as open to him. He behaves according to his perceptions of himself and his world. Each child sees himself in a context of other people. The kindergartner, even the one with limited prior experience with others of his age group, learns to deal with others. He inevitably feels ambivalent: he wants to be himself, yet he wants to be like others he sees around him.

Each of us, throughout life, experiences this conflict between identity and characteristic behavior. I cling to what I know and what I am used to, what I consider to be the core of me. Like Linus with his security blanket, I may cling to my "safe" emotions and be parsimonious in revealing myself to others. At the same time, I feel a desire to be a different self, a better self, a more wholesome self, a more outgoing self, a more authentic self. I seek ways to behave as I see I might behave, to become the authentic me.

The individual who gets injunctions is not to be regarded as a helpless victim. It's true, the very young child lacks an adequate range of experiences to compare his own feelings with. Increasingly, as he gets older, he adds to his observations of others and how they handle various situations. Increasingly, he gains control over aspects of his life. Increasingly, he becomes responsible for his life. Yet many do not find authentic ways of dealing with life situations—rather than facing them squarely, they cop out. Cop-outs include reliance upon the gene theory ("I've got poor protoplasm—you can't expect me to do any better") or the predestination theory ("I have no power over my life"). They are expressed by "I can't" which can be translated as "I won't," or "I'll try" which may really mean "I don't expect to succeed," or "You make me nervous, angry, and so on." Since *I* can't make *you* feel anything, such a statement is a cop-out. An example of how a teacher dealt with a boy used to copping out is found in *Maintaining Sanity in the Classroom* (Dreikurs, 1971, pp. 60–63). Active approaches by the teacher can help the child to move toward becoming self-directed.

Loving has to do with my feelings about myself and my abilities to share intimacy with others. I can now say in a class, "I love you, Hazel," and feel that I am being honest as well as stroking Hazel for being. Learning has to do with changing my behavior in ways that facilitate my expression of myself as a multifaceted personality and my ability to approach and become a sharer with other people in the world around me.

I know some people with outgoing personalities who always seem able to say a friendly word or evoke a smile which makes being near them pleasant. A friend of mine used to give compliments to almost every woman and usually got at least a smile. This man had learned to use words in positive ways to stroke others and to influence their behavior. He frequently succeeded in achieving intimate relationships, and he had many sensitive feelings to share. His early learning of the power of stroking helped him greatly in making friends and enjoying love. His loving relationships made possible a greater depth of learning about himself and about those with whom he experienced intimacy.

A third grade class in the northwest had the privilege of working with a student teacher, Mr. Hudson, who had lost an arm to cancer. During the first day of class he encouraged talk of his handicap and the reasons for it, and by the end of the first day he had established himself as a member of the "family." Two weeks later, he returned to the hospital for further treatment. His promised letter to the children was late in arriving. When he did write, he acknowledged severe pain, the only time he ever mentioned it. The students began to become aware of the seriousness of his illness and to consider his future and that of his wife and three children. Several families of class members volunteered to serve dinner to the Hudson family and to baby-sit. When Mr. Hudson came back to school, the students organized a party for him. Soon he returned to the hospital. The children wrote letters to him every week, and the whole class visited him in the hospital. He died, but the children were prepared. They appreciated the pleasure of having known him and of being able to help in small ways. They also gained understanding about serious diseases and the need for research to overcome them.

Involvement with people requires facing the tragic. "To love means to open ourselves to the negative as well as the positive—to grief, sorrow, and disappointment as well as to joy, fulfillment, and an intensity of consciousness we did not know was possible before" (May, 1969, p. 100). We expect much from love, but tragedy casts its shadow: I shall one day lose this loved person, unless I die first. This foreknowledge of tragedy helps me give of myself NOW while the possibility of reciprocal loving does exist. As a teacher I "lose" every June a number of loved students.

I want to talk about sensuality and the classroom, for too long a taboo subject. Each of us experiences many physical pleasures in his life. One of my special favorites is walking and looking at blue sky and white clouds. The blue looks as if it extends to the end of the universe, the white clouds look every way from fluffy to funny to majestic. Chicken cooked with white wine and herbs, broiled salmon, crisp celery, a green salad with vinegar and oil dressing—these are a few of the taste treats I appreciate. We all have sensual pleasures: the enjoyment of a person we see, music we hear, food we taste, a sculpture we can freely touch, the aroma of wildflowers. Some of us exchange thoughts or feelings with others without speaking. The world of sensuality encompasses a wide range of experiences. Bernard Gunther's *Sense Relaxation* (1968) contains a number of wholesome ways of tuning in to those experiences and thus expanding our enjoyment of living.

Sexuality is only a part, though an important part, of sensuality. Mature sexuality involves the learning of sex play that pleases one, that fulfills *his* or *her* sense of sexual pleasure. It also involves continued sexual awareness of other people, though not a constant compulsion to go to bed with others one sees as attractive.

Sexual interest is a factor in teaching in elementary school as well as in high school or college. Each teacher notices attractive students and, trying not to be swayed by this usually uninvited feeling, may betray his ambivalence. The attractive student is often aware of the teacher's distraction and may enjoy the teacher's discomfiture in such a situation. There's no sense denying it happens, but each teacher can build security against psychological misery and possible censure by other teachers by having viable loving relationships with a number of other people, family, and friends, so that he's not so vulnerable to upset because of a classroom reality he must live with. He may also enjoy a healthy nonsexual loving relationship with the student to whom he's attracted. The teacher will, naturally, experience the attraction. It can be enjoyed as a pleasant feeling, and as I expand my ideas of attractiveness, I can appreciate the beauty of many students. This does not require a kind of generalized attraction to everyone alike but can take due notice of individual and unique features. Just as I appreciate being noticed, so does everyone else. When we mutually celebrate our own attractiveness as people, the whole world begins to look different and we find it easier to have fun in our lives with all those other fun people.

Parenthetically, I remind myself that there are solutions to what seems to be an insoluble problem: a strong attraction (or antipathy) to a student in my class. The student can, in many cases, be transferred to another class on the very solid grounds that his or her education is being impaired in my class. Occasionally, the teacher may need to apply for transfer to another school within the district or in another city. However, if he finds that intense sexual attractions for students continually interfere with his judgment as a teacher, he should seek employment in some other line of work. For he has a responsibility to himself, to his students and to teaching as a way of life. Teaching as a profession owes him nothing. He as a teacher owes everything to himself, to be the kind of teacher he believes he must be. It's a question of his commitment to himself.

I make the distinction between sexuality and sensuality. A distinction must also be made between being *in love* and *loving*. To a large extent our semantic difficulties grow out of the evolution of views of love and loving. In the twelfth century, men made the distinction between sacred and profane love. The latter was idolatrous—the lover (usually a man) was by definition inferior and the loved one (the woman) was superior. However, this superiority was celebrated much more in literature than in real life. As our western civilization evolved, the role of the woman continued to be subservient to the man. Various societies, east and west, have provided for arranged marriages. Yet, especially in the west, the idea and the ideal of romantic love has persisted. Most of the American popular songs between 1890 and 1950 had to do with some aspect of idealized love between man and woman—or with its failure for the singer who continued to believe in the ideal. Even after Bob Dylan, Simon and Garfunkel, and the Rolling Stones, a substantial number of songs continue to speak of yearning for a one to one relationship that is substantially romanticized.

One part of the problem has to do with "falling in love," surely a significant event in one's life, but we can't maintain the feelings at the fever pitch of falling forever, perhaps not past the honeymoon. The husband goes back to his eight to five job and the wife takes care of the house or works, or both. During the early years of marriage the individuals can develop a sense of loving or can come to despair because the ideal each experienced has not maintained itself. This is likely to be especially true in cases where there was, as there so often is, a discrepancy in the degree to which the two individuals worshipped the ideal or experienced the falling. When disillusionment sets in, I may say love has failed, and my marriage has failed, and the only solution I can see is to fall in love again with a new partner. In a society in which we sell houses and buy new cars with great frequency, it seems natural to trade in a wife or husband for a new model. Before doing so, notice how often the new model turns out to be very much like the discarded one.

There are viable alternatives. One is giving up the magic of falling in love as a way to begin a love relationship. Or, one could go through the falling with more realistic awareness that it will end. I can learn to think of my partner as a unique individual with a life of her own, a substantial part of which is independent of me, instead of demanding "the obliteration of two people into one." I can learn that loving includes thought about and respect for that other person in addition to a yearning for stroking from her and sexual pleasures shared with her. The loving can include shared hobbies, travel and friends, as well as companionate cooperation in the upbringing of children. I hear some saying: That's an awful load to put on a marriage in times like these. It is. But for many the pay-off will be well worth the effort and the risks in a relationship which involves recognition of "the autonomy of the other person," the only basis on which loving can live for long (Mitchell, 1972).

Loving, then, is a new ideal, a more comprehensive ideal than love. I talk about love a lot in this book. I generally use it to refer to a relationship involving loving—a reciprocal relationship between two people based on shared enjoyments and mutual acceptance of the integrity of each as an independent person. Such relationships may exist between two young children, two teenagers, a child and her parent, two lovers, two male or female adults—as well as between wife and husband. I admit that I still have trouble with my own thinking about love and loving, and I encourage you to see if you can make sense out of it for yourself.

I believe that love and loving have enormous potentials to motivate other healthy relationships in society and to assist men and women in solving social problems. Here's where learning comes in: I can learn to love and to enjoy loving relationships of many kinds. Falling in love may have been romanticized for so long because it seems to absolve the individual of responsibility—as though I surrendered all my me-ness to an overwhelming force from outside. This force, strong as it is, usually does not sustain itself in the give and take of a long relationship. Hence, each of us needs tools for building more comprehensive loving relationships for a lifetime with others. Education at every level must face feelings, because feelings determine behavior. In nursery school, in kindergarten, and all the way through college, we need to encourage children and youth to learn about the complexities of human feelings. Each of us has the ability to learn more than we usually think possible.

Wertheimer (1945) tells of seeing two boys playing badminton. One, by virtue of superior size and agility, is easily beating the other. Gradually, as the psychologist watched from his window, the boys changed the game. Pretty soon the object of the game became to keep the bird in the air as long as possible, a game both boys could enjoy winning. In a highly competitive society, we stress winning, but winning can be interpreted more than one way. From this experience, both boys learned more about games and how to enjoy them. And both discovered something of the love that contributes to and grows out of human cooperation. Each of us has so much to give to others. A loving teacher appreciates that fact and allows opportunities for pupils to give to each other. Each of us can thus learn about varieties of loving we want and varieties we are able to share. But we only learn through experience.

Love increases both the quality and the quantity of the individual's potentials. As an example, the loving individual can look at his job more honestly and perhaps even decide: this is not the job for me. I cite this as an example for a very specific reason. Teaching is a job into which many people go without awareness of its demands. If they are aware, many of them are reluctant to try to meet those demands, or unsure of their ability to succeed in risky relationships. Too, they hear many disparaging remarks from other teachers about teaching, kids, and parents. Many of these people find themselves feeling guilty about not giving to children what they need; this means children get turned off, and some teachers become bitter, concluding that children are no damned good. Some of these people would be far better off in another field of endeavor. At the same time, many teachers have a good deal of interest in and ability for teaching, and what *they* need is an increasing capacity to give and receive love and to appreciate some of the beauty of learning about themselves and others.

I noticed Ted, a student in a summer workshop on self-directed learning, because of his reticence, his closed look. Ted had gone through teacher training without enthusiasm, aware at the time that teaching did not greatly appeal to him. Yet he continued to listen to his father's injunction, "Don't be like me." The father felt unsuccessful because he lacked formal education, and he constantly hammered at Ted about the importance of getting a degree and entering a status occupation. When Ted finally faced up to all this during the workshop, he decided to leave teaching. He had no other strong bent and was unrealistic about job hunting, but at least he overcame apathy and began to live his own life for himself. Perhaps he'll return to teaching some day. If he does, it will be his choice, entered into because of his own inner motivations. Why did you go into teaching? Do you feel you made the right choice? Do you still feel that the reasons for your choice are as valid as when you made your choice?

An increased capacity to give and receive love may result in an ability to begin long-deferred projects. For example, a teacher may find it is suddenly no longer traumatic to learn to folk dance if he wants to learn so that he can dance with his pupils. The experiencing of dance and music can then be more pleasurable for the teacher learning to teach it, and for the teacher and children in the classroom, because the children really love it when the teacher is obviously a learner. The quality as well as the quantity of joy is likely to increase. And dance and music enrich social studies—and so on through the whole curriculum.

Potentiality implies something that is not here but may be within reach. It is not only in science and technology that we are uncovering new techniques. Much has been learned about how we feel and how we can feel in human relationships if we will reach out. "Affection and trust, belief in the unrealized potentialities of other human beings, call into existence not only what is waiting to bud, but what never could otherwise be; and others, responding in their turn, lift those who reach out to them to a level which they themselves could never have defined" (Murphy, 1958, p. 313). Such affection and trust build loving relationships in the classroom, relationships which lead to learning and becoming.

CONCLUSION

Each human desires learning and loving as an integral part of his life. I want to love and to be loved. I really dig learning as a way of finding out about myself in my world. Many forces militate against loving feelings and personal learning in our society. Large scale organization, bureaucracy, living patterns, growing impersonality, increasing specialization—these are some of the apparent blocks to intimacy and love. Often they take the form of injunctions: Keep off the grass, or Uncle Sam Wants You. But it is the individual who, aspiring to love and learn, also fears to take risks. From childhood, he has learned the ways to play it safe and has experienced substitutes for love, such as pastimes and games. Habit persists, and habitual patterns fill time and tend to push love aside or at least leave little time for love. The result is that few of us have as much loving and learning as we'd like as a vital part of our daily living. Yet we can appreciate, though sometimes only dimly, the bounty of love, the beauty of love, the opportunities of love. For love adds to and enriches every other aspect of life. Giving and receiving love adds new dimensions to each life. And there's more than enough to go around, for love, like the loaves and the fishes, grows with human capacity to experience it—it is truly boundless. Each time I learn something about one of my fellow humans, I learn to appreciate him more as one who faces the complex problems of being human. I am his loving and learning brother. Each teacher has daily opportunities to give and receive love in his personal and his professional life.

NOTES TO CHAPTER 2

One of the great psychologists I caught up with in the past two years is Gordon Allport. His *Becoming* (1955) is a gem, and his *Pattern and Growth in Personality* (1961) represents his mature conclusions on the individual's evolution in Western society. I borrowed from *Becoming* the example of Roald Amundsen.

I think that *Games People Play* (1964) is Eric Berne's best book, and I refer to it often. A book which carries the transactional analysis thinking several valuable miles down the road is *I'm OK—You're OK* by Thomas A. Harris (1969). I owe special debts to Berne and to Harris—their ideas permeate the entire book. Muriel James and Dorothy Jongeword, in *Born to Win* (1971), bring together TA and the gestalt ideas of Fritz Perls in a very readable book.

Eric Fromm has had a lot to say to us in the past thirty years. I regard *The Art of Loving* (1963) as a truly loving book because, without being patronizing, it talks of loving in ways most of us can understand.

Lois Murphy and collaborators wrote *The Widening World of Childhood* (1962) quite a few years ago. I was happy to see it reissued in paperback recently, for it goes into real depth in studying a group of children. I used ideas from pages 53–57 in this chapter. Harry Stack Sullivan was one of America's creative psychiatrists; his ideas have been enriched and updated by June Pearce and Saul Newton in *The Conditions of Human Growth* (1963).

In 1971, CRM Publications published an impressive new and comprehensive look at individual evolution in *Developmental Psychology Today*. A number of well known physicians, psychologists, psychiatrists, and child development specialists contributed to the book. On pages 139–143, there are reports on the relationship of stroking and child development. Research from Spitz, Bowlby, Goldfarb, and Skeels and Dye supports active physical loving by parents and parent substitutes. The recent research of Kagan (1972) on infants and children in a primitive Guatemalen village indicates that even infants who receive little stroking may not suffer irreversible damage to their mental and social development. This would encourage teachers to believe in the possibility of having a greater impact on the individual child.

Alice Miel has made many valuable contributions to teachers over the years. *More Than Social Studies,* coauthored by Peggy Brogan (1957), is one of her best. It offers a large number of useful case studies and shows teachers at work solving real daily problems in the classroom. The story of the teacher with cancer is found on pages 317–319.

Pitirim A. Sorokin in *The Ways and Power of Love* (1967) challenges us all to live our beliefs. If you can't read the whole book, at least read his preface. In it he tells how he came to write this book after being in prison in the Soviet Union.

As the world gets smaller, we get closer physically and psychologically to the Eastern world. One of the great thinkers of our generation, Alan Watts, points out some similarities and contrasts between Eastern and Western ideas and practices in *Psychotherapy East and West* (1969).

A good place to learn about new skills useful for the classroom is Mark Chesler and Robert Fox' book, *Role-Playing Methods in the Classroom* (1966). Role-playing is a vital part of *Gestalt Therapy Verbatim* by Frederick S. Perls (1969). Two books which tell of many experiences with children and youth in affective learning, are *Human Teaching for Human Learning* by George I. Brown (1971), and *Learning to Feel, Feeling to Learn* by Harold C. Lyon, Jr. (1971). Gerald Weinstein (1970) coedited *Toward Humanistic Education* with Mario Fantini. Many experiences of knowledgeable risk-taking by teachers are included in these books. Examples will appear later in this book.

Dorothy Lee has crossed various cultural boundaries in her private life and in her writing. I recommend her *Freedom and Culture* (1959), a collection of her studies of various cultures.

Among the periodicals I've used is *TIP (Theory Into Practice)*, published five times a year by the College of Education, Ohio State University. The issue of April, 1969, entitled "Teaching the Young to Love," contributed to my thinking. Robert E. Bills, of University of Alabama, wrote "Love Me to Love Thee" for this journal. Bills speaks of the evolution of love in the young infant and child and of ways others may assist a young person to improve his various abilities to accept and reciprocate in intimate and loving relationships.

Another magazine I often use is the *Phi Delta Kappan.* It is always filled with solid controversial articles and frequently contains pioneering recommendations.

Richard and Patricia Schmuck wrote a very helpful book called *Group Processes in the Classroom* (1971). An article which explores dimensions of feeling and behavior about physical attractiveness is one by Ellen Berscheid and Elaine Walster in the March 1972 issue of *Psychology Today.*

Education is *the way in which each person becomes aware of himself and his place in the world at large, and learns best how to conduct himself in it and contribute to it.*

Harold Taylor (1970)

Three

LEARNING AND LOVING

LEARNING: WHAT WE KNOW, AND WHAT WE DON'T KNOW

So many teachers are depressed in late May and June, because they are deeply uncertain about whether they have succeeded. Whatever the official curriculum demands and whatever the teacher sets out to accomplish, he realizes, at some level, the importance of individual growth in self-understanding. Perhaps many of his students do not feel truly OK about themselves and so cannot make real, sustained progress in academic or social skills. Memorizing a few arithmetic facts or the dates of some battles or the technical names for a few parts of the body does not make a man or a woman—and usually such information is forgotten in a short time. After all, we've known about the curve of forgetting for eighty years. So the teacher has good reason for doubting his success—unless he has reached and touched the feelings of his students.

We know so little about learning. For learning is internal, private, and idiosyncratic. Each child learns for himself, whether he is working in a group setting or alone. The teacher acts as a facilitator but never knows for sure *how* the individual learns. And often he does not know *whether* the individual learns. The teacher accepts the mystery, the tantalizing truth that *he can never know exactly how another individual learns.*

How do you learn? For example, how do you learn to play a game, such as a card game? A sport, such as bowling or volleyball? Be as thorough as you can in your description of what you believe happens in such cases.

Alan, an active learner, became fascinated with the eye and vision. He took apart and put together a plastic model of the eye many times. He asked a question of the optometrist who spoke to the class as the guest expert on vision. Alan drew a diagram of the way the eye takes in patterns of light and wrote an accompanying description—six sentences which contained a lot of facts. Ms. Holmes found that Alan had learned a great deal about the eye and human vision, but she couldn't be sure how his learning came about. A child learns, a child doesn't learn, and I as a teacher learn to live with mystery. If I can live comfortably with mystery, I can relax more often in the classroom. If I can relax, students can more easily relax and learn. As I relax and focus on my own learning, I can be loving to students more spontaneously and can encourage their loving behavior toward each other. Thus I can replace the May–June depression with confidence that my students are experiencing a loving environment in which their learning is greatly encouraged. And I'll have evidence of their learning as well, for in such an environment many students will show me their valued products—stories, diaries, pictures, poems, things which might never be produced in a conventional classroom where expressions of true feelings are avoided.

No matter how I learn, sometimes I forget how I learn and sometimes I overlook something obvious—as the following example shows. One spring I was preparing for a summer demonstration school to be held at an elementary school. One of the demonstration teachers planned to fire the Alpha rockets which the students would assemble from kits. I wanted the cooperation and advice of a college official, and this hasty note was the result:

Dear Mr. K.:

As part of a summer demonstration school for teachers, we will be firing small rockets at the John Reed Elementary School in Rohnert Park. I plan to contact the Rohnert Park Fire Department to arrange for their cooperation. If there are other procedures I should follow, I will appreciate your letting me know.

My alert secretary sent me the following note:

Do you think it would be appropriate for me to send a copy of this letter to the John Reed Elementary school, or did you plan this to be a surprise attack?

Unless I am sunk in apathy or seriously restricted by my own parsimony, I seek understanding of myself and my relationship to the world in which I live. Unless I am largely withdrawn, my mind reaches out through my senses for meaning: "Where do clouds come from?" "Why does Andy distrust all white people?" This is a desire for *closure*, for completion, for an understanding of a phenomenon which I want to make sense to me *now*.

My friend bats right-handed. One day he bats left-handed and makes a hit. I observe his behavior, and I infer that he has somehow learned to bat left-handed. What I cannot see is the process by which he achieved this. In so many instances, we note a short-term behavior change in another person and infer that learning has taken place. We test some students on school learning tasks in May and again in September, and often we note that their scores decline over the summer. Have they in fact *un*learned? They have forgotten many of the details memorized during the previous year(s) in school, for the tests measure remembrance of details rather than understanding and ability to deal with major ideas. Our concern must always be with pupil learning of more consequential things than facts. And I always seek better ways than tests to evaluate pupil progress.

In so many cases, what we observe when looking for learning is short-term behavior change: Eddie learned his spelling words this week. What we seldom see is whether the change persists. Even if my friend hits four home runs left-handed this summer and Eddie knows all those words on a test four months from now, I still am uncertain about persistence of change. For I am interested in long-run changes which truly affect the individual's ability to deal with real life problems. It's not enough to spell words correctly. What does Eddie *do* with his correctly spelled words? The world may disintegrate tomorrow. What Eddie and I have to do is act as responsible individuals to see that it doesn't. It's the long run that counts —real learning results in changed behavior in the long run. Such changed behavior may mean that man *has* a long run.

Yes, education has a mission—the liberation of individuals so that they can see and act now as human and humane members of the living community on our tiny planet. Many teachers feel uncertain about their own success as teachers, in part because they sense the futility of being able to teach Eddie his spelling words but being unable to help him to act on his own behalf as an aspirant to loving relationships with others. I can hear the counter argument: "Yes, but he must know his spelling words in order to get along in college, work, life." Nonsense, some of the poorest spellers can act very effectively on their own behalf and on behalf of others. I favor the learning of the three Rs as important tools for further learning, but teaching the three Rs in isolation (as is so often done) is unloving and futile.

It is precisely because we teachers set our sights so low and risk so little that we accomplish so little. To teach, I risk, I dare, I often lose, but when I win, I win something that is worth the effort and the risk—I help a person win himself.

As a teacher, when was the last time you risked, really took a chance on a relationship or an individual? Did the risk pay off? Are you learning to take additional risks? Write down an example and look at it a week later to see how it looks then.

Earl C. Kelley (1965) says that "*how a person feels is more important than what he knows.* This seems true because how one feels controls behavior." I am aware that each student I meet has his own dreams and his own goals which influence his contemporary feelings. If I can be a nonthreatening resource to him, he may tell me his goals and even his dreams. In this way, I modify my own goals as I interact with others. My own personal goals have a value to me partly independent of the goals of my students. But my goals as a teacher include helping students to reach their goals, and to do this I behave as an authentic person available to them. Because I know Maris wants to improve her skills as a dancer and an actress, I encourage her to read and write about these topics. So student goals in fact influence my teaching behavior. When I am dealing in this way with the reality of student needs, I feel more OK as a person and hence am better able to deal with my problems and to help students deal with theirs.

The child wishes to become competent. Even a two-year-old boy seizes a baseball and throws with all his might. This is natural. Each child sees the people and objects of the world around him as opportunities to *do*. A small child says, "A hole is to dig." An adult says, "That mountain is to climb." This is the expectant Child talking, a child that goes out to meet the world. The small child may be frightened of an electric can opener when it first buzzes. This is the scared Child who can cower in fear. When he notices Adult reality—that the buzz doesn't bite—he seeks to know the machine and control it, to extend his competence and power.

The child wishes to become a competent adult in his society. The child seeks to learn how to do things which he sees older children and adults doing—pushing a lawnmower, mixing ingredients to bake a cake, smoking, driving a car. The parent encourages the child's aspirations, gives him mini-lessons in how to do various things, gives him toy replicas of many adult machines—automobiles, stoves, candy and gum dispensers. At school, and in the neighborhood, the child meets others who aspire to adulthood in their culture. How can it be otherwise, for they know no other.

On Tuesday, Angela starts making progress on short division based on her breakthrough in learning her times tables up through the sevens. With the use of a tables chart such as this one, she discovered that multiplication and division are reciprocals. See Table 2.

Table 2
Basic Multiplication Facts

	1	2	3	4	5	6	7	8	9	10
1	1	2	3	4	5	6	7	8	9	10
2	2	4	6	8	10	12	14	16	18	20
3	3	6	9	12	15	18	21	24	27	30
4	4	8	12	16	20	24	28	32	36	40
5	5	10	15	20	25	30	35	40	45	50

She found that such examples as 28 divided by 4 and 4 times 7 are reciprocals. Delighted by this new power to manipulate numbers, Angela worked steadily and happily for several days. I glibly use the word *discovered*, but, as you will note, I am not confident that this is an accurate word. The closer we can come to accurate descriptions of pupil behavior, the better.

A couple of weeks later Angela's math group began to study long division. From the first, it was evident that Angela would have trouble. Her face had a closed look. Ms. Weldon reviewed short division, reviewed the reciprocal relationship, and reviewed also the estimating lessons which had preceded the introduction of long division. Many of the group members caught on pretty readily, but not Angela.

Ms. Weldon observed that Angela had mastered her times tables and thought perhaps the tables chart helped—but couldn't be sure. She noticed Angela's delight at understanding the multiplication–division reciprocity—but couldn't know how it came about. Ms. Weldon bumped against the reality that no amount of exhortation or practice could force the learning into Angela's head. A child learns for himself. Angela will learn in her own way, in her own time. The true teacher helps the child to feel that he is worthy enough as a person so that he will work to live up to this favorable image. At the same time, the teacher can hold on to his faith that the student will seek to extend his area of competence in many directions. Each teacher encounters students like Angela. Next time you do, notice your own behavior and also whether it seems to help.

LOVING AND LEARNING

The human child needs love. Spitz (1971) studied a group of babies who lived in an orphans' home where, because of a critical shortage of staff, the nurses did not have time to mother the babies, to show them real attention as individuals, to love them. Twenty-seven died in their first year of life, seven in their second year. Of the remainder, twenty-one were classified as hopelessly neurotic because of limited ability to respond to other humans in spite of proper physical care. Jerome Kagan's study (1972) of children in Guatemala questions the hypothesis supported by Spitz. The physical strokes of cuddling an infant can gradually be replaced by the verbal and symbolic strokes of words and letters. But grown-ups need physical strokes too.

The adult needs love. I am aware of the pull/push of eros to find out about things I see as interesting. Most of the things that interest me turn out to be people; I am naturally interested in my own species. The erotic pull/push impels me to act to find out about myself and other people. I am pulled by this aspect of love to find more love to experience. Kenneth Eble (1966, p. 3) says, "To learn is to love."

Carol, a high school senior with a history of promiscuity, was going steady with a young man who loved her. Her early feeling about the affair was that it was simply a further example of her own sluttishness. "I'm not OK, I'm a slut, and Tony, since I chose you, you must not be OK either." Her parents, she thought, had wanted her to do whatever she wanted. They did not communicate consistently with her about rules and boundaries, and so she had not learned to accept the importance of rules and boundaries nor how to live by them. Carol had liked being free. But because there was little interaction between herself and her parents, she wondered if they cared. She began to gamble with her life, to become promiscuous in relating to people long before she was sexually mature. She had a series of best friends, but the relationships often ended soon—and with little regret on her part and little understanding of why they failed. Tony saw that she needed boundaries and attempted to provide them. In their relationship, he learned to say "no." She was at first surprised by this, then indignant. Still later, she associated it with Tony's feelings of his OK-ness, and she saw it as another reason for appreciating him. She learned that he cared for her enough to provide leadership toward a more permanent and viable relationship.

Tony consistently behaved in loving ways toward Carol. As their relationship developed and Carol grew secure in his sustained love, she was able to regard herself as a changing person. Her feelings toward Tony changed to the point where she said to herself, "If my affair is to be truly loving, then I want to have a baby, our baby." She intentionally became pregnant. Tony asked Carol to marry him. Because she was feeling more OK about herself, she regarded his proposal as entirely separate from her pregnancy. She considered his proposal for a long while, and because her love for him had been growing, she accepted, and they married. The baby arrived as a wanted child and was helped to feel OK from his beginning.

Carol attended school while pregnant. The school administrators recognized that the young adult who is expelled from school can no longer be influenced by the school. They chose not to create problems by making a moralistic judgment. Throughout this episode, Carol's parents steadily supported her. They accepted their daughter's right to have an affair, to become pregnant, to decide independently on marriage. And encouraged her, regardless of her decision on marriage, to get proper health care during her pregnancy. They appreciated their son-in-law for himself and for what he'd done for their daughter. They had been aware, in vague ways, that she had not understood their true feelings about her growing up. They worked at building a new relationship with Carol and with Tony, and all four of them enjoyed the new child who seemed so right for them. Parents and grandparents loved as they learned more about each other, and they learned as they loved. Truly loving and learning are reciprocal.

Elliot Liebow, in *Tally's Corner*, describes the lives of black "streetcorner" men in a poor neighborhood in Washington, D. C. Black men and women in such an environment *hope* for much from each other—a successful marriage, a comfortable standard of living, competent parenthood—but *expect* much less. Their expectations mirror the reality of broken homes, poverty, and another generation of children turned out to think, "I'm not OK—you're not OK either." The education most urban blacks receive contributes little to their ability to achieve satisfying lives in our culture, because that education does little to build positive self-concepts and because other groups in our society tend to resent blacks regardless of education. I try to live my convictions of OK-ness by accepting each person as an individual with whom I may possibly enjoy a positive and even loving relationship. Many people find it difficult to wholly accept members of some racial, ethnic, or religious groups different from their own. The question is not "Am I prejudiced?" but "How do I deal with my prejudices?" How do you?

I need validation from others, to remind me that I'm OK and that my efforts on my own behalf frequently appear to others to be sensible. Here's where the teacher comes in: he strokes the child frequently by accepting the child as a person and by recognizing that what the child does makes sense. But, *especially* by recognizing that the child is an important person, the teacher encourages that fundamental self-regard which makes possible the child's investment of emotional energy in his own activities and in other people. I stroke others for being as well as for doing.

A class of sophomores was studying communication, using Miller's (1952) *Death of a Salesman* as the vehicle. The teacher invited one large and tough male student to work with him inside a circle of students. "I have 'it'," the teacher said, "and you try to get 'it' from me." The student entered into the spirit of the game, asking, arguing, demanding, threatening. Teacher and student put out their hands, palms against each other's, and push, and push, and it is the teacher who finally "gives." The teacher showed he was willing to risk and to lose in a physical encounter. So often, students feel that teachers are aloof and apart from real life. The boy, one of the least interested students before this activity, used the subsequent writing period to reveal some significant bits of himself—including the revelation that this teacher had helped him to see himself as a person of worth. Starting from this fundamental learning, he can find ways to become. Members of the class learned from observing this student-teacher interaction. They also gained insight into family relationships by considering the Willy Loman family. Each family, each individual has, after all, some tendency to listen to the injunction "Don't make it," and insight can come from open discussion of such a fact.

Ms. Holmes noticed that William spent free time playing with the gears in an old alarm clock which Ned, the college student aide, had brought into the classroom. William had taken the works out of the case so he could see better. Using a popsicle stick and a nail, he poked and pushed at every accessible part, trying to make the gears turn—but they wouldn't.

NED: Hm, won't work, huh? What have you tried?
WILLIAM: See, the darned old wheel won't push it, it's stuck. But I can't see anything in there—you know, like a rock or something.
NED: Yeah, a rock would stop it all right. But if there's no rock in there. ... Do you think that spring there has anything to do with what's wrong?
WILLIAM: I don't know ... maybe.

William began to examine the spring with greater care and Ned left him to this activity.

Ned appreciated the value of mystery. He declined to explain to William how the clock worked or how he might make it work. He realized that William might try harder because he was faced with a puzzle. Ned showed loving respect for William and loving responsibility toward his own role as a facilitator of learning. Ned had noticed that William functioned poorly in a competitive situation. A situation in which William was pitted against another student killed his incentive and dimmed his curiosity. But when William was working alone on a project only he was attending to, he often put forth some effort, although it was not always sustained. Patience, Ned found, helped. Patience proves one's loving respect for the integrity of another.

Love recognizes that the real competition in learning is with one's self. For if people are indeed the heart of curriculum, then we will not permit content or procedures in our schools to tear down children. Arbitrary curriculum ignores the realities of individual differences; it says, for example, "These are the math or social studies or reading skills to be mastered at grade four." And such a statement has only indirect relationship to the individual child. While curriculum specialists labor to device a curriculum that is "best" or "necessary" for William, the loving teacher says: "I respect you, William, and I know you will select worthwhile activities to work on." In the same vein, the loving teacher, rather than pitting William against others in the class, says, "William, I value what you do, and I will help you with it whenever I can." This respects William's integrity and shows respectful love of William as a person.

In the early years, the child looks to his parents for leadership, for clues as to how to move toward independence as an evolving individual. During the school years, the teacher becomes a big factor. Dinkmeyer (1967, pp. 310–316) wrote, "Evidence is mounting that a number of children learn primarily because of the relationships they develop with the significant adults in their environment. The teacher becomes the significant adult in the classroom. ... Teachers must constantly be aware that their goal is to help shape the child's concept of self as an achiever." The achieving child, instead of listening to injunctions he heard as a younger child, adopts standards for himself and grows toward self-direction.

What is it about your teaching that you would like to change? I invite you to write it down and save it, and I'll come back to the same point later in the book.

A high school principal wondered what to do with Randall. Randall was seventeen, healthy, and generally pleasant to work with, but he really couldn't hack an academic program. He had had some troubles with the shop programs—an accident he caused had frightened him, and the shop teachers were doubtful he'd succeed because of the continuing fear. The principal asked the custodian if Randall could spend part of the day helping him. The custodian soon found that what Randall really liked was gardening. So for two years Randall spent several periods a day as the assistant gardener for the school. He graduated and became a gardener for the city parks department. He benefited from the loving interest shown him by the principal and the custodian and by their respect of him as a unique individual entitled to be himself. Randall might have gone on to be a success as a shoe repairman or as an insurance salesman. The point is he was helped to feel OK about himself, and this encouraged him to make efforts on his own behalf.

Each of us has many potentialities for learning. All of them function better in a free atmosphere. Freedom starts with me. I may indeed be in an environment, for example, a place of work, in which my freedom is seriously limited. In America today, my personal freedom is still very extensive, although my awareness of that freedom is crucial. I am aware that, to a considerable extent, I am as free as I feel. Right now, I feel free enough to write, to express my real feelings in order to communicate with others. The real jails for so many people are of their own making. Sunk in apathy, they can't muster the energy to do more than daydream about a life they'll never lead. Yet each of us can learn and can grow.

I remember a six-year-old girl—Brigitte—from Belgium who arrived in first grade with exactly two words of English: *yes* and *no*. The resourceful teacher asked a very quiet but capable girl to be Brigitte's "big sister." This avoided making the girl a class pet, as she might have become if lionized by the more ebullient girls. It assured her the help she needed, but only what she needed. This arrangement produced a valuable by-product: It helped the "big sister" develop a more comprehensive self-concept, to better appreciate her own worth. And the young Belgian girl flourished. This is flexibility in the service of people. When loving teachers help without doing it *to* or *for* pupils, the freedom and competence of everyone grow. Others of us might have tried another way of getting Brigitte to learn English and to become involved with her classmates. Are there games which students can create for themselves to help each other to learn?

Mr. Landon took over a fourth grade class in the middle of the year. His ways of teaching differed from those of the former teacher, and he changed from workbooks to more varied materials and from a rigid schedule to a flexible one. These changes engendered a good deal of anxiety among many of the students. Mr. Landon decided to go back to the former teacher's ways of doing things for a time, and then to introduce his ways gradually. Thus he took a double risk: that he could eventually change the program to one he liked, and that the children would accept him as a teacher as well as they had his predecessor. He compromised in hopes of achieving his goals later. Over a period of time, he was able to help the children see that news reporting and participating in a Red Cross project were social studies just as much as reading of the text was. He helped the children discover that oral reading of the text was not the most efficient way to cover the material. He succeeded in both his efforts: establishing himself as the teacher, and altering the program. For resourceful teachers, there is always more than one way to reach one's destination, but there is likely to be some risk involved. I recognize the risk-taking involved in working with other learners.

Mr. Landon remembered how he had felt when he had to adapt to army living, and so he could imagine the feelings of the pupils when they were faced with his imposed changes. He shared his learning from the past by acting, by going back to the program with which the pupils were comfortable. He could feel the easing of tension when he did so. This set the stage for carrying out his long-range goals, for he could see ahead to possible ways of leading the children to accept a new system. He combined his wishes for a better program with his will to bring it about—and brought it about. Each teacher can imagine such improvements in the learning environment for children, and each has genuine opportunities to bring them about. I lean into a future I can make better. Mr. Landon showed care for the children in the class, a care that is one important aspect of love. When I love, I care and I show it.

Ms. Lacey's combination class in a crowded school contained fifth and sixth graders. Sixth graders expressed their resentment of the fifth graders by forming a club from which the younger students were excluded. The teacher's initial reaction was parental: those sixth graders are wrong. She battled the club, but she also attempted to reduce the hostility between the two groups by allowing open discussion in which pupils and teacher expressed their feelings. One day, however, she expressed a different view than she had before: acceptance of the idea of a club for sixth graders. This revealed her ability as an authority figure to change her mind. The pupils asked to have a series of talk sessions in which they ventilated their feelings. During those sessions, the teacher accepted what each pupil said. The group discussion seemed to help lower the intensity of the hostile and hurt feelings and led to the expression of more positive feelings. To a large extent, the hostile reactions disappeared. As a proof of their newly enlightened attitude, the sixth graders invited the fifth graders to join the club. The teacher showed her ability in facing this situation as a problem to be solved and proved her flexibility by changing strategy when her first strategy failed. She revealed her strength and security as an adult sure of her OK-ness in the group sessions in which she encouraged free expression of feelings, some of which she had previously rejected.

Ms. Lacey showed responsibility toward the school and toward the children. In her view, she was responsible for making the combination class succeed in spite of the problems encountered. Her responsibility also embraced the feelings of students. She imagined the resentment of the sixth graders, the hurt feelings of the left-out fifth graders. She was able to overcome her indignation and find a way out for all of them, an inclusive fraternity of learners. She behaved responsibly on behalf of all of the children, and her love for them paid off in good human relations in the classroom. By revealing herself as a person, she showed the students that it is OK for them to reveal their true selves. When the sixth graders recognized the extent of the positive feelings of the younger group about being in the class, they responded in kind by offering the fifth graders equal partnership. Such revelation of feelings, under responsible teacher leadership, often brings out the best in pupils: feelings of acceptance and inclusion of others. Such responsible leadership makes love come to life in the classroom. When I love, I am responsible and I live responsibly.

Mr. Strauss shook his head to throw off his discouragement as he walked toward the lunchroom. His fourth period English class, mostly juniors, was studying Shakespeare's *Hamlet*. Students had been asked to read Act II the night before and to be prepared to discuss it. Mr. Strauss had asked many questions this morning but had gotten few satisfactory answers. In desperation, he had asked the students to read the play aloud, with students taking the various parts. Even that hadn't been too successful. Half the class was college prep, so both interest and application could normally be expected of them. At lunch Mr. Strauss shared his discouragement with Ms. Leavelle, a member of the English department. She listened, then drew a distinction between a question-and-answer session and a genuine discussion. In the former the teacher asks almost all the questions—it's his ball game—while in the latter many students too may ask, ponder, contribute ideas, and exchange views. After considering this for a few minutes, they went on to other topics. A little later Ms. Leavelle said: "Walt, several of my kids felt that there was no chance for them to decide things for themselves at school—even their courses are set down in the catalog. And in classes they usually have term paper topics and almost all assignments set by the teacher. When students start making some choices for themselves, they have a different spirit. As they gain respect for themselves, they lose interest in bugging each other during the quiet reading time. I feel like it's a breakthrough, the classes are so much more fun."

Ms. Leavelle had learned that respect for individuals yields many dividends. More of her students worked harder because they had been given the chance to invest something of themselves in their education. When they did, they got a lot of psychological payoff, so each was ready again to come back actively into the encounter with learning. She noticed that students showed her a different kind of respect, a personal interest in what she thought and felt, rather than mere deference to her position. She came to enjoy this and to respect herself more too. When I love, I respect and show my respect.

Ms. Gerber found that white and black students in her tenth grade English class clashed. There was definite racial hostility, although it was expressed in inhibited ways. Ms. Gerber had belonged to an encounter group for a year and a half. She had learned a great deal about herself while in it and felt much more comfortable in her various teaching roles as a result of it. "Why couldn't we have an encounter group in the class?" she thought. She talked it over with the leader of her own encounter group, did some additional reading, and formulated a plan which she took to her principal. At first he opposed the idea.

"Joanne, there's a lot of prejudice these days about this sort of thing. It sounds like 'sensitivity training.' Some people would say sensitivity or encounter equals feeling which equals touching which equals sex. Others would say it's a kind of therapy, and they're just naturally opposed to that. Either way, there's bound to be opposition." But he didn't flatly refuse to consider it.

Ms. Gerber did some more thinking on the subject and talked it over with the students. She wanted them to fully appreciate what they would and would not do, and she wanted to relieve their anxieties as well as her own before any encountering began. She encouraged students to express their fears about it in their journals (private between each student and the teacher) and in class discussion. This resulted in a number of agreements and ground rules that the class decided upon in order to avoid getting into problems they and their teacher saw as beyond them.

When Ms. Gerber went back to the principal with this set of ground rules and with a letter she'd prepared to send to parents, he reiterated his fears of parent objections. But, seeing that the class had anticipated such objections and had plans to avoid them, he agreed to permit the class to encounter. "Thirty-eight sophomores—Joanne, won't you ever just teach grammar?" was the principal's parting shot as she left his office.

Ms. Gerber sent a mimeographed letter to each parent explaining her plan of operations and inviting parents to phone or visit prior to the time the class was to encounter. For three weeks, this class functioned as an encounter group. Because the class had prepared for the experience and because the teacher provided loving leadership, the encountering proved successful. All the students participated enthusiastically, and none of the parents complained. And the students gained understanding of one another, so that they were able to function much better for the balance of the year —as individuals and as a group of active learners. Ms. Gerber, a free person, extended the freedom of every member of that class. She risked in a relatively unstructured situation and showed respect for and faith in students. By actively putting her love into operation in the classroom, she made a contribution to the capacities of every one of the students.

Today teachers recognize that there are many practical ways to learn which might not have been considered practical in 1965 or 1968. Ms. Gerber's encounter group is an example. When I love students, I stretch my own thinking, my own imagining, about how students may learn and about how I may learn.

Group Processes in the Classroom by Richard and Patricia Schmuck

(1971) contains many classroom-tested techniques for dealing with the type of problem Ms. Gerber and her class worked on in the encounter group. Each person seeks to be effective in interpersonal relationships. In the words of Arthur Jersild (1955), "in the sphere of the self, each person, almost from birth, is a pioneer; he begins where primitive man began. He alone, through personal experience, can shape the substance of the self. He can know the limits of his powers only by trying them out; he can know the joy of mastery, self-help, and self-assurance only through putting himself to the test; he can savor the meaning of sorrow or fear or disappointment, hope, anger, pride, or shame only through firsthand experience."

Each pioneer has the potential of becoming an effective learner and lover who enjoys life among his fellows and recognizes the total natural environment as having value. I am *of* nature; I estrange myself from it at my peril. It takes courage to reject the apparent wave of the future in which many of our actions can be replaced by mechanical and electronic devices. Without action, without initiative, we will cease to be human, to reaffirm the elemental human values of care, respect, and responsibility— all based on knowledge. We risk because it is an affirmation of our humanity. Many have succumbed to the apathy-breeding mechanistic system which promises everything—everything but human dignity. I risk by inviting other human beings to risk. I risk by relating the close relationships of loving and learning along with their uncertainty and complexity. If you will join me, we can rebuild schools into environments which promote loving and learning together.

NOTES TO CHAPTER 3

One of the finest books for teachers is *The Authentic Teacher* by Clark Moustakas (1966). Moustakas has worked for years collecting examples of teachers' successes and failures, as well as cases in which it is hard to tell whether the teacher has succeeded. *More Than Social Studies* by Alice Miel and Peggy B. Brogan (1957) also reports many cases of pupil–teacher interaction which are worthy of consideration. I borrowed from both these books in this chapter.

A moving account of the evolution of a mentally ill child to health is found in Virginia Axline's *Dibs* (1967). A somewhat similar story has been told by Beulah Parker in *My Language Is Me* (1962). We need statistical studies of large numbers of students, especially longevity studies, so we can get better impressions of evolutionary directions. But we also must have the intimate reports of individual cases which help us face real children in the flesh, something an elaborate statistical study seldom does.

I have greatly enjoyed George Dennison's *The Lives of Children* (1969). Dennison and his compatriots at the First Street School created, with their students, a rich environment for loving and learning. Particularly when thinking of the minority student and the rejected student, consult Dennison.

Margaret L. Clark, Ella Erway and Lee Beltzer, in *The Learning Encounter* (1971), have brought together a series of actual class experiences which they tape-recorded. Verbal, nonverbal, and perceptual behavior and communication games are featured. A sample game (see pp. 130–131) starts with "My grandmother went to California, and in her trunk she packed. . . ."

Stu Jones and Joanne Gerber made generous contributions to this chapter. Stu allowed me to use an abbreviated and edited report of a client he assisted. Joanne contributed her experience with the encounter group and also critiqued incidents that I had recorded involving high school students.

Two psychologists whose books have been helpful are Sidney Jourard (*The Transparent Self* 1964,) and Everett L. Shostrom (*Man, the Manipulator* 1968,). Jourard says (p. v), "man can attain to health and fuller functioning only insofar as he gains in courage to be himself among others."

Another book which I use extensively is *Identity and Teacher Learning* by Robert C. Burkhart and Hugh H. Neil (1968), valuable for good ideas, amusing illustrations, and for conveying positive feelings toward teaching. I also appreciate Neil Postman and Charles Weingartner's *Teaching as a Subversive Activity* (1969) and George Leonard's *Education and Ecstasy* (1968).

Every teacher owes a debt to John Holt, for schools will never be the same as they were before the impact of his writing and lecturing and other propagandizing for the humanizing of schools. *How Children Fail* (1964), *How Children Learn* (1967), and *What Do I Do Monday?* (1970) are all great books. John Holt constantly gives us examples of how love is effective in the classroom as a means of showing respect for students and helping teachers gain more self-respect.

Alexander Frazier has made many valuable contributions to American education; one of them is *The New Elementary School* (1968).

One of the most useful of the collections of articles on learning and teaching I know about is *Readings in Elementary Teaching*, edited by Glen Hass, Kimball Wiles, Joyce Cooper, and Dan Michalak (1971). Among the contributors to this volume are many distinguished authors. Jerome Kagan has done a new review of child evolution and learning called *Understanding Children* (1971).

The finest book on educational psychology that I know is *Psychology Applied to Teaching* by Robert F. Biehler (1971). It contains a vast store of information and many references to and contributions from original sources. Biehler encourages a very active involvement by the reader. I borrowed the idea of response places from him.

Gerald T. Gleason edited a collection of articles on *The Theory and Nature of Independent Learning* (1970) which presents background material to support the teaching-learning environment I advocate.

Games and simulations are being used more and more widely at all levels of education. Alice K. Gordon's *Games for Growth* (1970) tells about games available, especially at upper elementary and high school levels.

A recent book which contributes to teaching and also to related people-oriented professions is *Helping Relationships—Basic Concepts for the Helping Professions* by Arthur Combs, Donald Avila, and William Purkey (1971). This is an important and compassionate book.

Robert Sande has done a series of three films for BFA on guidance for the seventies. The one I like best is "Kids, Parents, and Pressures," a down-to-earth film dealing with contemporary issues involving students of ages eleven to eighteen and their teachers and parents. Concrete and very usable techniques are illustrated.

On the subject of love and its relationships to learning, I find *Love* by Rosemary Haughton (1971) to be instructive. She tries "to build up in the reader's mind a certain sensitivity to the occurrence of love" (p. 166).

Robert Coles, writer, psychiatrist, activist, has made many valuable contributions to educational thinking. Among them is *The Desegregation of Southern Schools: a Psychiatric Study* (1963). He notes that the strongly enraged person—teacher or student—is relatively rare in the south. We have, he says, "eloquent testimony to our stubborn ability as humans to survive nature's accidents and disasters as well as the folly of man's making" (p. 25). This is partly because, "Above all, a teacher heals." (See Paul Brandwein, *Notes on Teaching the Social Sciences: Concepts and Values* (1970).)

The Affective Development Program of the Philadelphia public schools produced several very interesting films on the nature of a city, personal expression through drama, and intergroup relations and communication. The titles are *Prelude, A Lot of Undoing to Do, Making Sense, Build Yourself a City*, and *It's Between the Lines*. For more information, see Terry Borton, *Reach, Touch, and Teach* (1970, pp. 192–198).

The striving to find a meaning in one's life is a primary motivational force in man.

Charles Frankel (1955)

Humanness results from being raised by people. . . . Since we live in a grossly irrational society, it is a part of the parents' responsibility to teach the child the rules of the game.

June Pearce and Saul Newton
(1963)

Four

I LEARN IN MANY WAYS

Both loving and learning are active processes. The man says, "My wife doesn't show me any affection." To this the TA group leader may say, "I hear you saying you want her to change." This reminds the man that waiting for the other person to change is likely to be futile. The true existential questions are: What am I willing to do to encourage or facilitate the different behavior I desire from another? Or: How long am I willing to wait for her/him to change? Indeed the other person may change, but I can't sit around hoping for that to happen. There are too many opportunities waiting for me which I can enjoy without waiting for anyone. I am in command and I've got living to do!

Each of us finds ways to love and learn. Each of us goes through many experiences, many approaches, with some successes and some failures. We continue to seek new ways. At fifty, I am finding out a lot about myself and ways I can achieve things I've yearned for for years. For example, I am learning to overcome the injunction, "Don't be close" and to see the beauty in more people than ever before.

1.   *I learn in part by imitating: learning involves my awareness of the perfor-*

mance of others. I notice and imitate, often unconsciously, behaviors I recognize as providing me with good models.

Each of us began in large part as an imitator, especially of parents or parenting ones. In addition to stuffing objects in his mouth, the infant watches and listens—and imitates (see Roe, 1971, pp. 165–166). The experiments with infants reported in Chapter 2 show the inherent desires of the tiny human being to reach out to his world and to be a part of it. We probably have been underestimating human potential in many ways at various ages, but we don't need to continue doing so. The studies also show that the young child has at least some understanding that he is responding because he is human and because of the presence of other humans in his universe.

What kind of model are you for your students to emulate? What phrase do you hear coming "back home" from your students? Are there things you notice your students doing without any help from you? Do you notice the influence of the peer group on individuals?

Nursery school children learn by imitating. Children who were given an aggressive adult model displayed more aggressive behavior afterwards. This was especially true of boys imitating an aggressive male adult. Both boys and girls acted aggressively after exposure to an aggressive female model, but to a lesser extent. Clearly, sex role models were already differentiated by these children: a girl was supposed to behave like " a young lady," and the aggressive adult female was *not* a model girls could readily accept.

Imitative behavior accounts for a good deal of learning. Some boys eager to improve their baseball skills will spend nonplaying time watching others play, anxious to see examples of skilled play which they can emulate. Girls imitate the hair styles found in magazines or on the heads of other girls. Miller and Dollard found that imitation is itself a learned behavior tendency; without the learning of the tendency, imitation does not occur. Children differ enormously in both their exposure to models which they could emulate and in their tendency to imitate models they see. The child with very passive parents who, for example, spend many evening and weekend hours in front of the television set, has very little help in learning imitating skills for activity—and may tend towards passivity.

Yet the child and the adult may almost always break out of a pattern of inactivity by seeking and imitating new models. In kindergarten, Rafael began to look around to see whom he wished to imitate. By second grade, he was choosing boys he considered successful, especially in sports.

Sara imitated Marlene in various operations at the hot dog stand during her first days on the job. She noticed how Marlene wrote down orders, called out to the short order cook the items to be cooked, mixed the drinks, and put napkins and utensils on the tray. She observed the way the other girls used the cash register and how they cleaned up the kitchen area, and she modeled her own actions after theirs.

It is important to notice that some children do not imitate as much, especially at particular times of their lives. Some will express the "Please, mother, I'd rather do it myself!" feeling, and they may break a few dishes, or even a bone, in the process of doing it their own way. When I love pupils, I notice which ones imitate and look for clues as to how they imitate, so that I can encourage successful imitative behavior. I also imitate constructive pro-people behavior myself, so that I stand as a model to be imitated by my pupils.

Did you imitate anyone when you first began teaching? Do you still imitate the same people?

2.   *I learn in part by practice. I vary in my need for practice.*

Sara learned by practice to put the right amount of milk in the container—so that she would end up with a full-measure milkshake but there would be no excess for the blender to throw around the counter. Rafael practiced throwing the ball from second to first base until it became a smooth performance and until he became the best fielding second baseman in fifth grade.

But in the classroom the student is asked to repeat many experiences over and over again. A fourth grade teacher complained to the principal that a boy declined to finish his arithmetic. When the principal came to the classroom to see what was happening, he found that the student had completed twelve out of thirty-six long division problems, had checked and found them all correct, and had said to himself, "How many do I have to do to show that I know how?" An arbitrary assignment requiring a lot of repetition may be largely dysfunctional. This is one reason self-selection can be so functional. The student really wants to know, to accomplish, to master. Only he, looking out through his twin turrets, knows how much he understands and what he still needs to understand—and his comprehension of his understanding is often piecemeal. How can another person understand what the learner himself only partly comprehends? (See Tanner and Lindgren, 1971, pp. 143–145, 198–199.)

When I see the child declining to practice, I figure he has a reason. Perhaps he's resting. Perhaps he's asserting his independence of an injunction he heard a long time ago or recently. The teacher who reiterates "Do it so you'll succeed as an adult" may find that the refrain progressively loses its potency as the student tunes in to his own feelings. This is exactly what a substantial number of people under twenty-five have learned to do in the past ten years. They are learning to love themselves and in doing so they are loving more and more of their fellow men. And they are learning a lot about themselves in the process.

When I love pupils, I notice which ones need practice and how much practice they need, and I encourage practice which will lead the individual to independent success in learning. Do you keep track of how much practice each student usually needs to master a particular thing? Spaced practice? Much repetition?

3. *I learn by self-initiated efforts.*

Each child brings a great deal with him when he first comes to school. He knows many words and can express himself in at least one language, perhaps two. Twins often come to school with a private language in addition to English. In a practical sense, the pupil knows quite a bit about people and how to get along with them. The extent of the child's knowledge is seldom known. And yet when we present the child with curricular experiences, we usually make assumptions about what and how much he already knows. Usually we underestimate what the child knows and what he is capable of understanding. We also underestimate his abilities to make learning efforts independently.

The efficacy of self-initiated efforts is supported by a number of research studies, which show that teachers who encourage self-initiated efforts by pupils get more such pupil efforts, and that the pupil with a strong self-concept ventures forth in his world. When he ventures, it increases the likelihood of his learning. The pupil's curiosity and interests lead him, when he has freedom, to find out for himself, in some sense to learn. The pupil with many opportunities to work independently develops self-confidence and skill in the areas in which he works independently. Specifically, pupils allowed to explore do explore.

To the extent that I feel free, to the extent that I feel worthy, to the extent that I do feel OK, I venture out to love and learn in the world around me. As a teacher, I take initiative in many ways.

Midway through the year, an overload in the fourth grade classes at

Grant School was alleviated by creating a combination third-fourth grade class. Ms. Holmes, who had been Nick's third grade teacher up to that time, took the new combination class, and Nick was assigned to Ms. Rogers' third grade for the rest of the year. The following conversation about Nick took place at lunch between Ms. Holmes, Ms. Rogers, and Ms. Wagstaff:

ROGERS:	I just don't know what to do about that Nick Carbone. Everyone else in my low group has ....
HOLMES:	He was improving in my room.
ROGERS:	Sometimes he's just like—like a nothing! If he'd only try, he might learn. ...
WAGSTAFF:	I had Nick in second grade. I found that going to see his mother helped, seeing his home environment. I figured out some of his behavior during that year.
HOLMES:	When did you find time for that?
WAGSTAFF:	I made time for it. And I discussed Nick with the principal, who suggested some techniques for helping him. I found that Nick needs a lot of love, but less direct talking to him or at him—then he will try on his own.
ROGERS:	Well, you may feel you're qualified, but I'm no trained psychologist. What this school needs is a full time psychologist to handle these kinds of kids.
WAGSTAFF:	Oh, I couldn't agree with you more, Margaret, but we don't have the psychologist.
ROGERS:	Well, I'm willing to try, but what can I do by myself?
HOLMES:	He likes my volunteer aide. You can send him down to my room every Wednesday from 9 to 11:30 in the morning when Ned's there.
WAGSTAFF:	I've tried several things. I often praised Nick for what he did —then he'd do more. Talking with his former teachers, consulting with the principal, visiting with his mother, gave me insight. I even got to talk to his dad once at open house. I kept notes on Nick's behavior, a kind of anecdotal record. It paid off several times—I came to realize what he was feeling and sometimes I could help. Come over this afternoon and I'll show you the notes I kept on Nick.

Ms. Wagstaff and Ms. Holmes recognize the reality of *now:* here's Nick as he is, and we don't have the school psychologist we need. So I deal with *now, as I can deal with it,* using my abilities to build toward a different future. That future will be different for me as well as for Nick. I intend it to be so. I accept the mystery: I will never know exactly how that different future will turn out for Nick. Loving respect for the student and loving responsibility toward him require me to make effort on his behalf —which is also effort on my own behalf. Helping a student makes me feel more OK: a person who helps others is an OK person.

4. I vary in my ability to respond to learning opportunities; I learn in spurts. I am aware of variations in my abilities to be aware of, to tune in to, to use, and to apply tools and methods of learning for my own benefit.

Physical change and change in circumstances alter one's pattern of learning to function within one's life space. A professional athlete stricken with polio learned to live in a wheelchair and to develop alternate talents for earning a living. Some individuals go through noticeable stages in their learning, others rather quickly arrive at a plateau where they remain for years. Many jobs in contemporary America call for rather rapid learning of specific clusters of skills (for example, operating a billing machine or installing a telephone), but then there may be relatively little demand for the person so trained to advance to new or more advanced skills. The rapid evolution of our economy is likely to alter this pattern for many workers in the near future. More efficient production methods will decrease the number of man-hours required and will provide more people with more time for leisure activities.

Variations in perception of a problem, in approach to a task, and in practice and persistence in working on it characterize the pupils I see in classes. Rodney loafs on Monday but turns out a lot on Wednesday, while Wilma works steadily through each day and each week. When I love pupils, I notice the ways in which they work and plan my operations within the classroom to make myself optimally available to those who need my help, and to be ready to help according to the immediate needs of the pupils. Because I do not lecture and I give whole-class or group assignments infrequently, I have time to observe and help those who need it. More on this later.

Communication between teacher and students can be encouraged by student journals. Students of many grade levels, beginning with grade two or grade three, are invited to write each day in a journal or diary. The teacher agrees that he'll read each journal and respond in some appropriate way. Teachers of high school students can stagger the reading of journals so that Period one and Period two are read on Monday, Period three and Period four on Tuesday, and so on. Each student's journal is private between him and his teacher. The writing serves many useful purposes: catharsis for students, varied writing practice, feedback for the teacher, a source for curriculum (especially for information about individual student interests and needs), and a possible way of reaching intimacy which enables more subtle teacher assistance to the learning efforts of the student. For example, the teacher who finds out through the journal that a student still obeys an injunction such as "Don't be important" can find ways of letting the student experience the feeling of importance.

Students in the 1970's, more than ever before, need to learn how to learn, to learn various ways to learn. Only then will they be able to train or retrain for new jobs, many of which have not yet been created, some of which have not yet been imagined. For some individuals, retraining or totally new training may be necessary two or three or more times within a working life begun in 1975 or 1985. Even more important, I help students realize that learning to learn is a way to expand freedom to be and become because it increases options. Learning about hobbies and recreational activities may be even more important than job-oriented learning.

5.   *Serendipity and the Aha! phenomenon.*

I got the idea for this section in the shower one morning. Each of us gets ideas at various times and places. Ideas are where you find them. Learning as I've described it is manifest when the individual behaves in accordance with his understanding of his situation. Yet there may be moments of insight when one comprehends something that had—until that moment—been unclear. Each of us experiences such moments—the second grader who realizes why he "carries" over from the one's column to the ten's column, the medical researcher who grasps a new relationship of an enzyme to the absorption of a particular nutrient. We all figure out things, sometimes slowly, sometimes with a rush. It is the individual with the prepared mind, the mind used to loving and learning, who is ready to utilize data in new and creative ways for his own benefit and for the benefit of others. Eureka!

6.   *I seek the most loving possibility in each situation. I know that, while I may perceive a number of possible ways to behave, I will choose one—and thus eliminate alternative possibilities. The fact that I cannot know how "it might have been" if I had chosen a different alternative is one of the mysteries I live with.*

Mr. Landon looked back into his past to seek understanding. He used that understanding in dealing with the anxiety of pupils whose program he had disrupted. He reverted to his predecessor's program to restore the psychological comfort of the pupils, meanwhile planning ways to introduce his own program a little at a time. He could have dealt with the situation differently; one way would have been by revealing himself verbally as a means of including the pupils in a new partnership. Part of my becoming is becoming transparent, open to others. From the beginning, I let pupils in on who I am and what my goals are. That way, I am not working on any hidden agenda. Pupils know what I seek, and thus they are free to tell me what they seek, both in public discussion and in private conferences. This helps to make education a personal venture for each of us. I seek my goals, each pupil seeks his goals. My transparency has one further advantage. It encourages pupils to reveal themselves so that more of our discussions, public and private, deal with real wishes and real aspirations. I allow individuals to free themselves as they become more uniquely themselves. Thus I help each individual to develop self-love.

Mr. Landon dealt with the disrupted classroom situation one way. I would deal with it differently. You might deal with it a third way—and still give students freedom and opportunity to learn as they deal with their own mysteries. Each of us acts, although we cannot know the results of the alternative ways of acting.

7.   Cognitive and affective learning.

The dichotomy between cognitive and affective learning is a paper tiger. As a whole person, I engage in complex relationships within overlapping environments. How can I be, at any one moment, wholly rational or wholly emotional? I am both emotional and rational. When I consider how to teach a math lesson tomorrow, I consider content, technique, and kids. In all three of these areas, my emotions are engaged. I choose, for example, to deal lightly or not at all with division of fractions—because division of fractions has hardly any usage in real life. Other teachers will teach division of fractions for what seem to them good reasons. Similarly, I have both cognitive and affective considerations when I decide which teaching techniques to use with individual children.

Traditional formal education in the western world focuses on cognitive learning. This includes the teaching of basic skills—such as the three Rs, and bodies of facts and their relationships—such as botany as the systematic study of plants and their life cycles in their environments. This learning serves a number of purposes pretty well. Knowledge that has been gathered by experts in a field can be put together and presented in organized patterns designed to help the recipients discern basic generalities useful in dealing with the real world. To plant or not to plant, that is the question. A student of botany can apply his knowledge to plant, transplant, graft, feed, prune, and harvest plants in ways designed to serve human purposes and to help plant species survive.

But any effort to focus exclusively on cognitive learning overlooks an entire spectrum of human experience which has an immense bearing on what is learned and on what effect the learning has on the individual. I still recall a few words of Latin memorized over thirty years ago. But I also remember that my Latin teacher was a fun person, a person who really cared about each student. Cognitively, I memorized little Latin; affectively, I grew fond of a man who cared. Overall, I liked him and tolerated Latin because of him.

Many teachers at all levels from nursery school through to graduate study are afraid of affective involvement. It seems poorly organized: what do we do with it? It seems unpredictable: how can we interpret it? Above all, it seems threatening: how can we control it? The feelings of human beings do present each teacher with a great potential for ambiguous difficulties. Yet feelings offer the means to integrate human learning and to help individuals achieve a wholeness altogether beyond the limits of strict cognitive comprehension.

In studying life patterns of the Netsilik, in a segment of a course entitled "Man, A Course of Study," students' emotions were deeply involved. Some actions of the Netsilik were repugnant to the students because that behavior was unlike our way of life (killing animals in an almost public way), and other activities were distasteful (eating raw fish or fish eyes). Yet the students appreciated the humanness of the Netsilik. And to a considerable extent, the students realized the bitter necessities of survival in an environment that differs so greatly from the ones we are accustomed to. The films and the discussions led to an integrated feeling about the Netsilik, as people, that went far beyond the usual "compare and contrast" of social studies instruction.

This and much more is found in *Fantasy and Feeling in Education* by Richard M. Jones (1968). In this book, Jones challenges teachers to utilize the affective domain along with the cognitive, to achieve a different level in the quality of what the student learns about human experience and his involvement in it.

Love endows human relationships with increased worth. As beauty is in the eye of the beholder, love is in the heart of the lover. A collection of loving people in a classroom is able to see clearly what is important and valuable, and what is for them worth doing. What is worth doing for me is learning, creating, and loving.

NOTES TO CHAPTER 4

One of the most valuable books for elementary teachers is *Curriculum for Today's Boys and Girls*, edited by Robert S. Fleming (1963). On the flyleaf is a bill of rights for kids which comes from Gladys Andrews, who also contributes a chapter on releasing creativity. Alice Keliher, Fannie Shaftel and Jeannette Veatch also contribute. Another worthwhile collection for teachers is *Individualizing Instruction*, edited by Ronald D. Doll (1964).

Alexander Frazier has written or edited many valuable books over the years. Two of them which contributed to my thinking in writing this chapter are *New Insights and the Curriculum (1963)* and *Open Schools for Children* (1972), both edited or written for ASCD.

Two valuable articles helped me in this chapter: T. Christie's article in the *Journal of Creative Behavior* (Winter 1970), and one by Ashley Montagu in the *Phi Delta Kappan* (May 1970).

I'd like to pay tribute to another major contributor to American education, Pauline Sears. Through her teaching, her leadership to doctoral students, and her writing, she has helped immensely. One of her useful writings is "Research on Teaching in the Nursery School," a chapter in N.

L. Gage's *Handbook of Research in Teaching,* coauthored with Edith M. Dowley (1963).

For two unusual books by psychiatrists, I suggest Allan Wheelis' *The Quest for Identity* (1958) and Meyer Zeligs' *Friendship and Fratricide* (1967). The former tells a lot about the human problems of getting to be and being a psychiatrist. Wheelis contends that most psychiatrists are in that field for largely the wrong reasons. The latter tells of the author's explorations into the lives of Whittaker Chambers and Alger Hiss. Whatever you believe about these two complex men, read the book.

I strongly recommend *Fantasy and Feeling in Education* by Richard M. Jones (1968). Jones in turn acknowledges his debt to several people, Erik Erikson and Lawrence Kubie among them. Erikson's classic is *Childhood and Society* (1963). Much of Kubie's work is reported in several of the journals, and a list is found in the bibliography of Jones' book.

Research to support my contentions in this and adjoining chapters also comes from the following sources:

1. W. W. Charters, Jr., "The Social Background of Teaching" (1963, pp. 715–813).
2. M. L. Cogan, H. B. Reed, and W. W. Cooley and H. B. Reed: All reported in "Research on Teaching Science" (in Gage, 1963, pp. 1031–1059).
3. Barbara Ford Grothe, "Transforming Curiosity Into Learning Skills" (1964).
4. Sarah G. Longwell, in *Selected Readings on the Learning Process* (in Harris and Schwahn, 1961).
5. Abraham H. Maslow, *Motivation and Personality* (1954).
6. Willard C. Olson, "Seeking, Self-Selection, and Pacing in the Use of Books by Children" (Spring 1952).
7. Sidney J. Parnes and Eugene A. Brunelle, in *Journal of Creative Behavior* (1967).
8. Hugh V. Perkins, *Human Development and Learning* (1969).
9. Pauline S. Sears, "Self-Concept in the Service of Educational Goals" (1964).
10. Leonard Steinberg, "Creativity as a Character Trait: An Expanding Concept" (1964).
11. J. Richard Suchman, *The Elementary School Training Program in Scientific Inquiry* (1962).
12. Norman E. Wallen and Robert M. W. Travers, "Analysis and Investigation of Teaching Methods" (1963, pp. 448–505).

Walter B. Waetjen and Robert R. Leeper edited *Learning and Mental Health in the Classroom* (1966), which deals with the individual's mutuality of experience and his struggle for competence. It reports on the uselessness of undue repetition and on the importance of imitation.

Biehler's book, *Psychology Applied to Teaching* (1971), helped once again. In *Freedom to Learn*, Edith E. Biggs and James R. MacLean (1969) have done an interesting job on the teaching of math. But the book, which is well illustrated, also makes suggestions that go far beyond math.

For a film that sets out to present math concepts and ends up as a mind-blowing experience, see *Flatland*, produced by the Canadian Broadcasting Corporation.

Jerome Bruner's *Toward a Theory of Instruction* (1969) gives a number of ideas based on Bruner's rich store of experiences. Bruner served as senior advisor on the project from which developed "Man: A Course of Study" (Bruner, *et al.*, 1963) surely one of the most creative of the recent crop of new social studies programs in use. I've seen very worthwhile outcomes of the program when used in classrooms.

Neal Postman and Charles Weingartner, in *Teaching as a Subversive Activity* (1969), delineate several ways in which the teacher can be a facilitator rather than a controller. They encourage the teacher to be oriented toward *now*. Their sense of humor is delightful. A very useful resource, especially for secondary teachers.

I have been much impressed with how often in teachers' conferences and psychologists' seminars it is exclusively the needs of the children that come into discussions of how to improve learning, when it should be obvious to all that the needs of the teacher are as germane to the problem.

Richard M. Jones (1968)

Five

I LEARN
ABOUT ENVIRONMENTS

What I learn depends on what I see in what Kurt Lewin (1935) calls my "life space"—the area of my total perception. If I do not imagine the possibility of space travel, it cannot be a part of my life space. The three R's remain an important part of my life space, for I see them as important tools which I use to learn other things. Clearly, my life space is an enormous smorgasbord of knowledge, ideas, impressions, fears, hopes, and regrets. That's what I have with me right this minute—a summation of who I am and where I've been and some indications of where I may be going. When I feel OK about myself, I can better select from the clutter in my psychological closet those things which will be genuinely useful to me today. Then, as success builds on success, I meet each today with greater ability to love myself and others.

Imagine a child born in the early months of a seven year voyage to a distant planet. He might well grow to adulthood and live out his life without ever seeing a tree or a running stream of water. A ghetto child may never see a mountain. An Australian aborigine may never see a car, although the chances of this are changing daily. Each of us has many unique opportunities to see and to experience. By the same token, each of us misses out on a multitude of other opportunities—we cannot be there, we cannot experience what another experiences. *There* and *here* are basically psychological descriptions rather than physical descriptions. When you role-play and then reverse roles, you see how true this is.

In the same way, I use what I see in my environment as useful to me. I will see some things and completely over-look others. Terry Borton (1970, pp. 32–33) tells of the self-conscious seventeen-year-old girl who built an object out of "space substance."

> Within seconds it was obvious that something extraordinary was happening to her. Her movements became graceful and spontaneous; her eyes were focused on something in the space before her; her tongue edged into the corner of her mouth. A shape began to emerge before the eyes of an astonished audience—first the body, then the tail, eyes, ears, whiskers, nose, and mouth of a living cat. When the cat was finished, her concentration broke, and she returned to us with flushed cheeks and shining eyes. Over and over, bouncing on the grass, she said, "I did it. I did it." She was laughing with the joy of herself, and the delight she had created in us.

Young people enjoy imagining and creating with themselves and their environment, especially when they feel OK about themselves. So do I.

Have you seen *Making It Strange,* a series of four booklets developed by Synectics, Inc. (1968)? *Creative Learning and Teaching* by Torrance and Myers (1970)? *Put Your Mother on the Ceiling* by DeMille (1967)? *Improvisation for the Theater* by Spolin (1963)?

I LEARN ABOUT CONTRIVED ENVIRONMENTS

I live in many contrived or arranged environments. A house is one. A city is another, a concert in an auditorium another, and a school still another. Every contrived or arranged environment exists as well as and as long as particular expectations are met—such as expectations that I can live there safely and comfortably. Those expectations are met when ground rules, stated or implied, are followed. In every school we have some set of rules. Ideally, those rules give each person a wide latitude for behaving as a free person and yet limit behaviors which threaten the life, the physical well-being, or the freedom of others who live in that environment. The high school student's freedom of speech, like that of any citizen, should include opportunities to speak at a student assembly, but it does not include the right to yell "Fire!" in a crowded auditorium.

Pupils who grow toward adulthood in a loving/learning environment develop a sense of responsibility toward human life, and that sense of responsibility supports legitimate rules and adult laws. Much of today's youthful protest is against laws and procedures which are unnecessary or are actually damaging to human life. When rules or laws or government actions are challenged, a responsible response is an examination of those rules and laws and actions and their effects, to see if they can be improved or dispensed with. How about the rules in your classroom?

Dreikurs and his associates in *Maintaining Sanity in the Classroom* (1971, pp. 148–185) present some specifics about the making and supporting of classroom rules.

One part of our arranged environment which displays our appalling ignorance about ourselves and other people is that collection of rules, laws, and procedures which seek to hold members of minorities—including women—in a lesser status. These inhibitions and prohibitions are ending—not rapidly, but they are ending. Meanwhile, there's a heap of learning for you and me to do. As I have suggested before, each teacher can play several roles in helping to increase the real freedom of America's minorities.

OVERLAPPING ENVIRONMENTS

Just as P–A–C (of transactional analysis) is an oversimplification of a human personality, so "an environment" is an oversimplification. At any moment I live in a series of overlapping environments. At the moment the television is on in the living room—the Democratic National Convention, a friend is playing a guitar, outside there are insect noises, and I am writing—tired, but joyful because I truly like to write. I am simultaneously conscious of various noises, sights, sensations, and feelings which I will deal with in some combination. In this case, the desires of my Child to have fun writing serve as a way to organize my Adult abilities to concentrate on the play/work of writing. It works.

Similarly, in the classroom, I strive to be aware of feelings and to meet those feelings with my own so that communication can deal with important things. In that way I exercise my freedom to be and to become, because my being and becoming are involved with people. My keenest desires are to play with others I choose. As teachers, we have such a wonderful variety of choices each day. As I become more self-directed, I find that I can imagine having fun with more people in more ways.

We play the Road Game. Each team has a territory of the floor covered with butcher paper. Each team attempts to build as many roads as possible on the land of its neighbors during the time allowed. To do so, the temporary team captain negotiates with the adjoining team captains for rights of way, so that the road builder can build the roads by painting with a long-handled brush. At intervals, the captain and road-builder duties pass to others in the group. Only limited verbal conversation is permitted. At the end, complaints against other teams are duly heard and voted upon and the team with the greatest number of legally accepted roads wins.

The similarities to ordinary relationships within schools and communities seem very real. The teams are comparable to groups within a classroom, to departments within faculties, or to the faculties within a school district. Some verbal and some nonverbal communication takes place. Inevitably, there are disagreements and conflicts, some with substantial merit, others which are trivial. In a group, a department, a class, or a faculty, effective communication and effective teamwork can lead to markedly better accomplishment of group purposes. Like many contemporary games and simulations, the Road Game is a collection of valuable opportunities for learning by people of various age groups. What learning games are your students playing?

Learning and loving depend on my realistic appraisals of the shifting complexities that surround me and on my willingness to risk dealing with those complexities. No wonder some people throw up their hands in despair when asked to define *freedom*. I think of freedom less as freedom *from* the controls of other people and circumstances and more as freedom *to* act on my own behalf in ways that prove to be satisfying and fulfilling to me. My freedom depends on my selecting from among available choices as I see them. I learn to make choices, to observe the consequences of those choices, and to accept the inevitable limitations on me as a collector and evaluator of data.

Suppose a white teacher has to decide whether to vote for or against a plan to desegregate his school district—a vote by his union or professional association that may have a decisive influence. He may think, "This is a white district, we're the majority, why can't they be happy in their schools?" He may tell himself, "Change must come gradually, perhaps they're not ready for it," and "Leave well enough alone—it's not my responsibility," and "People live where they choose; the schools can't solve problems caused by housing." These rationalizations may mask suppressed beliefs: "Negroes and Puerto Ricans are inferior—God made them that way," and "We've got to keep them in their place—or you can't tell *what* may happen!" Many people in recent years have voted entirely in accordance with such primitive racial fears. Do you know how you would vote?

There is an alternative to voting in obedience to what may be childhood injunctions. A dispassionate consideration of the data can recognize the situation of several minorities in America, such as blacks. Grier and Cobbs (1968, p. 167) wrote:

> (Thus) the dynamics of black self-hatred are unique. They involve the child's awareness that all people who are black as he is are so treated by white people. Whatever hostility he mounts against white people finds little support in the weakness and the minority status of black people. As it is hopeless for him to consider righting this wrong by force, he identifies with his oppressor psychologically in an attempt to escape from this hopeless position. From his

new psychologically "white" position, he turns on black people with aggression and hostility and hates blacks, and, among the blacks, himself.

Racial prejudice, therefore, is a pitiful product of systematized cruelty, in which frightened people climb onto the stand with the oppressor and say, "Yes, we hate them too!" They are opportunists, wretched and terrified, but going with a winner.

I want to see what I as a citizen and a teacher should do about it. Among blacks and other minorities, powerlessness is a relative truth. By whatever measure we use, members of minority groups do not share equally with whites in what we often think of as the good life in the United States. Now, what is to be done about it? It will take, above all, a commitment of human spirit. I start with me, and with whatever prejudices I retain. As a teacher and as a member of my community, I must live my beliefs about extending opportunities to various minority groups. I must encourage efforts—by legislatures, employers, government agencies, and my fellow citizens—which result in jobs, housing, and equal educational opportunities for members of minority groups. Cleveland, Gary, and Newark have shown that a black can be elected mayor of a major city. Los Angeles elected a Mexican-American as president of the school board. A black woman actively sought the presidential nomination in 1972. Any man or woman should be able to run for any public office in the United States and be judged by his fellows on the basis of those human qualities and beliefs which have a bearing on how he will serve them—and on those factors alone. That is far from reality today. So we—and I mean all of us, including minority group members—have to make much greater efforts. Tokenism and the slow pace of gradualism will lead to further bitterness and further violence.

Many minority group members, including Mexican-Americans and Native Americans, are in the position Harris designates Position 3: "I'm OK —You're Not OK." Many blacks and others currently in Position 3 are, for them, in a better position from a mental health standpoint than they have been in the past, because Position 3 lets them openly take pride in their own heritage and openly express their resentment. Those who recognize and use their freedom are more likely to take active steps in their own behalf—such as confronting white people to demand opportunities for themselves. Minority group members have a wider area of freedom than many recognize. Effort on their own behalf will lead to greater actual power and hence to greater self-respect. So it may not only be a matter of short-term expediency but also of long-term advantage to them and to the nation of which they are a part. Minority group members who achieve by their own efforts will prove themselves to themselves. Then many of them can move to "I'm OK—You're OK" because they will feel OK about themselves without feeling the need to put anybody else down. This is one reason for a teacher to avoid the temptation to give a minority student a higher grade than he would give a Caucasian student for the same achievement. In the long run, such an act depreciates education. Individuals who achieve for themselves value themselves and can better appreciate the efforts of others. Valuing will always be relative, but if more of us have more feelings of positive self-esteem, more of us will honor our fellow men.

EXPECTATIONS AND MYSTERIES

I have expectations about myself and my future experiences. I wish to continue loving and learning, and I act to make these wishes into self-fulfilling prophecies. I also have expectations of others. What is my expectation about the student as a learner? Do I look at him as a bundle of potentialities waiting for me to push buttons and start the learning process? Or do I look at him as a person already striving, already interacting with his various overlapping environments, a learner who has his own goals and who needs encouragement and assistance in achieving them?

When I look at an individual student for the first time, seated in the classroom, I wonder where he is on the continuum I just suggested. I don't know. That's a piece of the mystery I start with. At the beginning of a year or a semester, at the beginning of the first class meeting, I can be pretty sure of one thing: I have his attention, because he wants to know who I am and what I will be like as a teacher. A college student may be looking me over, deciding whether he chooses to take the course with me or with another teacher. The elementary school child, alas, seldom has any choice in the matter, so he's looking at his teacher to determine his fate for the year.

But back up a few years to the preschool, nursery school, and kindergarten child. Where is he? Well, he's tentative too, a bit uncertain in many instances about how to respond to new situations or new acquaintances. However, my impression is that children at ages three, four, and five are willing to commit themselves quickly and eagerly to learning. They want to learn to slide down the slide, to make things with clay, to draw or paint, to communicate their ideas verbally to others. One clear evidence of this readiness to participate in learning is question-asking behavior. If young children are given freedom in learning opportunities, they show the same eager readiness for reading and arithmetic.

I believe the pupil to be, potentially, at the active end of the continuum. He is, in some way, always learning. For example, the pupil is getting the "feel" of a new desk, perhaps noticing the particular smell of this room, reading the features and facial expressions of other pupils. His interest is likely to be attracted to a new pupil who has just arrived in the neighborhood. This learning is not the same as writing a story or solving arithmetic examples, but it may be more central to the pupil's interests. As a teacher I can have great influence on the learning that does take place by being aware of the natural interests of the pupils—in a newcomer, for example. I can also give each pupil opportunities to seek answers to questions he has about the world and its people—which really means the world as he sees it, and the people he sees as significant in his world. I tell him what my goals are and he may tell me what his are, and we interact on goals and their attainment. I start with me, where I am *now*, with my perceptions and my feelings. Each pupil, similarly, starts where he is *now*.

Now sounds very definite and precise, but it isn't. In any *now*, the tiny bit I know is much less than the vast ocean of what I do not know. While I can see that Jim is messing about with the Mystery Powders, I cannot know what he sees as interesting or worth knowing. I can help to provide a variety of materials with which he can interact. I cannot insure his memorization of facts or comprehension of relationships. *Now* always has more mystery than clarity. As a teacher, I am learning to live with mystery.

Ms. Monroe's second grade class had some unusual learning opportunities. Among the class members were two educable mentally retarded children, a noncommunicative boy who had been held back, and one girl who was half blind. The realities of individual differences came to life in this class, as its members found that these atypical students each had much to offer. At mid-year a new boy entered the class, a boy who stuttered. One day when he was out of the room, the teacher asked the class members if they wished to give him the same opportunity they had to "share and tell." The class said yes, and yes, they were willing to be patient while he struggled with his speech. The teacher then asked the boy if he would like to have a turn with the sharing and he said yes. The first time he participated was painful. He took nine minutes to say three sentences, but he got through them and the students showed him more than courtesy—they were supportive of his efforts. Over the weeks, his stuttering abated markedly, returning only in times of stress. He carried on conversations with others. He later undertook a census of science projects in the various second and third grade classes. To do this he had to visit each classroom and speak with the teacher and with each student preparing a science project. He wrote up his report as a newspaper. One way he improved his oral reading, as well as gaining confidence in his speech, was by reading to the tape recorder. He learned from listening to the tape, and he erased the rough spots and redid them. He built greater faith in himself, partly as a result of the faith the others showed in him. The other class members learned firsthand of the power of faith, which they can always extend in support of a fellow human being. But some stutterers continue to stutter. And mysteries continue to be mysterious. Is there a mystery with which you are now living? One which really bugs you?

"Because concepts are built by each individual according to his own idiosyncratic ways, progress along a conceptual arrow cannot be planned in a series of logical steps—in a way each child will follow" (Lansdown, Blackwood, and Brandwein, 1971, p. 186). Or, as John Holt says, a student needs time to "mess about" with materials and ideas to find his own individual meaning. As a teacher living with mystery, I give students time to mess about with what they see in the hope that they will come to their own conclusions and will then be more willing to exercise their freedom in ways they find successful. As a teacher I am an available resource with the patience to let it happen. Then students can bring about their own self-fulfilling prophecies of loving and learning. *I act in spite of the complexity, the mystery, and the threat of existential reality.*

What I can do is reexamine Parental data taken in a long time ago. It is possible for the whole person to review the data and change his attitudes and behavior. As Harris (1969, p. 57) says, "At age three he cannot change reality. But at forty-three he can." Racial fears and hatreds are found among *all* racial and ethnic groups; individuals so afflicted cannot act effectively in their own behalf or as loving friends to others. The individual can reject old data, take into account contemporary data, imagine a better social order in the future, and participate in bringing about that better order. That is an exercise of his freedom to love himself and others.

The struggle toward confident OK-ness takes place within each individual in his life space. The individual who has experienced enough hurt, or enough boredom, or who has discovered that he *can* change may find sufficient energy to overcome parsimony in given instances. Or as Shostrom (1968) says, the manipulator can become an actualizor.

Suppose our teacher faced with the decision decides to vote for the plan to desegregate the schools. This would be a decision based on current reality and real social needs and would overcome ignorance and fear. Perhaps at the next meeting of the teacher association or union he lets others know how he feels about it. This takes guts in our world today, when so many people simply go along with the establishment viewpoint —in this case, that school integration is unnecessary or possibly undesirable. But teachers listen to other teachers, and progress often begins to occur when a few will voice the underlying feelings of many. This risk-taking self-affirmation and self-validation can make self-love possible: "I really *do* believe in something, I really am willing to commit myself to a cause which will help others, and me along with them, so I'm truly OK. Since I'm OK, I deserve self-love." The ability to love one's self is necessary before one can love others in positive, non-manipulating, non-exploiting ways.

We live with mystery yet we wish to abolish mystery, to settle it once and for all. A settlement in favor of desegregation, which is a move to include other human beings, lifts our spirits and enables us to enjoy the other mysteries with which we continue to live. I'll never forget the good feeling I had years ago when I picketed a major corporation demanding equal employment opportunities. I dealt with other life problems more lovingly as a result.

I teach for survival. There is polluted air forty thousand feet up, there are residues of pollutants at the north and south poles, there are millions of pounds of DDT lying around waiting to be absorbed into plant and animal tissue and then into human tissue. We are using up resources such as iron, copper, coal, and petroleum at a staggering pace, while the world population climbs at an alarming rate. Meanwhile, in such popular living areas as California, open space for leisure and recreation, as well as valuable orchard and farmland, is being filled with houses, shopping centers, drive-in movies, and freeways. Each such usage is irreversible. True, we can break up the pavement on a parking lot and plant grass and trees, but that is tough to do when people come to think of a parking lot as useful. With such a value system, we hasten the extinction of human life on our planet.

We must act in two ways: affirmatively to provide viable alternatives to present practices, and negatively to prevent further disasters to our fragile ecology. In the San Francisco Bay area, a rapid transit district is an example of a viable alternative to more freeways and bridges. Obviously, too, our technology makes possible today the electronic movement of ideas, information, images, human voices, and features, and so less movement of human bodies is required. The setting aside of land for parks, for camping and recreation, and for preservation of wilderness is also necessary. Negatively, we must prohibit the killing of endangered species, the use of dangerous pollutants, and the continuation of the human disasters known as wars.

In addition, we must show respect for future generations by not making all the decisions now. So many decisions are irreversible, reducing our own choices and drastically reducing the freedom of future generations. It just won't do to say that our advancing technology will always rectify our mistakes and create new wonders to replace old ones. I don't want to live in a treeless world!

I teach as though my life depends on it. It does. I encourage students to recognize their own OK-ness so that they can stop smoking, drive their cars less, recycle bottles, cans, bags, and newspapers, eat healthy foods, and insist that their legislators at local, state, and national levels show respect for human life and for plant and animal life while there is still time to preserve life. I am learning to set an example in these ways and thus be a loving resource to others.

CONCLUSION

An environment for learning is a collection of people dedicated to learning what is important for them. The key person is the teacher, a teacher who is comfortably sure that he is somebody and is able to help students who are becoming. Physical surroundings, materials, and equipment can be very meager if the human ingredients are there and are interacting. I have visited one-room schoolhouses which were dilapidated and short of the latest teaching materials. But their environments were positively dedicated to learning—and much learning took place.

In any environment, natural or contrived, human values come first. This does not mean human comfort or human convenience, but the expansion of freedom and dignity, the continuation of human life, and the preservation of other living things on our planet. As a teacher, I have faith that I can live harmoniously with man and with nature and that I can help others to learn to do so.

Faith in myself and faith in my fellow men encourage me to stay committed to active life, to seeing and acting toward a better life for all. Alan Watts (1958, p. 38) writes that,

> if there is to be any life and movement at all, the attitude of faith must be basic—the final and fundamental attitude. . . . This is another way of saying that toward the vast and all-encompassing background of human life . . . there must be total affirmation and acceptance. Otherwise there is no basis at all for caution and control with respect to details in the foreground. But it is all too easy to become so absorbed in those details that all sense of proportion is lost, and for man to make himself mad by trying to bring everything under his control.

I teach students today of the interrelationships of everything we do in our daily lives: I teach today as though my life depended on it. It does. Faith in ourselves, faith in children, and faith in the child's faith in his ability to grow up will help us make our daily contribution to living and learning and loving more relevant and also more enjoyable.

NOTES TO CHAPTER 5

Philip Jackson has written a sociology of the classroom called *Life in Classrooms* (1968). He reminds us that school attendance—which we may think of as a great privilege—is compulsory for most attendees, and this inevitably colors the child's perceptions of teachers and the curriculum. Jules Henry, in *Culture Against Man* (1965), gives some dramatic examples of the plight of the student in a teacher-dominated and competitive classroom.

Richard M. Jones has edited a collection of articles, called *Contemporary Educational Psychology* (1966), in which he reprints several memorable articles; the ones which impressed me most were by Howard E. Gruber and Lawrence S. Kubie.

Another powerful influence for improving the education of human beings is Arthur T. Jersild. His *When Teachers Face Themselves* (1955) is a great book, showing the human side of teaching and the feelings teachers have which influence their teaching. I wonder if teachers today feel as did the teachers surveyed in Jersild's study.

In my exploration of minority feelings, I have used William H. Grier and Price M. Cobbs, *Black Rage* (1968); *The Autobiography of Malcolm X* (Little, 1965); Claude Brown's *Manchild in the Promised Land* (1965); and Elliott Liebow's *Tally's Corner* (1967). Each author presents a powerful plea for agape, for man's humanity to man.

Have you ever read any of Loren Eiseley's books? I've enjoyed *The Immense Journey* (1957), *The Firmament of Time* (1960), and *The Invisible Pyramid* (1970), and there are others. Eiseley has the ability to talk of vitally important human concerns and to write of them lyrically and poetically. A new Eiseley is a cause for celebrating—with Eiseley—our humanness.

Kurt Lewin started lines of inquiry which have been followed by many others and which have led to useful insights into the human condition. In *A Dynamic Theory of Personality* (1935) he reviews research (largely German) and presents his views about the environments in which we live. His use of simple diagrams adds to my understanding of his points.

Another original thinker I have encountered in recent years is Robert Jay Lifton (*History and Human Survival*, 1971). Lifton, a psychiatrist, has made a special study of Japan which started with a psychological study of Hiroshima survivors. He gives insight into the mechanistic fallacies which Lewis Mumford talks about and also into problems of apathy and dependency dealt with by Rollo May.

There have been many recent reports on British elementary schools. One that I have used is *Learning How to Learn* by Robert J. Fisher (1972). He brings out several of the significant differences between the environment for learning in British schools and that in American schools. Among these is the ways in which English teachers are encouraged to a greater extent to use their freedom to try variations in the classroom. Fisher also lists a hundred features he considers potentially transferable from England to the United States. You may want to refer to this book when you are reading Chapter 10.

On the subject of mystery in teaching, I have written an article entitled "Teachers Live with Mystery," which appeared in *Educational Leadership* (1971).

Education is living, not a preparation for living.

Bernice Goldmark (1968)

Six

ACTING FOR CHANGE

Through encounter, through meeting and interacting with others, each of us has daily opportunities for learning and loving. In spite of the risks involved, encounter offers two great possibilities to the person who goes out to meet others as equals. He can learn to focus on and to be guided in his behavior by what is real for him. And, using this learning, he can become more and more independent of the crowd, more and more able to live with his own judgment. Thus he can become more self-sufficient and more self-directed. I am becoming more self-directed as I learn to study students as individuals.

Any description of "a child" suffers from two handicaps: one, it is bound to be piecemeal, and two, it is inevitably static—a still picture when only a moving picture will come close to reality. Nevertheless, much benefit can accrue to each of us as teachers from recording the visible behaviors of individual children. As has been stressed before, I view the child as "engaged in a process of transaction with his world" (Gordon, 1966, p. 5).

What the child can become is unknowable, but the ceiling in many areas of performance is extremely high. The student in school, unless he has been severely mistreated or utterly neglected, will work at activities which appeal to him. Fader, who wrote *Hooked on Books* (1968), found that even very turned-off teenagers read with delight when given freedom to select what they want to read and no busy-work assignments to spoil their pleasure. It's hard to kill curiosity about one's self and about all those other odd people one encounters in life. Curiosity is erotic, an expression of loving desire to know.

Two school staff members went out of their way to help Chester, a boy who felt very inadequate, did poorly in school work, and aggressed against other students. The teacher made a detailed case study of Chester and used insights from her study in modifying her behavior toward him. She spoke to him as matter-of-factly as she could, praising and reprimanding in ways she hoped conveyed her continuing regard for him as a person.

The principal invited Chester to help her on various projects which were within his abilities, and she praised him generously for his help. As an example, Chester stapled the PTA notices and delivered them to each room. With the principal and with his teacher, Chester developed pleasant relationships. Through them he steadily built his own self-regard and gained in abilities to get along with his peers. As he felt more OK about himself, he could accept himself as lovable and could express love to others. His neurotic anxiety abated.

What children can become is apparently unlimited—certainly in our present state of knowledge we are seeing more emerging possibilities and fewer closed doors. Such books as *A Hole is to Dig* (Kraus, 1952), *The Me Nobody Knows* (Joseph, 1969), a vast number of Haiku and other poems, the annual output of thousands of science fair exhibits—these are all examples of the immense creative potential of youth. Each teacher helps students realize their potential by watching to see how students behave and finding ways to support them in their producing.

LEARNING BY DOING: CHILD STUDY

In the classroom, the teacher observes as well as participates. He cannot help observing, and he can use his observations of individuals and of groups within the class. I adjust my teaching on the basis of feedback from students.

Children know they're being observed by the teacher, and so they wonder what the teacher is like and if they can be themselves. The reciprocal relationships between teacher and student and between student and student can succeed much better when there is a substantial degree of authenticity. As Bugental (1965) says, the authentic person is aware of himself though not conventionally self-conscious; he accepts choice and decision-making as the vital stuff of learning and takes responsibility for his decisions and their consequences. Children accept and respond to authenticity with authenticity. If I express my contemporary feelings, students tend to express their contemporary feelings. From authentic students, one gets observed data which is relevant and worthwhile: you can depend on it. But in five days—or even five minutes—the living data changes, so observation must be frequent.

What I most want to know about a child is his personality as revealed by his behavior. Approaches to knowledge of the individual can be through self-report, inference from observation of the child's behavior, and inference based on projective techniques, as well as other data, such as the work the child produces. (Only the second of these will be described here in detail; for the other two, I suggest you read Chapter 3 of Gordon's book (1966, pp. 52–88) or Chapter 4 of Burkhart and Neil's book (1968, pp. 62–79).

The fifty-minute period simply does not afford the secondary teacher enough time and enough variety of performances so that he can get rounded pictures of all the individual personalities with whom he lives. The suggestions which follow will be more difficult for secondary teachers to use, although they *can* be used. Student journals, suggested before, can supplement direct observations.

How do teachers get adequate data about individuals, data which they can use in making inferences? They keep written anecdotal records or specimen descriptions based on brief observations of a given child. The teacher behaves as though he were a movie camera, recording as precisely as possible what he sees: "Picks up pencil, writes words on line, gazes out window, turns to look at friend J. across room, smiles, turns back to writing. . . ." Teachers are not movie cameras, and so they may fail to observe what may well be significant aspects of the child's behavior and will tend to select and possibly overstress some details. But practice will lead to improvement, and the fact that records are kept over a period of time will increase the probability of significant details accruing in the continuing record. If I record Ann's behavior at spelling time today, I will choose physical education or math period to record tomorrow. The day, hour, and any especially noteworthy influence (such as a fire drill) should be noted in the record, which should be filed for future use.

The secondary teacher, cramped for time during class period, should still be able to make occasional notes of pupil behavior. Teachers can observe pupils on the school grounds at lunch period to see who associates with whom and to note clothing and hair styles. Similar observations can also be made at extracurricular events. Knowing who's in the dance band, who's on the basketball and cross-country teams, also helps. Alert teachers I know tune in to the radio stations the young listen to and note what those songs say. The lyrics are often a reflection of how youth feels—or at least have an influence on the feelings of youth. All these clues can help the teacher to understand his students and to plan class work that takes into account the changing teen perceptions of reality. The teacher may use part of his preparation period to catch up on the writing and filing of notes on pupil behavior and the necessary thinking about their meanings and implications for instruction.

After ten or twelve anecdotal notes about a particular student have accumulated, the teacher may be ready to reread all of them and look for hypotheses. They may shout at you from the record, as in the case of the child who constantly looks pleadingly in the direction of another child, or they may resist your first and second look. In any case, you may be able to make some tentative hypotheses on the basis of this first run-through of your first set of data. But resist the temptation to jump to conclusions— or to behave next day, in interacting with this child, as though your hypothesis were proven true! Hypotheses may be stated in question form. For example, "Could it be that Carl is really afraid of me?" "Could it be that Mary already knows that skill?" Such questions incorporate a healthy caution. Later, after more records have been made, and with due consideration for variations in time of day, the subject being studied, and other circumstances, you may be ready to run through the entire record again, again looking for tentative hypotheses. In addition to direct classroom observations, teachers add other notes which may contribute to understanding of the child. These could include notes on conferences with parents, with other teachers who have the student currently, or with teachers who previously had the student in a class, and with other school personnel such as the nurse.

There are alternatives to making such studies as one lone teacher. For years, the University of Maryland has sponsored the Child Study Program. Individual teachers in the Maryland program follow the steps outlined above. The chief difference in the Maryland procedure is that a group of eight to fifteen teachers conducting such studies (each teacher studying one child at a time) meets together once a week to exchange ideas and insights and to get guidance from a trained leader. I participated in such a group for one year and still recall the rewarding experience of observing, sharing, hypothesizing, reobserving, rethinking, and rehypothesizing. Obviously, much can be gained from the pooled perceptions and hunches of a number of teachers about each child being observed. In this process, each child becomes more and more vividly individual, more and more vividly alive as the weeks go by. The group ordinarily lasts a full school year, although some teachers continue in the program for many years. On the basis of carefully evaluated data, teachers plan and carry out modifications in class programs for the children studied. They also improve their abilities to observe and work with other children.

You can conduct the study of an individual child in concert with one or more friends or colleagues who are teachers you know and who will enjoy such sharing. This may be a way several high school teachers can work to help a problem student. Each of two or three teachers can make anecdotal records, collect other data, share from time to time, and make hypotheses as seem appropriate. Or each teacher can use one or more of the survey techniques listed in one of the books described at the end of this chapter. If one or two teachers in a school start such a program of child study, it may prove so interesting that all or most of the faculty will decide to join. There is a rich harvest of love gained from a more complete understanding of children. However, child study, even thorough and thoughtful child study, may fail to give you answers to questions you need answered. That frustration is a part of the reality we live with.

LEARNING BY VENTURING: HOME VISITS

Ms. Guintoli rang the bell and waited, half hoping no one would be home. Soon she heard footsteps inside, and the door opened to reveal two girls of elementary school age. Right behind and bearing down on them was a woman calling out loudly, "What is it?"

MS. GUINTOLI:	I'm Lara Guintoli, Albert's math teacher. Could I talk with you?
MS. CAIN:	I'm Ms. Cain, Albert's aunt. I guess you can come in. You girls, go on, get out, can't you see we're busy? Sit down, Ms. Guintoli.
MS. GUINTOLI:	I had Albert last year in the pre-algebra class, and he did quite well. And he started out doing well this year, but in the past two months his work has dropped off. He does very little work, and he doesn't seem to care. Do you know why he's stopped working? He won't tell me.
MS. CAIN:	Well, you see, it's like this. I guess you got a right to know. A while back, that would be about four months ago, Albert's mother took off, just up and gone. I work at the plant where Albert's father works, and him and me's been friends for a long time, and bein's my old man left me—that's been four years ago—Mr. Williams asked me to come over and help out. The plant changed my shift so I could be here days. Tell you the truth, Albert don't care for me. I don't know why, but he don't. Him and his mother were pretty close, I guess, and he and his father don't get along too good. Albert's mother told him he could live at her new place. ...."

The two women talked for a half hour and then Ms. Guintoli left. She could guess at injunctions Albert may have received as a young child. Now that she knew a bit more about him, how could she use the information to help him?

When I get information, even very pertinent information, I may not see ways of using it to help the student learn, at least not immediately, so I file it away for future use. I live with mystery, and I also live with frustration. I can't always do what I would like to do, but I never stop trying.

Ms. Guintoli thought again about Albert and her visit to his home on her way to school next day. This Ms. Cain was not her idea of an ideal mother for Albert, but then the woman did seem to care about Albert's father and seemed aware of Albert's feelings about her. She decided to talk with Albert's counselor and managed to see him at lunch. He agreed to talk with Albert and to point out to him the option that he could go and live with his real mother. She talked with Albert that day also. She knew he'd be curious about her reaction and was open in saying she felt Ms. Cain cared for him. She let him know she was interested in him and was willing to discuss his problems with him. She also suggested he talk his situation over with his counselor.

Albert took his time in setting up an appointment with his counselor. The counselor, on his side, planned his talk with Albert carefully. He first talked with the father, and he also verified, through the school nurse—who knew the family and was acquainted with Albert's real mother—that Albert could return to her if he chose. When the interview occurred, it was inconclusive, but the counselor laid the option in front of Albert and asked him to think it over. Albert came in three days later to say he'd decided to stay where he was.

Although his math didn't improve appreciably, Ms. Guintoli noticed that Albert seemed a bit more interested and responded more to other people in the class. Maybe he needed friends more than he needed algebra, she thought ruefully. Students as people, she saw, come first, ahead of algebra. She learned, increasingly, to use that understanding. She also found out a lot about herself by her contacts with Albert, Ms. Cain, and the counselor. She found out that she could make successful home visits which would yield usable data for her teaching. And she learned that such visits would leave a residue of goodwill in the home visited, something on which the parents could build better support of their children in school. A loving teacher, who visits a home as Ms. Guintoli did, helps *all* the children from that home. Just as the teenager's parents want to know they are loved, so every parent wants to know their child's teacher really cares about that child. The home visit is a form of proof of that caring. We all benefit from the good feelings generated by those around us. Ms. Guintoli realized that her own self-confidence rose as she added to her repertoire of skills in working with people.

Many a teacher sighs as he turns off the engine of his car when he arrives at school, and then he assumes his teaching role as he walks toward the building. Many a teacher looks forward joyously to the afternoon bowling or the Saturday fishing, and this is not a sign of irresponsibility. All of us relish good times—whatever we consider to be fun. But it is the extent to which so many teachers separate their teaching selves from the rest of themselves which concerns me. My students need all of me, the best and the worst, but above all the real me, the whole me. As a whole and unified person, I serve as an example and as a loving resource to my students. They respond to my authenticity. I expand my freedom as I become more authentic.

LEARNING BY ASKING

One form of teacher risk was described in Chapter 4 when Ms. Holmes, Ms. Rogers, and Ms. Wagstaff talked about Nick. My fellow teachers know a lot about my students; by asking, I can find out, especially if I am willing to risk by admitting that I'm stumped. This invites Adult to Adult exchange of information and nurturing Parent to nurturing Parent transactions regarding a student—or happy Child to happy Child exchanges.

Figure 4. Teacher-Pupil Transactions

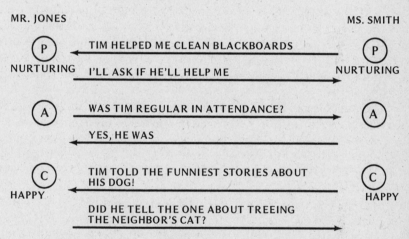

MR. JONES — MS. SMITH

P NURTURING — TIM HELPED ME CLEAN BLACKBOARDS — I'LL ASK IF HE'LL HELP ME — P NURTURING

A — WAS TIM REGULAR IN ATTENDANCE? — YES, HE WAS — A

C HAPPY — TIM TOLD THE FUNNIEST STORIES ABOUT HIS DOG! — DID HE TELL THE ONE ABOUT TREEING THE NEIGHBOR'S CAT? — C HAPPY

All these are complementary transactions in which information or enthusiasm is shared. Each teacher shows willingness to risk in ways which are potentially helpful to the student. Not all teachers will be willing to reciprocate in such situations. Many teachers prefer to play the game "Ain't it Awful," in which other teachers, the principal, the parents, and kids are blamed for the failure of the learning environment. I have heard teachers say, "Mrs. Brown dislikes all teachers, so how can Cindy know any better?" as though Cindy were a carbon copy of her mother. Or "Mr. Johnson won't let me use *Words in Color*," as though the speaker was thereby rendered utterly helpless. Or "Chuck always leaves his books at home," as though there were no solution to this problem. Each teacher has the freedom to give up useless time-wasters of this kind and focus on productive possibilities such as: "What can I say that will reassure Mrs. Brown that I accept her as an OK person?" I focus on what *I* can do. This helps me to deal with current reality and to encourage those changes in the attitude of others that may well result in progress for the student.

LOVING IN PRACTICAL WAYS: PUPIL-TEACHER TEAMWORK

In Chapter 5, the events in Ms. Monroe's class were described. She enlisted the best feelings of her class members in helping each student to appreciate himself and his peers. Still another example of risking and of pupil-teacher teamwork is found in Chapter 3, where Ms. Lacey's fifth and sixth graders learned to get along together with mutual respect. Later, I will discuss teacher–pupil planning and class meetings as ways of reaching higher plateaus of understanding and cooperation among human learners. Have you seen *Schools Without Failure* by Glasser (1965)?

LEARNING AND LOVING WITH TRADITIONAL ACADEMIC MATERIALS

The knowledge explosion brings quantities of new material on the market daily. My students and I deal with the avalanche of materials and develop selecting and "dealing with" modes which help us to get where we want to go. My capacity to read and to assimilate data is limited. Even computers are unable to handle overload. What I do is to select what I will read, select a way of reading it (such as skimming), and decide how (if at all) I intend to use what I read—whether I will make extensive notes on it, reproduce copies for students, or simply put it on the shelf and forget it. This is one of the reasons why self-selection by pupils is of such vital importance from kindergarten through graduate school—only *I* know whether something is interesting, useful, relevant, or important to me *now*, because I am the consumer of knowledge.

My role as a loving teacher is threefold in regard to knowledge. First, I make knowledge available to students by having books, games, films, records, newspapers, and other materials available for their selection. Some materials I order from nearby resource centers. Second, I am ready to deal with any bit of knowledge which the pupil chooses at any time (within reason); this means he can come and ask me or challenge me about any item he wishes to talk about. I respond openly during class and group meetings, and I set aside time for individual conferences.

Third, I always am seeking syntheses and relationships for and among knowledge as I encounter it. For example, I suggest hypotheses as ways of looking at facts. A recent hypothesis I offered college students asks: Could it be that many students of various ages suffer from some degree of claustrophobia when sitting in a classroom?

I am not interested in manipulating students, but I know that as an honest and open person I can contribute in wholly legitimate and loving ways to pupil interest and pupil action. I am not interested in sitting on the sidelines; I want to be part of the action. I use the syntheses I make in two ways: to work more effectively with pupils, and to contribute to their thought. I offer an hypothesis, not as an end product but as a stimulus to further thought. Often the offering of my own hypothesis to a pupil leads *me* to further thought and further research about it. My learning, like my becoming, is everlasting. I learn most about myself.

Children produce as well as consume. I encourage the pupil's productivity by stroking him. Each day I reassure each pupil that he is somebody, and one way I do so is by praising his products. Obviously, I cannot do so indiscriminately, because, over a period of time, that would depreciate the value of my praise. But I surprise myself with the way I'm increasing the positive qualities I notice in the products of other people. When I say I like a pupil's picture or essay, I'm not saying it's a masterpiece. But I am saying something which helps him. I overcome stinginess with largesse.

I stroke the student for being as well as for doing. It's easier, I grant, to say, "I like your dress" or "You did a great job as class treasurer" or "That's straight A work," but I'm learning to give "being" strokes also. Here are a few samples:

> What a neat person you are!
> I like you.
> That shows the kind of a person you really are.
> He asked for *your* help.
> I like being around you.
> You remind me of one of my favorite people.
> You are kind/honest/fair/sincere/friendly.
> I like the way you enjoy running/painting.
> I love you.
> Or, your suggestion: _____

A number of suggestions for "congruent communication" between teachers and students are found in *Teacher and Child* by Haim Ginott (1972, pp. 79–121). Ginott goes on to discuss the perils of praise in the next chapter.

Praise isn't a simple thing psychologically. Some students resent it or fear it as a way of the teacher's gaining a hold over them (I'll have to do good work forever to pay her back for praising me!). Dreikurs, Grunwald, and Pepper discuss this area very thoroughly in *Maintaining Sanity in the Classroom* (1971, pp. 71–80). They suggest, for example, having the student who is in need of encouragement be a helper to another student or to a group. If a student is fearful of inability to do something, the teacher might sit beside the student and do part of the work with him, showing the teacher's empathy. Another way to enlist the student in his own appraisal is to say, when he shows a painting, "Hmm, what do *you* think of it?" Or, "Purple is one of my favorite colors, too."

As the teacher gains in ability to tune in, he will find that he is often conscious that the student is pleased with his accomplishment. The teacher can then say, "I'm aware that you are satisfied with your work," or "I'm aware that what you did pleases you." This acts as a recognition and sharing of good feelings and as a powerful reinforcer of the student's

pleasure. It encourages him to take future risks. The teacher whose awareness statement is accepted by a smile or a nod is encouraged to take future
risks in his conversations with students.

Outlandish or not, poetic or not, creative or not, some of each child's
products must be accepted by someone so that he will come forth again
and risk again. It is the student's evolution as a person that I am concerned
about, not the potential genius of a Vincent van Gogh or a Thomas Edison
or a Loren Eiseley or a Doris Lessing or a Brock Chisholm. Love puts
people ahead of curriculum content. People, including children, *produce* the
content of real curriculum, and we cannot afford to reject any of it out
of hand. When our concern is with people, we find that a considerable
proportion of their products justify our appreciation because they have
intrinsic merit. When we have positive images of what they can become,
children and adults tend to produce materials which have intrinsic merit.
Some of the most satisfying poems and pictures I've seen were produced
by school children.

> *Who Looks*
>
>> *Beneath the sidewalks*
>>   *to tunnels—*
>>   *merging*
>>   *separating—*
>>   *searching out the*
>>   *earthy blackness;*
>> *Behind the neons*
>>   *proving*
>>   *camouflage*
>>   *for purple-veined faces;*
>> *Past the faces—*
>>   *hiding selves.*
>
>   Neil Moore, age 14, in Joseph (1969, p. 82)

> *If you touch me soft and gentle*
> *If you look at me and smile at me*
> *If you listen to me talk sometimes before you talk*
> *I will grow, really grow.*
>
>   Bradley, age 9, in James and Jongeward (1971, p. 41)

LEARNING BY DOING: COMMUNICATION SKILLS

In a sophomore English class, Ms. Gerber was working on communication
skills: communication first with the self, then with others. She found an
opportunity to allow the students to explore the idea of acting on their
feelings when the discussion turned to family relations.

> *MARK:*   It's getting so I can't stand to be around my house any
>   more. My parents both hassle me all the time.

SUE:	Mine too. "Do the dishes. Clean your room. Put away the laundry." I'm a slave around there.
MS. GERBER:	Do both of your parents work, Sue?
SUE:	Well, yes, but after all, I'm a student. I have my own work to do. Plus I'm a cheerleader this year. That takes up a lot of my time.
TED:	Yeah, parents don't remember that we have our lives to lead, too. I never get to do anything I want. I hardly ever get the car—only a couple of nights a week.
KAREN:	And the hassles! "Pull your hair back out of your eyes. You can't see a thing with it hanging down in your face!" How do they know what I can see and can't see? Do they even ask me?
MIKE:	My old man says I can't go with them to Nebraska this summer if I don't get my hair cut. He says my grandparents will think I'm a hippy. Why can't he just let me be myself and let me look like I want to look?
MS. GERBER:	Do you like it at your grandparents? Do you usually have a good time there?
MIKE:	Sure! Of course I haven't been there for three years. But there are lots of relatives and animals and fruit trees on the farm. My grandfather used to let me run the tractor for him. He's pretty cool for such an old man.
BETTY:	Do you think your long hair would upset him?
MIKE:	I don't know. Yeah, probably. Come to think of it, he did send me a newspaper article about a "hippy dope raid" in the high school there. He said he hoped I hadn't gotten in with the "wrong" crowd at my school.
MS. GERBER:	Perhaps your parents could be showing love for you by trying to help you to be comfortable and well received in Nebraska.
JUDY:	Don't give us that! They're doing it for themselves. They're afraid of what people will think of them if Mike shows up looking like he does. Parents don't care how we feel. Showing love! I can't remember the last time my parents showed any love for me. All they ever do is criticize me and my friends.
TOM:	Wait a minute. I can't just sit here any longer. I may be weird or something, but I get along fine with my parents. Any time I have a problem—school, sex, clothes, sports, anything—I just say, "Hey, Pop, I need to talk with you," and he always listens. And I listen to him too. Most of the time he really helps me figure out what I want to do about things. I really love my dad.
SUE:	Well, sure, I love my parents too. But I sure don't *like* them very much.
MS. GERBER:	What do you do to show your love for them?
SUE:	Everything! I told you, I work like a slave around there.

BETTY: No, Sue, you said *they* work you like a slave around there. What do you do, voluntarily, to show your love?

SUE: Not much, I guess. But every time I try to show love they take advantage of me. If I offer to do something they load twice as much work on me.

MS. GERBER: Do you love your mother?

SUE: Sure! Everyone loves their mother. No matter how much they hassle us, we still love our parents, I guess.

MS. GERBER: Are any of you ever consciously aware of love for your parents?

KAREN: Sure! Sometimes I remember when we all really got along well. Every once in a while it happens again for a few minutes. We all laugh at something together or go somewhere together. It happens especially with my mom.

MS. GERBER: When you have this feeling, do you mention it? Do you say, "Mom, I love you?"

JUDY: If I said that to my mother, she'd drop dead from shock!

SUE: Mine would say, "Now what do you want?"

LARRY: Parents just don't know how to receive love.

BETTY: Maybe we don't express it well sometimes. Judy said they don't care how we feel. Maybe we don't really tell them how we feel—especially the good feelings.

JUDY: I sure can't see myself expressing my true feelings to my parents. They're in another world and I don't like their world.

MIKE: Yeah, it's hard to explain my feelings to my parents. Even when I really want to.

MS. GERBER: Do you want to? Do you feel a need or desire to have a better, more loving relationship with your parents?

SUE: Boy, I sure do. I'm so tired of being hassled at home.

TED: Me too.

KAREN: And I guess I do sort of miss having fun with my family.

MS. GERBER: Then, perhaps, at least for those of you who feel the need, it's time for you to make your actions back up those feelings. Your homework assignment for tonight . . .

SUE: Homework! How could you?

MIKE: Homework? In a communications unit?

MS. GERBER: Your homework for tonight, for those of you who feel you want to try acting on your feelings, is to tell your mothers —or fathers—or both—that you love them.

JUDY: Are you kidding, Ms. Gerber?

LARRY: Did you tell *your* parents you loved them when you were a teenager?

MS. GERBER: No, I'm afraid I have to confess that I carried around a lot of resentment for my parents for years. I was a hassled teenager too, but I see that, in a way, their hassling me was their way of showing love for me. They tried to help me to avoid their mistakes and their sufferings. They tried to get me to do the things that would make them happy—

assuming that those same things would make me happy. The only knowledge they had was what they had experienced. And I didn't bother to tell them of my experiences, needs, fears, feelings. So all they had to go on was their own. I believe they didn't understand or accept me because I didn't see to it that they did.

LARRY: Well, maybe that's true for you. But you don't know my parents.

MS. GERBER: You're right, Larry. Like your parents, I, too, can only relate to you my own experiences and feelings.

BETTY: Then how can we "see to it" that they do know and understand us, Ms. Gerber?

MS. GERBER: I sure wish I could tell you that, Betty. I only know how it worked out for me. You are a different person, and you have different parents. And you are a teenager in a different and new time from my experience. You have to decide for yourself how to work it out in your own family and in your own life.

MIKE: I can just hear myself now. "By the way, Dad, I love you." It would blow his mind!

TOM: But he'll love it. I say it to my dad all the time.

KAREN: And he doesn't laugh?

SUE: Or ask you what you want from him?

TOM: No, he knows it's true. And he likes to hear me say it to him.

MIKE: You're really lucky, Tom. But it could never happen in my house.

BETTY: We never know until we try it.

Like Ms. Gerber, I express love in my teaching. This involves me in reciprocal relationships with pupils: giving, receiving, mutually supporting and enriching our lives, enjoying what we have, creating more of what we need, and learning. Living with mystery, sometimes creating new mystery. I learn in many ways through other people. Each pupil in Ms. Gerber's class learned, by comparing and contrasting his home experiences with that of others, and by becoming aware of the nature of his existential freedom to learn and to love. Ms. Gerber lives.

LEARNING TO LOVE THROUGH ROLE-PLAYING

"Jeff, come here!" called his mother. Reluctantly, Jeff turned from the ball game and walked across the street and into his house. "Mom, we're having a good game. Can't I play, Mom?" "No, you can't play now. I need some things at the store right now, so you go down there quick. Here's a list and here's money. Now, git!" Ms. Allen returned to her phone conversation. When Jeff returned twenty minutes later his mother was still on the phone. When she hung up he said, "It's about time"—and this got him a cussing out from his mother and later a spanking from his father.

The next day at school, Ms. Orton noticed that Jeff seemed sadder than usual. She knew she would have to wait for him to say something—if, indeed, he would. Just before school was out he asked if he could stay to help her with the blackboard and erasers. He cleaned them with care, all the while making only monosyllabic replies to her comments. Just before the last bit of make-work was completed, he said, "Can I ask you about something?" "Yes, of course, Jeff, what is it?" He told her the story of his interrupted baseball game, his trip to the store and his comment to his mother, plus the aftermath.

MS. ORTON:	Well, Jeff, what's your question, what do you want to ask me?
JEFF:	I think it's unfair, that's what! Don't you see how unfair it is?
MS. ORTON:	You think it's unfair?
JEFF:	Yes, she made me leave the game.
MS. ORTON:	Made you leave the game?
JEFF:	Yes, and then I got punished.
MS. ORTON:	Punished?
JEFF:	It's her fault—she could get the stuff at the store.
MS. ORTON:	Get the stuff at the store? Hmm—Jeff, I have an idea. Let's role-play. You be you, and I'll be your mother. Let's start when I call you in from the ball game. Let's make it happen just the way it did yesterday. (They replayed the previous day's incident.)
MS. ORTON:	Now, Jeff, how do you feel about it? Feel the same as yesterday?
JEFF:	Yes, it's all her fault—course, maybe I shouldn't of said what I did, but—course I wouldn't say that to you, Ms. Orton.
MS. ORTON:	It's OK to say it to your mother but not to me?
JEFF:	No, I mean yes—but I like you.
MS. ORTON:	You like me?
JEFF:	But I like my mom too, sometimes.
MS. ORTON:	Jeff, suppose we play the scene again, only this time you be your mother and I'll be you. Think you can do that? OK, here we go. (They replayed the previous day's incident again.)

In the ensuing discussion, Jeff faced up to some problems with freedom: my freedom is often related to someone else's freedom. His mother, he remembered, did have Victor and Diane to take care of, the house to clean, meals to cook—and not too much money to spend. Alice was her best friend, and his mother's chosen freedom could include a twenty minute conversation with Alice. Jeff walked home thoughtfully. The next day before he left for school he gave his mother a hug and said, "I'm really sorry I said that to you, Mom." Ms. Allen realized what Jeff was saying and hugged him in response.

When I love pupils, I help them learn about the nature of their own freedom and the freedom of others. When pupils love themselves, they can make immense efforts on their own behalf—and hence on behalf of all of us.

THE BIGGEST RISK OF ALL: STUDYING TEACHING

There are other ways of releasing potential and improving service to students. Teachers who study their own teaching risk—and they grow. It's time to study teaching in more objective fashion than we have in the past. No matter what my pattern of teaching, it can be improved with self-study. A recent advance in teaching and in coaching sports uses video tape recordings. These are available for instant or later replay, so that the person can see exactly how he performed. Teachers of all subjects can use a tape recorder or the video tape for this purpose also. If these devices are not available, ask a trusted peer to record your teaching behavior on one of the available tally sheets. (See reference in chapter notes to the work of Flanders and of Medley and Mitzel, 1963.) Later you can make thoughtful hypotheses about your behavior and student responses to it. Teachers in many schools are learning that video tape doesn't lie. Some prefer to watch the replay alone, at first, but before long they willingly share their tapes with other teachers. I have long thought of the ideal faculty as a community of scholars. Honest exchange of knowledge and opinion about teacher performance in the classroom can help bring this to reality. Teachers show their love for each other by sharing their less successful moments as well as their triumphs in the classroom. They grow by continuing to define varied ways in which good teaching *does something for the learner.*

A high school English teacher found himself dissatisfied with what his students retained. When he talked with the students about it, he realized that morale and involvement, as well as retention, were weak. He asked a colleague to observe several classroom planning sessions, and the two decided to use Flanders' (1970) interaction analysis during the sessions. The observer found that the teacher relied on lecturing, asking questions, and giving directions, while student activity was limited largely to responding. Even when the students made useful suggestions to the teacher in their responses, he tended to neglect the suggestions and to go on following his pattern. The teacher seldom accepted student feelings, praised or encouraged students, or accepted or used student ideas. No wonder the students felt left out! Interaction was basically a one-way street: "You respond to me the way I want you to respond, and only that way." The lack of trust, the lack of love, was evident.

The teacher, when shown his behavior as recorded on the Flanders interaction analysis, argued about the instrument and the validity of what it showed. But later he began to accept the data and to modify his behavior. By then, however, the students had come to expect his former pattern of behavior. It was not until the following semester, with a new class, that he was able to use his new knowledge to establish a more positively interactive environment. Students, too, must recognize that successful interaction requires effort on their part, including the effort to modify their behavior in response to modified teacher behavior. This will not happen automatically.

All teachers feel they do not have enough time for individual students. The teacher who cares, especially the secondary school teacher, must show his own uniqueness. He must ask for feedback, for student responses to what he does and about the nature of the curriculum the students get. If he doesn't get responses he considers close to what he wants, he should ask the students why he isn't getting them: "Can you feel a difference when you're in my classroom?" He should, of course, avoid invidious comparisons between himself and other teachers—he should focus on his intention of having a loving/learning environment in his classroom.

Barbara Shiel had thirty-six sixth graders, including several educationally handicapped and emotionally disturbed children. In January and February she faced the fact that her teaching was not succeeding; she considered change to be essential. She took the students into partnership with her in making changes. Their student-centered program was succeeding within two weeks of its inception.

Barbara held conferences with each student about his learning needs. Each student learned to write his own daily work contract—specific learning activities for each subject, listed in the order in which he would do them. Students checked their own completed work, using teacher manuals or answer books.

Two major benefits grew out of this experiment. The students, by any measure we have, gained. They gained academically, but also as individual human beings: in self-understanding, self-acceptance, self-discipline. The students learned the difference between failure and making a mistake —that mistakes are a valuable part of the learning process. Children in Barbara Shiel's class learned "to get to *know* one another—the children learned to communicate *by communicating*" (Rogers, 1969, pp. 11–27). Barbara Shiel lives.

Many school districts have in-service training programs. What better subjects to include than child study and the study of teaching? Many conventional in-service courses focus on bits and pieces of subject matter, such as primary math, instead of tackling the tougher problems of child study and teaching. Most districts encourage teachers to request topics for in-service study. Similarly, many colleges provide opportunities for teachers, individually and collectively, to request courses or workshops. Tooling up for tomorrow starts with the basic human factors.

LEARNING WITH OTHERS: EVALUATION

I learn with others. True, I may come to some understanding about myself or about a relationship while I push a cart around the supermarket, but much of my important learning takes place while interacting with others. As a teacher, I recognize that my most valuable attribute is to be an open, aware, and interested participant/learner in all that occurs around me. In that way I can more often serve students because of my readiness to serve.

After school one day, Ms. Holmes was making entries in the cumulative records of her students and noticed the charts on physical growth printed on the outside of the folder. The average third grade boy is four feet, three inches tall. Jimmy is four feet, four inches tall, and he talks less than other boys in her class. The average third grade boy throws a baseball a short way and not too accurately—Jimmy throws further and more accurately.

Over a period of days Ms. Holmes played with some ideas about what success is, what a mistake is, what failure is. Gradually she saw ways of showing students the differences and the relationships among these ideas. It was time for the annual physical checks, which included weighing and measuring each pupil and conducting the physical fitness tests. She needed a parent to help with record-keeping. Ms. Holmes invited Jimmy's mother to help, and was glad when she accepted.

After the height and weight of each pupil had been recorded, Ms. Holmes told the class she would like to make a graph of their heights on the board. She listed each child's name with his height beside it and then drew the two axes of a graph. With pupil help, she placed the range of heights along the horizontal axis and then put in appropriate numbers along the vertical axis. The pupils assisted her in deciding where to place the numbers and entries.

The ensuing discussion covered the nature and utility of graphs and the non-judgmental nature of the data arrayed in a graph. "From the graph, we can see that Stephanie is taller than Ardyce. Does this mean she's a faster runner?" The class warmed up to the idea. "Fred is the heaviest and he's also the best speller, but the two things aren't at all related. . . ."

The following day the class was given some data and asked to see what could be inferred from it: Tommy (fictional) brought home a geography paper with eleven errors on it out of a total of twenty-six items. His father said that this was a failing paper, even though no grade had been given by the teacher. Tommy knew that four of his friends in the class had gotten between eight and fifteen errors, and only one pupil that he knew of had gotten fewer than six errors.

The pupils spent some time in individual thinking and then worked in pairs for about fifteen minutes before discussing this information. The discussion disclosed the following points:

1. The teacher had not defined *pass* or *fail*.
2. The teacher had corrected but not graded the papers.
3. Possibly this was a trial test or an exercise which would not be graded.
4. Several in the class had done no better than Tommy.

5. Should there be an arbitrary dividing line between pass and fail? What if everyone had less than three-quarters of the answers correct, for example?

6. Errors or mistakes do not mean failure—possibly Tommy learned a whole lot of geography.

7. Maybe tests don't always show how much you know or what you can do with what you know.

The class decided this was an important set of ideas and delegated two class members to write up a report on the discussion for their wall newspaper. Three other students were delegated to invite the other third grades to send representatives for a continuing discussion to be held the following day.

In succeeding class discussion, students noted that when two teams play a game, only one team can win. Losing a game or even a long series of games could be called a losing streak but did not have to be called failure. A student who was out of school for eight weeks with illness might repeat third grade because he needed to learn all that he missed, but this was not failure. Students then remembered that several of the Indian societies they have studied in social studies stressed cooperation rather than competition. This led to a listing of possible ways people could use alternatives to a competitive system. The students complained about some of the effects of competition on them and agreed that when one of them didn't compare favorably with others it made him feel less OK. Ms. Holmes and the class agreed on some processes they could use to avoid making students feel less OK. They agreed, for example, that each student's scores and grades would be private between him and his teacher—unless he chose to tell others. They also agreed that the teacher would talk over grades with each student frequently, and that the student would take part in grading himself.

Ms. Holmes found that she benefited from this sequence of experiences as much as any student. Previously she had felt uncomfortable about grading, especially about giving low marks to students who appeared to have less academic aptitude than others. She had been aware that students feared and resented the grading process but had not realized how universal or deep-seated the feelings were. Several times she remembered she had said to herself, "I didn't make the system, I just live in it. The people who set it up must have some reason for separating the able from the less able." During the sequence of lessons having to do with public and private ideas about evaluation, she recognized that when the apparently less able student got a D or an F, this could easily become a self-fulfilling prophecy for him: "I'm a D student, I can't do any better." She saw that this was grossly unfair and could hamper his self-image and his accomplishments for years of his life. What we need, she decided, are loving achievers, individuals motivated to find out for themselves, to *do* for themselves. Even though the world of work may stress competition, the schools are not compelled to follow suit. If we give students many success experiences and positive self-images in school, they will be able to cope with a competitive system better in later life. Maybe they'll work to change it.

Ms. Holmes also realized that she, as an individual teacher, had more freedom than she had previously thought. She had freedom to explore the whole area of evaluation, within herself and with students. She had a wide latitude in interpreting the district grading policy. She began to use that freedom. At the next faculty meeting, she suggested that the faculty devote a whole meeting to reviewing the present grading policy. That afternoon as she drove home she realized that she was growing and changing as she learned, and the idea delighted her. She greeted her own two children joyfully.

I recognize the importance of evaluation, and I know how to do it. I utilize feedback of various sorts as a means of deciding whether a particular product or process meets my need(s). Few of the humanistic critics of traditional public education deny the importance of evaluation. What we do question is the arbitrary nature of evaluation. Each of us naturally evaluates himself daily, hourly, even second by second. As my hand moves the pencil across the page, I evaluate to see if each word is in fact legible: immediate feedback. The basic evaluation then, is by me. I evaluate my effort and my product in terms of my needs and aims as I see them. You cannot evaluate me—because you don't know what I set out to do. You can only guess, unless I tell you, and even if I tell you, I may fail to communicate to you more than half of what you need to know to evaluate me with any degree of fairness.

What I do is listen to pupils, talk with them, and help them build more comprehensive ideas about self-evaluation. They evaluate. I help. When I love pupils, I encourage their recognition of the great importance of their own evaluation. I help them trust themselves and their evaluations of themselves.

I can estimate: I am aware of approximation, of fit, of the degree to which my behavior or product comes close to meeting my contemporary need. Sara learned to estimate the amount of material needed for a dress so that she could buy material with confidence. Larry learned how to estimate a throw to first base. He also learned to estimate an answer to a long division example so that he had a built-in partial check on his answer: he could tell if it was in the right range. We all estimate whether it is safe to cross a street in the face of an oncoming car. Each of us makes many such estimates each day. It is important that I, as a teacher, am aware of the estimates made by pupils and of the way those estimates are used. They always should serve the need of the individual as he sees it. By helping the pupil make and use estimates, I am helping him to increase his competence and his feeling of OK-ness.

I can alter goals, revise process, redirect learning effort. As I learn, I am aware of my ability to redefine my goal, redirect my learning efforts, and revise any process I am using.

The real existential question Sara faced was: What person am I willing to become? As she completed her high school credits and took courses at the junior college, she constantly evaluated her own progress, as she saw it, in achieving her goal, as she saw it. As she took more courses and learned more about herself, her goal began to change. She was no longer sure she wanted to be a beautician. She began to dream of other possibilities. When I love pupils, I allow them to dream. I encourage them to evaluate their own current needs as well as their dreams.

I LEARN AS LONG AS I LIVE

Ronald Laing (1968, p. 76) says that "we have to realize that we are as deeply afraid to live and to love as we are to die." I can spend six hours a day with students, lecturing, assigning, testing, grading, or I can teach by observing, listening, being available, responding in group discussion, facilitating, encouraging, conferring. The former mode would be nonteaching to me now.

I choose to live. Along with breathing and eating, I learn. Today I confirmed my learned ability to talk with one person and to focus a great portion of my consciousness on him right now. I choose to teach. Today I learned more about listening to one of my students in the everlasting effort to hear what he really was saying. I choose to learn things about people and human interacting which will help me to be a better teacher, a more useful human resource to students. I choose to go on learning about myself as I continue becoming. This is my answer to the question: What am I going to do with the life that I have?

CONCLUSION

When I dedicate myself to loving behavior in the classroom, when I show care, respect, and responsibility to students and interact with them in knowledgeable ways, then I am contributing to a better school. I am electing to teach human beings and am inviting, by my example, other teachers to do likewise. Together we can rebuild schools into environments which promote loving and learning.

NOTES TO CHAPTER 6

As you may have noticed, I suggest a number of activities that may be regarded as old-fashioned, such as home visits. Although the idea has been around a long time, I feel teachers need to be reminded of the potential value of visiting a parent (or parents) at home.

The child study movement owes a great debt to Daniel Prescott, professor of education at University of Maryland for many years. His *The Child in the Educative Process* (1957) is a classic which insists on the uniqueness of the individual and shows the practical values of persistent child study applied in the classroom. Hugh V. Perkins has added many significant points in *Human Development and Learning* (1969), which puts child study in a larger framework of growth and development. Ned A. Flanders has devoted over two decades to the study of teaching behavior in the classroom. His book, *Analyzing Teaching Behavior* (1970), brings together his work and that of others. Ira Gordon, author of one of the standard texts on the evolution of the infant and child, has given many specific suggestions on observing and evaluating individuals in *Studying the Child in School* (1966). In a booklet for ASCD, Gordon (1972, pp. 9–22) stresses basic understandings that help teachers deal realistically with students:

> What the child may become is strongly influenced by the way he is brought up from the moment of birth.
> Both heredity and environment are important.
> Cognitive and affective learning occur together, not separately.
> Intervention by teachers and others may succeed at any stage in the individual's evolution.
> There is no single "culture of poverty."
> Intervention (as in Head Start) generally shows little long-run gain by the subject students; those not included catch up as a result of schooling.
> "We know for sure that the human infant is able to learn far more than we previously thought."

This booklet, is an excellent brief report on recent research, ideal for your faculty library.

Ronald Lippitt, whose doctoral study in the late thirties compared reactions of young boys to authoritarian, laissez-faire, and democratic leadership, has continued to contribute leadership in the field of education. He and his associates at the University of Michigan have learned much about the psychology of the classroom and have made many very practical suggestions to teachers. One of the books this team has produced is *Diagnosing Classroom Learning Behaviors* by Robert S. Fox and others (1966). Another is *The Teacher's Role in Social Science Investigation* by Lippitt, Fox, and Schaible (1969).

The Association for Supervision and Curriculum Development (ASCD) publishes many useful books in addition to their yearbooks. One of those used in this chapter is *The Unstudied Curriculum*, edited by Norman Overly (1970). Chapters deal with the middle-class values in most public schools, school philosophy, authority, and the impact of the school on the student.

Daniel Fader and Elton McNeil proved that the intensity of student interest survives years of deadening experiences in school. *Hooked on Books* (1968) is one of the best testimonials I've ever read for adapting to the needs of students.

One periodical I enjoy greatly is *Educational Leadership*, published by the ASCD. The December 1971 issue has an article by Nicholas P. Georgiady and Louis G. Romano entitled "Ulcerville, USA," telling of the ways in which schools at all levels bring pressure on students with often tragic results.

Benjamin Bloom, associated with the taxonomies, has also done *Stability and Change in Human Characteristics* (1964). It presents evidence on physical changes, IQ, achievement, interests, attitudes, and the environments in which human evolution occurs. The preface gives his basic conclusions in a nutshell.

Robert J. Schaefer wrote a slim volume called *The School as a Center of Inquiry* (1967), which I believe never got proper recognition. It is well worth reading.

The Place of Love in Education, by Shakti Datta (1960), was published by University Publishers, Jullundur-Delhi-Ambala, India in 1960. Mr. Datta has read about experimental schools and has visited many schools, and he has interesting things to say on love and its utilization in education.

The Italian TV network did a careful documentary on the life of Leonardo da Vinci which I saw on CBS-TV in August of 1972. It stresses how little we know of the life of this creative genius and does not overdramatize what we do know. Hopefully, films of this quality will be made available to schools and colleges.

Fannie and George Shaftel wrote a book called *Role-Playing the Problem Story* (1952) which is especially helpful in interracial and intergroup schools.

Fred Wilhelms edited the 1967 ASCD Yearbook, *Evaluation as Feedback and Guide*. If you feel threatened by behavioral objectives or performance criteria, look at this book. Clifford Bebell considers the reasons—such as inertia—for the continued use of the grade system of evaluation. Rodney Clark and Walcott Beatty relate evaluation to individual becoming and state that evaluation must be made by: (1) the individual student, (2) the teacher, concerning each student, (3) the teacher and students, concerning the class, and (4) all the resource people (administrators, lay boards, and so on). Dorris Lee gives classroom examples. I find much to encourage me in this book.

On page 86 I discuss the value of studying teaching. Ned Flanders has been one of the most persistent students of teaching. His *Analyzing Teacher Behavior* (1970) brings together many of the recent studies on teacher behavior and presents ideas about how to make systematic studies, including (on pp. 54–86) samples of coding of classroom interaction. Donald M. Medley and Harold E. Mitzel have a chapter on this in *Handbook of Research on Teaching* (1963), although a lot of work has been done since publication of this paper.

A book which I recommend especially for high school seniors and college freshmen and sophomores is *Those Who Can, Teach*, by Kevin Ryan and James M. Cooper (1971). It raises many of the most significant questions about public education and suggests several ways of answering each. The young person who is considering teaching will find it a realistic introduction to American schools. This book has beautiful photos. It also has excellent lists of contemporary films on education.

Learning (behavioral change) is a consequence of experience. *People become responsible when they have really assumed responsibility; they become independent when they have experienced independent behavior; they become able when they have experienced success; they begin to feel important when they are important to somebody; they feel liked when someone likes them. People do not change their behavior merely because someone tells them to do so or tells them how to change. For effective learning, giving information is not enough; for example, people become responsible and independent, not from having other people tell them that they should be responsible and independent, but from having experienced authentic responsibility and independence.*

Angelo V. Boy and
Gerald J. Pine (1971)

Seven

DO-IT-YOURSELF

This is a do-it-yourself chapter. What do you feel like doing at this point?
Do it.

NOTES TO CHAPTER 7

The best how-to books in the area of personal growth are the following:

Joy, by William Schutz (1967).

Ways of Growth, by Herbert Otto and John Mann (1968). A number of possible ways to learn and grow are outlined. A good place to start.

Born to Win, by Muriel James and Dorothy Jongeward (1971).

I'm OK—You're OK, by Thomas A. Harris (1969).

The Shared Journey, by Terry O'Banion and April O'Connell (1969).

Notes to Myself, by Hugh Prather (1970).

Awareness, by John O. Stevens (1971).

Sense Relaxation, by Bernard Gunther (1968).

I Ain't Much Baby—But I'm All I've Got, by Jesse Lair (1969), available from Jesse Lair, 509 South 9th, Bozeman, Montana, 59715.

Enjoy!

It startles teachers to see pupils carry out a lesson without their help. But when this does happen, they see their meaning as a teacher—a meaning determined by the things they have to contribute to a pupil that a pupil cannot do for himself. This meaning or purpose is the one and only reason for having a teacher. Therefore, it is important for a teacher to see what a pupil can do on his own without the teacher's help. Then the teacher can determine the kind of help that is actually essential.

Robert C. Burkhart and
Hugh M. Neil (1968)

Eight

NATURE AND NURTURE IN THE CLASSROOM: SELF-DIRECTED LEARNING

During her first year of teaching, Ms. Weldon had tried some self-selection in reading and self-pacing in arithmetic, and she was pleased with the results. She decided to talk with her new principal about self-directed learning before the opening of school.

"Hmm. I don't know much about this sort of thing," said Mr. Thomas. "I've never had a teacher who used these methods. But tell me more about it." Ms. Weldon described how her program had worked. It was agreed that Ms. Weldon should start out teaching her fourth grade as she wished, that Mr. Thomas would visit her several times early in the year, and that if he detected too many problems they would confer again about modifying the program.

Self-directed learning (abbreviated as SDL) is not a single idea or formula. It is based on specific attitudes toward teaching and child growth and development, attitudes which have been discussed in previous chapters. Different teachers work out different combinations of ways of working with students. I have devised my own plan, which works better for me than any formula I could adopt from someone else. This program could be used in junior and senior high schools, and in college, although it may need to be carried out differently than in an elementary school.

In ideal form, SDL consists of some combination of the following:

(1) Pupils select what they will use from an array of available learning opportunities and materials. This is especially convenient for reading but will also work in social studies, math, science, health, language arts, physical education, and creative and vocational arts. Self-selection is the real hall-mark of SDL. It encourages the child to make his own commitments.

(2) Pupils work at their own pace—they are not slowed down or speeded up by being in a group.

(3) In order to get the greatest benefits from self-selection and self-pacing, pupils plan and organize their own work: the sequence of work to be undertaken in a given day, the length of time they expect to spend on each task, and also the approach they use to get at what they want to know. They have some say about how they work (alone or in pairs, for example), so that social learning skills are integrated with other skills.

(4) Pupils act as teachers in many informal ways. This happens when classmates ask for help and also at the teacher's request.

(5) Pupils are grouped or group themselves for various purposes at various times: social groupings, common interest groupings, and skill-building groupings.

(6) Assignments may be agreed upon between the teacher and each pupil: what is to be done, how, when it is due, and how it is to be evaluated. The *contract* plan may be used, even a written contract obligating the student to fulfill specified work in a specified time—although when this is rigid it conflicts with the ideal of pupil freedom.

(7) Pupils, singly and in groups, report their findings or show their products to part or all of the class. This may be done in many ways besides the traditional oral report.

(8) The class holds meetings each day. Please see Chapter 13.

(9) The teacher spends his time in many ways. The following are among the most important:

(a) He observes to see what is happening, to see what can be learned from pupil behavior that will help him in instructing pupils: "I see Janice moves her lips when reading silently."

(b) He assists pupils to get started on their self-assigned projects: Jack needs a pamphlet on how the post office works.

(c) He teaches groups, sometimes in the same manner as in a conventional classroom, using the teacher manual to give a very specific skill-building lesson: I prepare for a group lesson on "the main idea" of the story, at home the night before.

(d) He diagnoses individual learning difficulties, applying child study as discussed in the last chapter.

(e) He confers with an individual pupil to find out how the child sees the problem he's working on, to help him, to counsel him in his work, and to encourage him. On Friday I talk with Ted about the wooden salad bowl he's making.

(f) He keeps records, making notes on what he observes and on what happens in group sessions and in individual conferences. I note that Mel's enthusiasm outstrips his basic skills—I plan activities with him to build needed skills.

(g) On the basis of what he learns in the activities listed above, the teacher makes lesson plans. Mine includes three groups I will meet with, conference time, and reporting time.

Each of these practices will be developed more fully in this and the following chapters. Are any of these practices found in your classroom?

What I have called self-directed learning has for several decades been called individualized instruction. In my reading I have found descriptions of individualized instruction written as long ago as the 1920s. Articles appeared in the thirties, and since the fifties there has been a substantial increase in the number of reports from practitioners. Why then, do I choose to change the name? In the last ten years and most especially the last five, a whole rash of educational programs, many of them offered by profit-seeking corporations, have claimed to provide individualized instruction. Upon examination, most such programs allow, at best, self-pacing by students as they go through a succession of tasks established by the adults who devised the program. Frequently, too, the programs are dull and uninteresting; they have given individualized instruction an undeserved bad name. Self-directed learning may be a happier and more accurate description: it clearly indicates that the student and his learning take precedence over performance by a teacher.

As Burkhart and Neil say at the beginning of this chapter, each teacher must find out what each pupil needs—and *then* he can serve that pupil. My *only* reason for employment as a teacher is pupils, and most specifically, pupils' needs. Pupils' needs come first, ahead of me and my needs. For if the pupil does not grow as a person, all the skills in the world will avail him—and the world—nothing. So I plan and carry out my teaching to meet pupil needs, to serve pupils as they need to be served. I can do so best by teaching individuals.

Charles worked away quietly in the corner, occasionally muttering to himself. Ms. Ramsey finished up with the group that was learning to extract the main idea from a passage, made some notes on their work, and then went over to see how Charles was doing. He had come into the class only a week earlier, a forlorn looking boy, reluctantly accompanying his older sister to school. He made odd noises and was sometimes needlessly rough with others in the yard. He would not read, would not even pick up a book. Yesterday Charles had noticed Ted carving a bar of soap and immediately showed an interest. Ms. Ramsay told him he was free to carve as much as he liked. She expressed her pleasure at what he was carving. Charles carved twenty-seven bars of soap. Then, one day, he picked up a comic book.

SELF-SELECTION: THE WISH IN ACTION

It is reading period in Ms. Weldon's fourth grade. John walks over to the bookshelf and picks up a magazine. He turns the pages to see what is in it, yawns, puts it back, looks at the teacher to see if she is watching him. After a while, he chooses a Dr. Seuss book, returns to his seat, and reads. Soon he tires of the book, returns it to the shelf, and repeats the browsing process. He does read a *Mechanics Illustrated* article before the period ends. He finds an article about clock mechanisms, becomes interested, and his face brightens as he reads.

John confirms an area of his own freedom by rejecting some books —which he may later choose to read. He confirms his own OK-ness by enjoying reading what he selected: "My choice turned out to be fun—and I made the decisions."

Perhaps you know a student who will browse all day or all month if you let him. Browsing has its own benefits, scanning many books and getting impressions from them, examining a few books in detail and choosing one, relaxing without pressure from the teacher to perform a stated task, realizing one's potentials in an area of freedom. At the same time, different individuals have different readiness to reap these benefits, and each teacher will watch to see how browsing occurs. You may decide to ask an occasional student if he wants help. This may be patronizing or it may be viewed by the student as a veiled injunction: "Get busy, or I'll take away your freedom." In classrooms in which there is freedom for the student, that freedom is always conditional, partial, and revocable. At any point the teacher may withdraw the freedom or some of it from an individual or from the whole class. Nevertheless, in many classrooms the area of real freedom is extensive. Each teacher desirous of granting it will decide for herself or himself what areas of freedom he will grant and how much— and also the limits of his tolerance of behavior that threatens his feeling of security. The teacher will also think ahead to ways in which he can talk with individuals and with the class when he is upset about what the students are doing. Ginott's *Teacher and Child* (1972) has many suggestions. Besides talking, the teacher may elect to communicate with a student through the student's journal.

In a feeding experiment done many years ago, Abraham, the young subject, could eat anything he wanted from a large selection of food. Over a period of time and without any coaching, he ate what was considered at that time a remarkably balanced diet. Each of us, at any age, at some level of consciousness knows what is good for him and what he needs. The child who starts out feeling partly OK will use learning as a means not only of validating but also of extending his own OK-ness. The child who, like John, feels less OK about himself, will venture more often in the freedom of SDL. But it will take time. John has to learn for himself that his teacher's real message is "Be yourself."

I consider a child's wish to be of value, just as he does. *Total value admission* means listening to each child's wishes. More than that, it means creating a learning environment in which each pupil feels free to express his wishes. Once expressed, the pupil's wish enters the marketplace of possibilities: it may be rejected, amended, adopted, or neglected. My responsibilities as a teacher include helping individuals and groups to consider wishes realistically. For example, I ask the dance committee how much money they have when they talk of hiring a rock band. An individual pupil's wish too, requires recognition by the teacher—that is a form of validation of the pupil: I recognize your wish, and in so doing, I recognize you as an OK person. But the wish of the OK person cannot and should not always be granted. In fact, sometimes the answer must be "No"—as when one pupil wishes to take home a book which is needed by many other pupils. I say, "I'm aware that others need that book," or "I'll help you find alternative material until you can use that book," or "Can you work on your science notebook until that book is available?" to give the student options instead of a closed door.

Wishing, expressing wishes, and interacting with others about one's wishes—all these occur at home, at school, and in the neighborhood. Experience gained in this way helps the personally involved pupil learn to deal with such varied situations as choosing which movie to go to and choosing a delegate to a union's state convention. The pupil participating in self-directed learning has many opportunities each day to choose, and so he gets lots of practice in this important skill.

To achieve the purposes we proclaim—effective participation in adult life as creative workers, citizens, and parents—schools encourage both convergent and divergent thinking. Each American child, desiring to become an adult in our culture, chooses to learn many of these things which we as adult representatives of that culture believe to be important. We hope that the process of choosing will be genuine, involving questioning and comparing by the individual before he accepts. SDL permits constant practice in choosing and—as the student becomes able to deal with more complex ideas—opportunities to try his hand with more sophisticated ideas and relationships. For example, the student in algebra today may learn not only to solve textbook examples, but also to consider applications of algebra to practical affairs outside the school. Each student in SDL, because he finds that learning is his own private enterprise, plays with facts, concepts, processes, and relationships in his own unique way—so that the outcomes of his thinking are unpredictable. The teacher in SDL finds himself going along with the student at appropriate times, opposing him at other times in order to provide contrasting points of view. The net result in some cases will be divergent thinking and creativity stimulated by an environment which invites fresh ideas and new solutions to emerging problems. We need them.

Each student recognizes at some level of awareness that school is a means by which each generation attempts to perpetuate a value system and a social system. But exposure does not guarantee acceptance. In practice, this is what happens most of the time: the end result of much self-selection is convergent behavior and thinking. What will be idiosyncratic are the sequences and configurations of learning undertaken by each student. They are already idiosyncratic; recognition of this reality will help us as teachers to go *with* the student instead of opposing his natural impulses to do it his own way. If in the process the student learns some divergent ideas, processes, and approaches, in addition to the convergent ones, this is a bonus for him and for society.

In math period in Ms. Weldon's class, four students are doing geometry, seven long division, five short division, three multiplication with a two-place multiplier, three are doing graphs, another elementary statistics. As they master one process, most children move on to another because of interest, curiosity, and peer influence. Most will follow the book from topic to topic, although some will skip around, which must be understood as also OK. Each will learn, in part, by failing at tasks he chooses. That's a part of real life, too, and no preplanned curriculum can avoid it. I learn to make choices by making choices. Are you aware of how you feel when faced by a choice-making situation? How do you make choices?

Becoming aware of one's wishes is healthy, and self-selection encourages such awareness. Self-selection also nudges the individual toward acceptance of responsibility for his own learning, a very necessary part of his evolution toward independent selfhood. He can learn to discard the old injunctions and to create for himself self-fulfilling prophecies of achievement. The teacher can enjoy presiding over a rich smorgasbord of choice-making, instead of prescribing work which many students will elect to do haphazardly or not at all. The teacher has the option of following tradition or breaking new ground.

SELF-PACING

The student in a self-pacing program works at his own speed. Instead of being slowed down by the pace in Group 2 or alternatively struggling to keep up with the whole class, he *is* the group, the group of one, the most important group. Whether he is drawing a map or using the dictionary or studying spelling words, he does it at his own pace—which may differ from time to time during the day. I questioned a large bill for mechanical repair of my car and was told that the shop charged a fixed amount per hour and did not keep track of the actual time spent on most jobs; they simply referred to the book which lists the standard time required. The foreman explained that this allows for the considerable variations of time required by different men to do the same job. When business and industry recognize such natural differences in working speed, how can I as a teacher do less? The foreman's aim is to see that all repairs are performed at a high level of excellence. My aim as a teacher is to encourage both convergent and idiosyncratic learning by a group of unique individuals. Loving respect for each individual student requires permitting him to work at his own pace.

In a high school chemistry class, each student can work in his textbook or in the lab at his own pace. Of course there are exceptions: an important film, or a problem of expense, storage, or set-up time may require all students to do one thing at the same time. If the teacher plans thoughtfully, these times can be infrequent, so that students can work at their own pace most of the time.

In arithmetic, Willie was three-fourths of the way through the second grade book, so Ms. Weldon started him at the approximate page where her checking out of his skills showed he could succeed. She noticed that he was out of his seat a lot and asked him to come for a conference to which he brought his work. The quality as well as the quantity of work he'd accomplished in the two days was unsatisfactory, she felt. They went over the work, noting that he hadn't marked all the errors he'd made, and she helped him with two things he didn't understand. She also encouraged him to work more consistently, pointing out how easily he was being distracted.

Willie appreciated her strokes, the individual attention and interest she showed in him. Also, he understood what she taught him and this helped make the next few pages in the book easier to do. So for a few days Willie accomplished more in his math. Before long, however, he slumped back into his old ways, doing less work, visiting with his friends, correcting his work carelessly. The teacher was anxious about Willie and about several others in the class: would they really get themselves together on the math?

Martin Covington and his associates (1965) have devised some intriguing verbal/visual problems for upper elementary pupils to solve. In each problem, the directions make it clear that there is more than one "right" answer, and pupils are encouraged to suggest many. A number of the problems are mysteries which a boy and girl work together to solve. They show ingenuity but often are stymied, in spite of a variety of verbal and visual clues. The booklets provide the clues for the students who are working to solve the mystery. After scoring hundreds of responses to these problems, I am convinced that only the individual knows how he sees a problem, its related aspects, and possible steps to its solution or solutions. The pupil needs opportunity to consider: what for me at this time is the way(s) to accomplish what I'm after? He can do this best by working at his own pace.

A group of students was working on Clay Boats at the science learning center in their classroom. Several students caught on quickly, realizing if they molded a fairly thin, concave shape, their boats would float. Others tended to imitate the early successes. One student, however, paid little attention to the others and went his own way. After a while he made a thin-shelled, hollow ball, and it floated. This pleased him; it also aroused the curiosity of the others. Several had found that a solid ball would not float. At first the maker of the hollow ball declined to tell them why his ball floated, but he later relented. Each of the others had, during this experience, at least a glimmer of understanding of why this student had marched to a different drummer. Self-directed learning, by encouraging variations in style and pace, helps to optimize the learning experience for each learner. Do you notice students who march to different drummers?

How do students working at their own pace compare in achievement with students working at a pace set by the instructor? In an experiment that involved learning paired-association items, a self-paced group did as well as a group to which the material was presented at fixed intervals. In fact, the self-paced group did significantly better on the first practice trial, although this difference faded on subsequent trials. Could it be that the subjects, especially the self-paced ones, were settling in and adjusting to the very narrow and limited demands of this learning situation? When we ask so little of the individual, he may well restrict his outlook and draw in his willingness to respond to a restricted environment.

Self-pacing, by giving freedom of pace and style, gives dignity to each individual. It encourages becoming. It allows the individual opportunities to love. He feels OK, appreciates his OK-ness, and can consciously as well as unconsciously contribute to the OK-ness of others.

THE PUPIL PLANS HIS OWN WORK

The ultimate beneficiary of the teaching-learning environment is the pupil. To optimize these benefits, he needs opportunities to plan his own work. Through planning he can find ways of better utilizing his freedom to select his own materials and to work at his own pace.

In one sixth grade class, the first period of the day is devoted to self-selected reading. The second period has five to ten minutes set aside for planning. Each pupil is to plan the way he will spend the rest of the day

—the sequence of tasks to be undertaken and an estimate of the time required for each. He writes down a schedule for the day which the teacher may ask to see at any time. This schedule serves as a guide to the pupil. When the teacher asks to see it, the pupil is reminded once again of the teacher's interest in his progress. This interest may take the form of questioning about where he is in terms of his own schedule.

A similar plan may work in a secondary classroom. The teacher may assign a brief task for everyone to accomplish in the first five to ten minutes of the class period, and then he may allow each student to plan for himself the rest of the period. Or, each student could plan on Monday his use of his time for the rest of the week. This will give students opportunities to work at learning centers (to be discussed below). Sharing of this type of responsibility for leadership gives each student an increased feeling of participation in and responsibility for his own education. It reminds him that, rather than listening to parental or teacher injunctions, he can bring about futures he envisions for himself.

Planning will be both conscious and unconscious. Conscious planning occurs when the pupil decides in math that he will work on geometry next, plans how he will go about it—for example, by deciding to make a set of drawings and measurements instead of simply doing the exercises in the book, or plans the day's sequence of learning experiences as suggested above. If class time is not set aside for planning, each pupil should be encouraged to give some time to it. He should also be encouraged to note the value of revising his plans on the basis of his experiences—just as he learns to evaluate his own work and make adjustments on the basis of that evaluation.

Unconscious planning occurs when, in the course of his work, the pupil alters an earlier plan in response to something he reads or some new idea which occurs to him. He may shift almost imperceptibly in the way he approaches a problem or task. When a pupil can do this without hesitation, he shows growth toward self-sufficiency, toward ability to stand on his own two feet as an independent learner.

GROUPING

Grouping economizes the time of both teacher and students. It also helps by giving individuals structured opportunities to learn both content and process skills and also to learn listening/pondering/contributing skills which increase the success and the fun of group work. Students enjoy working in groups which have clearly recognized purposes and which aim at meeting their immediate instructional needs.

Groups may be formed for several purposes. When several pupils have a common skill-building need, the teacher will invite them to come together to work on it. An English teacher notices that some members of his creative writing class have difficulties with free expression. Some students feel that a poem ought to rhyme, others describe scenes/events/-characters in the most pedestrian fashion. These students need help in letting go, and the teacher calls them together to work on this collection of skills.

Common interest groups, by contrast, form according to the impulses of the members of a class. Occasionally members of a team, such as a girls' volleyball team, may choose to come together to socialize as well as to practice outside of the regular established time. In individualized reading, some kids choose to sit together for no reason visible to an outsider—yet they work better and enjoy learning more because of this proximity. It is one of the mysteries of teaching which I am now content to live with. Spontaneous groups happen when students elect to sit together in the cafeteria or to play together on the yard.

How do groups function in your class or classes? Are there minimum standards or rules that should be applied?

The teacher will decide how best to work with skill groups. He will decide how often the group should meet and for how long. Some groups will need to meet every day, while others may accomplish all they need to do by meeting once a week. From time to time, groups will change the frequency of meetings or will taper off as they come close to completing what was planned. Length of meetings should also be decided according to needs of the group. Flexibility will help all members to optimize benefits and to feel OK about the group.

Common interest groups, social groups, and spontaneous groups will meet as often and for as long as they see fit. They will learn to make decisions for themselves. Only when they encounter discord within the group, or when the group activity interferes with the work of others in the class, should the teacher intervene. Even then, this should be done thoughtfully; the teacher must avoid being the heavy who spoils the fun. Often, kids can settle their own hassles, and they need opportunities to learn from doing so.

The teacher must always evaluate his priorities in making decisions about which groups to work with, the length of group sessions, the frequency of meeting, and the duration of a group (that is, when to terminate it). He may decide that a science group needs to meet right now and that a group to work on map skills in social studies can wait for a week or two —until some of the other groups have finished their work. Many times students realize that a group has served its purpose. Or an individual will know that he has gotten all he can out of the group. The teacher who tunes in to what is real will, many times, accept such gut-level decisions by students. If the same group needs to re-form a week or a month later, students may be better able to accept the teacher's invitation if they know he listens to their feelings.

How do I evaluate the work of a group? How do I decide when it's time to terminate a particular group? Both content and process need to be evaluated. For example, a chemistry teacher established a group to work on kinetic theory and its extensions. In evaluating this group, she had to ask herself whether the students had learned the skills they needed. Along with checking comprehension of the material studied, the teacher looks at process. How has this group worked together? Did the members show patience, did they listen to each other, did they make efforts to achieve rapport? Obviously content and process are inseparable, although progress in one may be more noticeable in a particular case. The teacher's evaluation of the students' content learning and process skills is made jointly with the students.

Mr. McVickers teaches a night school course in American government. During the evening, after the class met, he spent some time considering what the groups in his class were learning in the way of process skills. They were having some difficulty in defining their goal and hence in sticking to the point. Once started, many talked eagerly but not always to the point. He decided that each evening he would ask a member of each group to serve as process observer, to make notes on who said what and how he said it, but to abstain from the discussion himself. Then, the process observer would discuss his observations at the end of the group discussion period. In an in-service workshop, Mr. McVicker had served as a process observer four times in a two week period, so he felt able to explain what the observer's job was. By rotating this job among all the members of each group, he hoped to provide each member of the class with an opportunity to learn to be a better listener and to learn how he affected other members of the group. Hopefully, then, each member's participation would improve. The evaluation discussions at the end of each discussion period would then help the group members to see how much their group had accomplished and how it could improve next time. Studies have shown that such practice results in considerable improvement by the group members in achieving objective success. More information can be found in Warren G. Bennis, Kenneth D. Benne and Robert Chin, *Planning of Change* (1970) and in Matthew Miles, *Learning to Work in Groups* (1959).

In Ms. Weldon's class, Sue belonged to the "outlining group," in which she learned a great deal about outlining material in science or social science. Ms. Weldon said Sue was free to leave the group, because she had mastered most of the skills. However, the group had branched out into thinking and evaluating skills—such as comparing and contrasting, scaling, and frames of reference—so Sue chose to stay in the group. Harvey chose to leave when he completed his outlining. Ms. Weldon said the group could disband, but four members wished to continue. They did, for three more weeks, providing their own leadership.

Divide your class into groups for a particular purpose, such as to discuss an accident in the neighborhood. See how each group functions, and get ideas for a different grouping next time. Each teacher will learn by doing, will find ways of working with different groups, and will learn to improve his skills for working with groups.

STUDENTS AS TEACHERS

Each child serves as teacher and as learner in many activities inside and outside the classroom. Girls teach other girls to play jacks or jump-rope, for example. Teaching can be seen as demonstrating, behaving, and explaining on a one-to-one basis rather than simply telling or criticizing. Learning can be seen as trying, experimenting, altering performance on the basis of feedback—rather than as memorizing and regurgitating in response to orders from the teacher. The teacher's role and the learner's role are seen to be complementary and supportive of each other. Self-directed learning allows loving behavior in the form of friendly help and reciprocal relationships which aid individuals in imagining and bringing about more exciting futures for themselves. One group of ninth graders in a remedial class became tutors to third graders in a nearby school. The older students took pride in preparing by reading the third grade materials carefully. They learned a lot by helping the younger kids.

How do you select students to serve as teachers? There are various ways you can let it happen: Nick asks Janet for help and she gives it, or Mary notices that Freda is having difficulty and goes over to help. At other times the teacher will ask a student to serve as teacher, often for a specified period of the day. Occasionally I encourage a group working together to invite a student to serve as their teacher or resource person. Over the school year, I make sure that most of the pupils in a class have chances to serve as teachers.

Students serving as teachers (or they may be called helpers or teacher aides or tutors) may teach a great variety of things. A particular student in grade four may know more about a topic than the teacher. Mary's mother weaves and Mary has learned a lot from her mother, so she can serve as the expert on weaving. Teaching is a great learning experience for the student. The third grader who is going to help others with math will have to review what he is to teach, and he may come to a higher level of understanding through teaching it to someone else.

Evaluation of the work of a student-as-teacher may be done by the individual serving in that role, by the ones who are his clients or students, and by the adult teacher. All participants would consider the criteria discussed above, in the section on evaluation of group work. Evaluation should focus on the improvement of performance by students serving as teachers. Observation and conversation seem to be the most appropriate procedures for carrying out evaluation. Occasionally the teacher may find that it helps to jot down a note to include with other material in the pupil's folder. Such notes are useful in conducting individual conferences.

Many teachers say: "I'd try SDL if I could get some help," or "I just can't get around to all those groups and individuals at once—it bugs me to see kids needing help and me tied up with other kids across the room." Well, there's a way to get help: recruit volunteer teacher aides. In a first grade room, I recently saw two fifth graders from the same school, one ninth grader from the nearby junior high, and one grandmother—all serving as teacher aides at one time. Pupils got help promptly when they needed it. Also, each pupil had some choice as to which aide he asked for help. This greater freedom helps in many subtle ways: pupils *do* have preferences, and they enjoy expressing them. Aides are relatively easy to train and very available if you ask for them.

Each student must experience for himself times when he feels he needs help but cannot get it immediately. More and more often he will use his own wish and will to figure out a solution for his problem of the moment.

ASSIGNMENTS

In a conventional classroom, an assignment is usually a teacher-selected task given to students unilaterally. The teacher hands out the work to be done, and the pupils do the work required and turn it in. Giving an assignment may be giving students the injunction "Don't grow up." Assignments may be a way of saying to students, "You're not competent to make judgments for yourselves, so do what I say and stay helpless." In a self-directed learning classroom, assignments can be a series of self-selected tasks by which pupils work to master skills they recognize will contribute to their learning of skills and abilities they prize and which are also valued in our culture.

When possible, let individuals (or members of a group) decide on assignments. Self-assigned tasks carry an implied commitment to carry them out. When the pupil knows that he is thought of as able to make his own choices, he's more likely to make sound self-assignments. Also, there is likely to be greater pay-off for him through doing the assignment. He's more likely to remember how to do long division and more likely to behave differently on the basis of his learnings about his health. Here's where loving patience is so necessary as a teaching skill. Patience enables the teacher to wait for the child's natural impulses to work things out in an economical way for him. The teacher's role is that of a friendly and continuous supporter.

Assignments may be made or agreed upon at any of several times: during the teacher's conference with the pupil, during a group session, or in a more casual contact during the school day. An assignment made during a group session does not need to be a uniform assignment for every group member. To the greatest extent possible, I encourage the individual to pinpoint his need, to define for himself what he wants to know—and then to agree to work on that. Assignments should be as simple, clear, direct, and immediate—in terms of the pupil's need—as possible. I use conference time to encourage widely inclusive and also very specific consideration of what the pupil proposes to do, the sequence of learning experiences he expects to follow, and where he may end up. As my rapport with a particular pupil increases, I find that I listen to him more thoroughly and he likewise listens to me—so that decisions often reflect a comfortable consensus.

A particular approach to assignment-making is the *contract plan:* The student agrees with the teacher as to what work is to be done, when it is due, and how it is to be evaluated. Many times the contract will be in written form—a work sheet or job-card describing what the student agrees to complete. Sample job-cards are shown in Figure 5.

Some teachers who use the contract method say, quite correctly, that it has a kinship to SDL, because it includes self-pacing. Most contract assignments are teacher-prepared in the form of mimeographed or dittoed materials arranged in a sequence similar to that found in a textbook. Although these programs are indeed systematic, they have two serious flaws. First, they do not allow much pupil freedom for selection of topics or tasks. The sequence of skills provided by the teacher in math, for example, is a new lock-step, a new set of constraints for the individual—and these are constraints which SDL seeks to avoid. Testimony to this is teacher insistence that sheet No. 45 be done next after No. 44. Second, such programs usually involve the teacher in a fantastic amount of paperwork—selecting materials, cutting stencils, arranging the materials in the classroom, and correcting all the written work turned in by the student. My time is put to better use in planning for and working with individuals. Adoption of a program such as IPI is a cop-out.

If a student agrees to an assignment or contract, he should carry it out. One of my teaching goals is always to help the student arrive at independence—the ability to face tasks with confidence in his own skills and enough stamina to follow through. Hence I must be available to pupils as they do their work and as they seek to become more independent. Availability does not mean hovering over the student, but it does mean being near him, both physically and psychologically. When the pupil encounters difficulty in dealing with a problem or task, I, as an available and loving person, can give moral support as well as direct problem-solving aid. Similarly, a volunteer teacher aide can often give pupils much of the assistance they require.

How do I deal with the pupil who doesn't complete an assignment?

Figure 5.

Job Card 1 (Could be grade twelve or grade one)

You are a balloon that has always wanted to run away. One day you are free. A gust of wind has carried you over the circus tent and now you are on your own. Write a short story about your thoughts and feelings as you float through the air.

[Adapted from Synectics, Inc., 1968, p. 38.]

In kindergarten or grade one, card 1 could be used as the stimulus for an experience story, with the teacher or an aide serving as scribe for 3-6 students. In grade 2 or above, it can be independent or pair work.

Job Card 2 (Grade eleven)

From reading the attached newspaper clipping, can you get some insights into ways ITT and other large corporations attempt to influence the federal government? Please give examples from the clipping to illustrate your answer.

Job Card 3 (Grade two)

Read the story below. When you have finished, write a title for the story.

[Suggested by Valmont, 1972.]

Job Card 4 (Grade four)

Here are three paragraphs about trees. Each was written by a different person. Read each paragraph and then guess the profession of the person who wrote the paragraph. Also write the word or clue that helped you decide what his profession is.

[Adapted from Goldmark, 1968, pp. 98-99.]

Instead of making the pupil feel guilty about not accomplishing his mission, I help him figure out why he had difficulty and how he can avoid similar difficulty next time. As an authentic and empathic adult, I give the child opportunities to find out that adults don't always carry through on their responsibilities, can't always finish jobs they start, and sometimes experience downright failure!

Assignments should be evaluated and some record should be made of this evaluation. Traditionally, we think of assignments as ways of finding out what students can do, and we evaluate assignments and tests with a view to placing a relative value on each such sample of the student's work —a grade. Grades, as discussed in Chapter 6, almost always seem to be a threat to students. Evaluation is neutral, so I invite the student to evaluate his work *for his benefit,* so that he can appreciate how he is doing and how he can improve. An important part of my individual conferences with a pupil consists of his evaluation and/or our joint evaluation of his work. Occasionally I invite or ask the student to invite his parent to sit in on the evaluation of his learning activities. My comments in such conferences will focus on the facts: "You got thirteen answers right out of eighteen." "Your errors are due to not knowing your times tables." "All of your sentences are complete." I record notes on each conference and also keep records for grading purposes. All of my records are open to the student upon his request. That way, he knows what's in the records and they pose no threat to him. No threat, no worry! And the pupil can focus on his work rather than worrying about what the grade book says.

A teacher-made assignment has the quality of an injunction: "Do the exercises at the end of Chapter 11." Many students will feel somewhat obligated to obey and will feel somewhat guilty if they don't. Yet the usual feeling is either resentment at having it laid on them or resignation in the face of what is recognized as superior authority. Neither resentment nor resignation encourages enthusiastic effort. The usual result is partially completed or partially understood work. And, because the assignment is another person's demand on him, the student feels only partially responsible. Thus, the teacher-made assignment provides an easy cop-out for the student. I'm not letting the student off the hook: his existential freedom is almost always greater than he is willing to acknowledge, but an easy out is a fault in an instructional program.

The teacher-pupil contract occupies an intermediate position: the teacher will be watchful to see that there is genuine discussion of the nature of the work and any requirements about it. If he allows himself, in patronizing fashion, to pat the student on the head and say, "That's a good boy, do what I suggest," then he gives the student a potential out and the student's work may reflect resentment or resignation. But, as rapport develops, the teacher can participate in helpful ways in agreeing on assignments. Such help can be of real assistance to the student, without triggering resentment or resignation.

The pupil-chosen assignment is not a panacea. Many pupils of varying ages find it hard to accept the responsibility. But that's where the true responsibility is, and the sooner the individual accepts it the better. Each teacher has the power to move in this direction. What steps have you taken to move toward student self-direction?

REPORTING AND SHARING ACTIVITIES

In the course of their work, individual students and groups find, adapt, rearrange, or produce materials which excite them and which may be of great interest to other members of the class. To make such materials available to the others, there should be reporting and sharing activities. In a traditionally competitive classroom, learners may hoard what they get, seeking a good grade for their accumulated treasure. In a self-directed learning classroom, students lovingly give away what they find because its only real use is for human enrichment.

When should reporting/sharing take place? When appropriate. Often this will be at the conclusion of a learning segment. For example, if a group runs an experiment, the best time to report may be at its conclusion. In a junior or senior high class, part of a period one day per week should be available if needed. At least some brief span of time should be set aside each day in an elementary classroom for reporting. But that time should be used for reporting only if a genuine report is ready. When a student, a pair of students, or a group has done some work on why grass is green, the outcomes are often intensely interesting to them, and often they can communicate their enthusiasm to others. Reports by such students make a great contribution to the education of others. I'd have reports only when the students truly want to make them.

How are reports made? I encourage variety, not for its own sake, but because it can help individuals to "light their own fires" and hence to make their reports exciting to others. Here is a partial list of ways reports can be made:

dialogue
debate
pantomime
bulletin board

music
choral reading
demonstration
drama
dance
photos, slides, film
tape

Some form of illustrated record, such as graphs and charts, can be used to report data from a class weather station. Some combination of the above, such as transparencies explained by a tape, also could be used for reporting.

Some examples of interesting reports include eleventh graders in an English class using pantomime to portray feelings they get from poems they have read and some they have written; fifth graders "selling" books they have read to others, with the dialogue between the "seller" and the "buyer" bringing out many features of the book; third graders presenting what they've learned about occupations in Japan by means of a play they wrote.

To whom is a report made? To the teacher, to a group of pupils, or to the whole class. It is important to avoid using reporting time as an ego-trip for a few pupils who seek the spotlight or want to fill up time. Reports, real ones, arise naturally out of work pupils are enjoying. I have often written on the board a list of reports to be made during a given span of time and allowed students to choose those they wish to hear. Students who are absorbed in their own projects may choose not to go to any report. That's what freedom entails: a succession of real and meaningful choices made by individuals. Along with this, students learn to live without regrets for the inevitable lost opportunities.

How do I evaluate a report? Largely by discussion among the hearers. I hope that some of the following questions will be considered during the evaluation; I may raise one or two of them myself if no one else does:

1. When is a report useful: to reporters? to others?
2. What form of report is most useful for a particular purpose?
3. What standards are appropriate for a particular type of report?
4. Why was the report given?
5. To follow up on a report, what do you do with or about the material presented?

Such questions may help students in the process of selecting better class or student body officers, and later in evaluating a discussion at a city council meeting, nominating a person for the city planning commission, or evaluating a speech by a candidate for governor. Of such skills, gradually learned, is good citizenship made. The teacher will assist in evaluation and learn from it, as well as from the reports.

HOW DOES THE TEACHER SPEND HIS TIME?

The important thing the teacher does is observe—watch and listen—to see what he can learn that will help him understand his pupils. Some of this observing will be done on the run—in the process of performing services for students—but the teacher should find an occasional two or three minutes when he can observe and really focus without being distracted.

Another responsibility of the teacher is to research and round up materials. A teacher visits the county library after school to seek materials for the social studies program needed by students, and dispenses them the next day.

The key instructional activity of the teacher in a self-directed learning program is holding individual conferences. I ask several students each day to confer with me. Others who desire to talk with me may sign up for conference. So it's a two-way option. Conferences aim at giving the pupils validation as individuals. And conferences are also opportunities to give pupils very specific instructional help. Individual needs vary from time to time. The teacher spends some time observing students and some time preparing for each conference, especially by reading through the accumulated anecdotal records and samples of the pupil's work. When Tom is involved in his study of the Maya, he needs much help. His project involves consulting many sources—a type of task he hasn't tackled before. During the conference, the teacher listens to the pupil, because it is the pupil's opportunity and the purpose is to help that pupil. Harold Taylor (1968, pp. 126–127) has written:

> The student who is being educated is in fact discovering his own self and learning how to relate it to other selves. At its best, education is a series of private conversations in which all sham, pretense, and intellectual hypocrisy or name-dropping is stripped away and the student is free to respond with honesty to the intellectual and personal situation in which he finds himself. This is why it is so important to keep the student's situation as free of educational formalities as possible, to insist upon some version of the tutorial system, to resist all efforts to build an impersonal administrative machine in place of a fascinating intellectual community, to assure that the student and the teacher are known to each other and that the student may thus benefit by the fact that his individuality is known, recognized, and respected.

The scene is Mr. Cohen's third period French class. He has asked Sue and Conrad to be helpers today; other students who need help can ask them for it; when Sue and Conrad are not needed, they do their own work. Most of the class listens to tapes in the study carrels and puts their own voicing of the sentences on tape to compare with the original. Others are working in pairs or threes on dialogues. Some of those working with tapes switch from time to time to practice of dialogues. Mr. Cohen plans his conference with Alec, looking through his folder and listening to a portion of a recent tape. He then calls Alec to his desk and confers with him, almost entirely in French. Later, Mr. Cohen confers with two other students, works with a group on irregular verbs, and discusses the next week's work with the class.

I put the following ingredients into most conferences. First comes an opportunity for the student to express his interests and his feelings. I stroke the student and may praise him and his work. At the time when he seems ready, I give him precise help with one or more instructional problems. If he seems to need it, I give him an assignment to follow up on the skill or skills, or I consult with him about an assignment that would help. I close the conference on a positive note with some appropriate stroke for the student.

To assist me in my work with students, I keep records. Records must be kept to help the teacher provide instructional services to the student rather than to provide a justification for grading. I keep some brief notation on each conference: what was covered, and any follow-up that is needed. I may note particular words a student has difficulty with or particular skills he demonstrates. Such notes help me to plan and conduct better conferences in the future, provide better feedback to the student, and provide data which may be useful in conferences with a parent, the nurse, the guidance worker, or the principal.

I frequently involve the students in grading. Some need the reassurance of being consulted daily or three times a week, others less often. Many pupils can grade themselves and will learn to do so fairly; in fact, their self-evaluations will be very close to the teacher's evaluations of them. If they do not grade themselves, I would at least have a conference with each student before completing his report card so that he will be familiar with his grades.

I have found that I can remove most of the threat from grading. I never use grades as a put-down or as a punishment. When students feel comfortable about the grading process, they can focus on their work, secure in the knowledge that grades will never be used unfairly against them by their teacher.

High school and college students, too, react better to openness and involvement in the grading process. An important part of my responsibility as a teacher is to husband, to cherish, and to encourage human resources. I'm OK and I encourage pupils to feel OK, too. As teachers and as interested citizens, we need to exert our influence toward a more human and humane system of evaluation of people—for example, in hiring and promotion. In a situation in which the teacher is bound by a strict grading policy, he may have to decide whether to follow the policy, to work to influence the policy, or to seek a job elsewhere. When he's worried about such questions, it is difficult for him to focus on the needs of learners. He can behave more lovingly when he and each student cooperate on evaluation for the improvement of the student's performance.

LESSON PLANNING

Lesson planning has one purpose: to improve learning. Because self-concept is so important, formal coverage of subject matter must give way to pupils' needs. Hence I use data noticed while I perform all of the operations already discussed. I also consult the official curriculum: the state or county course of study, and the local district guides for such subjects as health or social studies. These guides suggest goals for me to seek through teaching, and they often give some clues about how I can tell if I am approaching those goals. I also pay a lot of attention to feedback from students, especially their expressions of interest and need. In planning, I consider ways of using time during the day: pupil use of time, and my use of time. I look at ways we are using our human and material resources to see if there may be ways we can improve. For example, if I have a teacher aide who comes in for two hours each week, I evaluate what he is doing in terms of his desires and abilities, and also in terms of the needs of pupils he serves. Along with some of these factual matters I also take some time to imagine, to speculate, to dream about what might be. Some of my ideas become wishes which I consider further until I will them to come into being.

Part of a daily lesson plan for a self-directed learning class might look like this:

Wednesday, January 28
 Before school, get science equipment for experiment with magnets. Observe children as they enter. Open with discussion of feelings—if appropriate.
 Individualized reading: Confer with Albert and Priscilla. Work with context clues group. Invite others to confer.
 Recess: Confer with teacher aide.
 Science: Whole class activities, then individual activities.
 Whole class: Review what we've learned about magnets (chart). Have Al and Martha do experiment. Arrange for each person to do it and write up results in notebook.
 Individual: Each individual or pair to work on own project. I circulate and help as needed.

CONCLUSION

I have watched first year teachers, and teachers with twenty years of experience, as they learn to teach individuals. And so I know that many teachers can do it as well. I start with myself in playing with ideas and with possible ways of working: I imagine myself dealing with a particular situation. SDL is not a panacea either for me as a teacher or for my students.

It will turn on many students, although it often takes time. My doctoral dissertation is based on a study of an individualized reading program. I found that—if fifth and sixth grade students have previously studied in traditional programs—one year in an individualized program does not give them enough time to substantially change their style of creative thinking and problem-solving. Many students did make gains that were evident to me and to the teachers, even though the testing program did not always show significant differences in favor of the students in the individualized program.

Barbara Shiel, struggling with some of the problems of making a self-directed learning program work, said, "I have to remind myself constantly that these pupils were 'failing' under the old program, and never turned in completed assignments .... They only *looked* like they were doing something!" Most teachers have less to lose than they realize by abandoning their present teaching program, and a great deal more than they can imagine to gain by adopting SDL! (Carl Rogers, 1969, p. 14).

Through a community involvement project, one of my students became a counselor to a group of junior high students. In her report, Anna compares her work with the junior high students with the school visits we made as a college class: "I learned more from those individuals than from any of my visits to the classrooms . . . each person is an individual who has something unique to offer the world. This idea is one of the basic tools by which to approach life." Anna is learning the value of individuals through loving encounters with them.

NOTES TO CHAPTER 8

Because of the number of useful references available on individualized instruction or SDL, I will comment on only a few.

I suppose individualized instruction was practiced among the Chinese, Egyptians, and others well before the Christian era, but I don't know of any sources. I'll start by paying tribute to a great person and friend, Jeannette Veatch. For years Jeannette has practiced and preached and fought for individualized instruction. She has been straightforward in pointing out the fallacious ideas on which basal reader programs are based. Her *Reading in the Elementary School* (1966) has a very detailed explanation of how to carry out an individualized program. She has also written articles for many of the educational journals.

Next I must thank the valiant teachers of New York City. May Lazar was the first I heard of. Marcella Draper and Louise Schwietert prepared the excellent *A Practical Guide to Individualized Reading*, which May Lazar edited (1960). This guide answers most teacher questions about "how to do it." As an example, there is a section on the teaching of skills in which the writer points out that not every step of every skill must be taught to every child.

Many periodicals bring me useful information on good classroom practices. One is the *Elementary School Journal*. A magazine which has many up-to-date reports on the most significant contemporary issues is *Psychology Today*. Articles by Irving L. Janis, Ralph K. White, and Jay Hall on group activities appeared in the November 1971 issue.

Here are other valuable sources of information: Walter B. Barbe, *Educator's Guide to Personalized Reading Instruction* (1961); Peggy Brogan and Lorene K. Fox, *Helping Children Read* (1961); Helen Fisher Darrow and Virgil M. Howes, *Approaches to Individualized Reading* (1960); Caleb Gattegno, *What We Owe Students: The Subordination of Teaching to Learning* (1970); John Holt, *What Do I Do Monday?* (1970); Virgil Howes, *Individualization of Instruction* (1970); Virgil Howes, Helen Fisher Darrow, Robert E. Keuscher, and Louise L. Tyler, *Exploring Open Structure* (1968); Bernice J. Wolfson, *Moving Toward Personalized Learning and Teaching* (1969); Herbert R. Kohl, *The Open Classroom* (1969).

References especially for secondary teachers include: Mary-Margaret Scobey and Grace Graham (editors), *To Nurture Humaneness* (1970); Terry Borton, *Reach, Touch, and Teach* (1970); Daniel Fader, *Hooked on Books* (1968); Norman K. Hamilton and J. Galen Saylor (editors), *Humanizing the Secondary Schools* (1969); Earl Kelley, *In Defense of Youth* (1962); Neil Postman and Charles Weingartner, *Teaching as a Subversive Activity* (1969); Viola Spolin, *Improvisation for the Theater* (1963).

Theodore W. Hipple, in *Secondary School Teaching* (1970), presents a series of classroom situations involving students and teachers, asks for the reader's solution, and gives several alternate solutions along with brief summaries on key topics (discipline, motivation). The problems ring true and summaries on the solutions are varied. A thoughtful teacher can make profitable use of this book.

Richard A. Schmuck and Patricia A. Schmuck, *Group Processes in the Classroom* (1970) is a useful reference on group work.

Philo T. Pritzkau, of the University of Connecticut, challenges teachers to deal with the world of opinions and feelings. His *Dynamics of Curriculum Improvement* (1959) is a gold mine of usable suggestions. His *On Education for the Authentic* (1970) brings together newer thinking on dialogue, inquiry, and investigation. As Pritzkau says, "The world has much to reveal and give to individuals if they will stand in its presence."

The ASCD Yearbook edited by James Squire (1972), *A New Look at Progressive Education*, is full of support for self-directed learning. I find the chapter by Robert Soar on teacher–pupil interaction to be especially helpful. Growth-producing classrooms, he says, are low in criticism of pupils; pupils' ideas are accepted and used, there is greater subject matter growth, and pupils have more spontaneity and higher self-concepts. Soar's bibliography to the chapter has fifty-five references. Let's remember that there is substantial research to support student-oriented classrooms.

Most classroom group research corroborates the view that a positive social climate in the peer group enhances a student's self-esteem and his academic performance. The warm support, encouragement, and respect which students express for one another facilitate the development of high self-esteem and a fuller utilization of intellectual abilities.

Richard A. Schmuck and
Patricia A. Schmuck (1971)

Nine

A CLASS IN WHICH INDIVIDUALS LEARN TOGETHER: Frank Carson and His SDL Class

The class troops in from recess, bringing some noisy excitement in with them from the playground. Frank Carson moves among them, asking questions, listening, exchanging ideas. Within three minutes, this fourth-fifth-sixth grade class has returned to its work without any reproving words from the teacher.

In one corner Alice and Marcia compile the class newspaper, which comes out, as they say, "when we're ready." Others contribute stories, poems, and reports, and the two girls write and rewrite until it suits them. Most items go back to the original authors for rewrite.

Louis works on his spelling and vocabulary cards. He has a cardboard box of three-by-five cards. Whenever he encounters a word he cannot spell or does not understand, he makes a card on it, and then alphabetizes the card in his box. Then he works on learning the new word, spending time on it each day. Mr. Carson may ask Louis to define or spell any word in his box.

Virgil and Al are outside making readings on the instruments in the weather station. The boys check the instruments to make sure they're working and record the data on a board, so that class members can follow the weather scene.

Carmen sits alone, reading *The Children of Sanchez*. Every now and then she nods her head in agreement. She has given one report on ways the book relates to the life of her family and is looking at other ways to utilize this information.

Alan, Adrea, David, and Felicia constitute the Navajo tribal group. They are continuing to find out all they can about the traditional Navajo ways and also about how Navajos live today. They have begun correspondence with the tribal council. They plan a booklet, complete with illustrations, and are considering a Navajo dinner if they can get hold of authentic foods. A young Navajo who lives in the next town has expressed interest in their work, and they hope to have a talk with him tomorrow. Now, they plan what they want to ask him.

Frank talks with Herbie for a few minutes. Herbie is an inventor, the kind who builds a model first before he's sure what it is. Slowly, Herbie is facing the fact that reading, planning, and thinking may result in better products, not only products that work but products closer to his image of what he wants them to be. Several he has done so far have been artistic successes but practical failures. Frank lives with the mystery that is Herbie, yet he continues to seek to understand Herbie better in order to serve him better.

Natalie and Robert, the two class debaters, talk over plans to debate a pair from Mr. Rinehart's class. Natalie and Robert want to debate: "Resolved: The UN should disband," but the Rinehart pair wants to debate equal rights for women.

The Navajo group calls Mr. Carson over to help them. They want reassurance that a parent can drive them to the nearby town. After this has been settled, Mr. Carson observes Alec and Roger, who are showing themselves a set of filmstrips on fractions. They pause to discuss interesting frames and occasionally to try examples on paper. Herman prepares a map to accompany a report he is doing on Malaysia. Three other students are at the listening center, two listening to a tape of Dick Gregory discussing *Black Boy* and one getting some science information from a record. Another boy is studying geometry with a simple teaching machine. Two girls are creating their own game based on the television program, "Marcus Welby, M.D."

Frank helps one boy with his math, another with a health study, and visits with two girls in the reading center. One of the girls is lying on a rug while the other is draped over and around a large pillow. Frank then holds a conference with John, who needs much assistance with reading. John tends to read very fast, skipping over many important points. Afterward, his impressions of what he reads are very incomplete and often do not reflect an accurate picture of the author's intent. Frank has engaged John in a series of discussions of what he's read—discussions which require John to justify what he says about the reading. John is learning to read with greater care and to vary the speed of his reading depending on the nature of the material. At one point in the process of helping John, Frank utilizes the controlled reader, controlling John's speed and forcing him to focus on what he reads rather than letting his imagination run free. At other times, as in creative writing, Frank encourages John to let his imagination run free. Frank believes in John and John knows it.

Frank occasionally returns to his desk to jot down a note about a book or a filmstrip that is needed or to make a note which will help him in working with a group or an individual. At times, too, he quietly observes what an individual, a pair, or a group is doing. Most of the time, though, he interacts with students in friendly and informal and supportive ways. Many of his questions and comments to students are neutral, dealing with facts. Examples are: "I see you found a new source on the Navajo," or, "What is the purpose of using this pulley?" These serve the purpose of assuring the student of the teacher's interest and his desire to keep up with what is happening in the room. They have the instructional advantage of helping the student to focus on what he is doing. Other comments by Mr. Carson are more qualitative, such as, "What a great idea!" or "I really think you've got it," or "I like it," or "I like you." For Frank knows that pupils need to be stroked, just as he does.

The class also works together several times a day. The class has physical education daily and music twice weekly as a whole class. In addition, Frank brings the students together for any one of several purposes. One student or a committee may have a report to give in which a number of students have already expressed an interest. Working together as informally as they do, students become acquainted with each other's work and often become greatly interested in it. So reporting time is looked forward to as a way of keeping up with progress on interesting projects. When a new type of barometer arrived and was put into operation, many class members wanted to know what it showed and asked for a report. The whole class also convenes to review either content goals or ways of working and to plan future activities, such as visits from outside experts or field trips. Occasionally, too, the class meetings consider some difficulty which Frank or one of the students sees in the way things are going. This sometimes involves a request for more or better teamwork. A final reason for an occasional get-together will be to discuss some business which affects the whole school.

That's life in Mr. Carson's room, and it is vital all day, at some times more than others. The stuff that makes it vital is human feelings: people pulling/pushing erotically in the direction of finding out about themselves and about things that genuinely interest them. Through learning and loving, they are becoming. What they are becoming varies enormously. This adds to the excitement in the room. I enjoy every visit to this room because I learn there, too.

Frank lives with mystery, yet collects data about individuals, knowing that he'll be able to figure out better ways of questioning, supporting, and encouraging them, but that he will remain in the dark about other facets of the students' personalities. He practices freedom by allowing individuals, pairs, groups, and the whole class to make choices about significant affairs in their daily lives. At the same time, the students give him freedom to be himself and to continue his search for himself and for satisfying ways to be human. Frank gives and receives love from students and parents each day. He remains open, and by word and example he encourages each student to remain open to frank discussion and decision-making about what is to be done. In these ways Frank stays on top of his learning environment—as well as any one man can. Frank, as the significant adult in an evolving learning environment for the whole class, contributes to the learning and loving that occurs there.

In Frank's class there are failures, too. Some projects never get completed. Some of those completed are of poor quality. Some students do not work up to their potential—whatever that is. However, Frank and I remind ourselves that adults manage to fail also. I can remember several lessons that were failures, even though I spent a lot of time preparing them. Success does not crown our every effort. Frank helps to reduce the number of failures by avoiding negative injunctions which inhibit student risk-taking and growth. Errors and mistakes, he knows, may contribute more to knowing than would commands or instructions from him which would reduce the individual's self-commitment to a particular learning venture.

Frank's class consists of twenty-nine students in grades four-five-six in a ghetto school. Twenty-six of the pupils are black. There are two white pupils and one Chicano. One other thing to note is that Frank's class consists of pupils who score average or above on IQ and achievement tests. However, I have seen SDL work just as well in classrooms with the normal distribution of ability levels, and in classes which contained mostly "low ability" learners. The magic comes from SDL applied by a teacher with heart, a teacher who cares about every pupil and shows it, a teacher who loves the teaching and learning process in the classroom. There are many such teachers.

My hunch is that many teachers will choose to use a plan different from Frank's. What techniques will you adopt or adapt from his classroom?

NOTES TO CHAPTER 9

An important group of supporters of SDL has been centered in Southern California. Virgil M. Howes has been the leading spokesman of this group. He has written, edited, and coedited a number of valuable books and has been an indefatigable worker in support of a student-centered curriculum. His able and articulate coworkers have been Helen Darrow, Robert Keuscher, and Louise Tyler. All have helped promote practices which encourage better teaching and learning.

When asked to recommend one *brief* source on what makes a good learning environment, my choice for years has been *Diagnostic Teaching* by Dorris M. Lee (1969). Dorris Lee shows, with down-to-earth examples, healthy ways for teachers to live and learn lovingly with students. Herbert Kohl's *The Open Classroom* (1969) also tells of many ways the creative teacher can join with students in enjoying learning. So do Jim Herndon's two books, *The Way It Spozed To Be* (1969), and *How to Survive in Your Native Land* (1971). From Kohl I get inspiration for ways to transform any physical setting into a learning environment. He and his students use the sidewalks and the stores of Berkeley as stages for impromptu plays. They want other people to see that they regard education as living rather than as a segregated preparation for living. From Herndon, I get irreverent commentary on many of our sacred cows and delicious examples of spontaneous humor. I laughed a long time over the junior high kids using the photomat booth to make pictures of their breasts and penises to be circulated in their own underground to fight the boredom of the standard curriculum. Who says American kids have no imagination?

The major publications by Virgil M. Howes (in addition to those listed in Notes to Chapter 8) are *Individualization of Instruction in Reading and Social Studies* (1970) and *Individualization of Instruction in Math and Science* (1970).

Another book which captures the spirit of SDL is *Teacher* (1963), by Sylvia Ashton-Warner. This is a true classic, a fiery testament to humanistic teaching. Sylvia has also written several lovely novels. Her newest book on education is *Spearpoint* (1972); an excerpt from it appeared in *Saturday Review* of June 1972. Her description of the teacher in the open classroom fits Frank Carson very well: "Here is the enlightened, skillful teacher strolling in the street (the classroom), agog with interest in whom he meets, engaging in conversation. An interesting person at the least, so that people from the houses, the native inhabitants (the kids), are disposed to come out and meet him, exchange greetings and ideas with him. Sometimes with him and often without him, they feel free to think and do things . . . outside in the world. A street named Variation."

*A rich imagination and creative impulses are not produced
in humans the same way we create space vehicles and cars.
Children need periods of incubation, time to turn to an inner
world of long thoughts, opportunities to become deeply involved with an idea or interest. They need to hear themselves
sometimes, over the din of the noises in the competition market. If every child has buried deep inside his own Shakespeare,
as anthropologist Loren Eiseley has said, he has slender chance
to discover it in the schools of the sixties.*

*. . . a child still needs time to grow up, to integrate what he
learns, to consolidate what he means to himself in his time of
ascendancy. And he needs time and desire to indulge in a little
ordinary child-like activity that is not organized by adults.*

Donald McNasser (1967)

Ten

STARTING SDL:
Getting Ready

You want to teach well, to make a difference in the lives of your students. Before you change to a program such as SDL, you want your principal to accept the idea of your trying it. I was an elementary principal for five years, and I have worked with several hundred principals as a teacher, as a principal, and as a curriculum supervisor and college teacher. Many principals are wary of proposals that deviate greatly from the three Rs and conventional teacher-dominated classrooms. However, a lot has happened in the past ten years to wake us all up to contemporary reality: that the majority of children and youth make very little progress in achieving selfhood in traditional classrooms. That is why so many young people create lives for themselves in out-of-school hours. Meanwhile, school costs continue to rise and the grumbles of the taxpaying public are heard across the land. The demands of minority groups for equal educational opportunities complicate the problems of harassed school boards. There may come a day when there are serious suggestions to abandon public education or to turn it over to General Motors to run "efficiently."

For all these reasons, I believe school administrators are more willing than ever before to listen to teachers who have plans that will better meet the needs of the young. Before you talk with your principal, you'll want to plan what you intend to say. That means having thought through what you intend to do in the classroom. Perhaps your principal will want to think it over before giving you an answer. That's reasonable. Be ready to discuss it openly with him and to answer his questions or objections. I have found that most principals say "yes" to teachers who know what they are going to do. Perhaps you may need to ask yourself: Is it my principal who is preventing me from changing—or is he my excuse for not changing?

GETTING ME READY

I ask myself one crucial question before I start an innovative program such as SDL: Am I ready? Before I ask about the curriculum guide, the supplementary textbooks, or the desirable remodeling of the building, I inquire of myself. Any change in my style of teaching begins with me. I must be committed to it. I believe in it, I am willing to work at learning as I do it, I must accept the idea of SDL as interacting and becoming. Further, I have thought it through: I have some definite plans for carrying it out in my classroom.

In order to optimize chances for success, I will plan in concrete terms —for space and its utilization, for time and time schedules, and for instructional materials and their use. I will clear my plans with my principal.

Another aspect of planning involves informing parents. When a new program is proposed, some parents will fear that their children will miss some essentials of their education. This doubt may be transmitted to their children, so evidence of parental worry demands thoughtful consideration. I would hold an open house in my room a few days before starting and explain SDL to all the parents. A mimeographed letter to each parent is not a satisfactory substitute—make time for a meeting. The meeting will be worthwhile for me, as it will be another chance to think aloud about how I envision SDL in my classroom. I will invite parent questions and reactions; I will also invite the parents to visit the classroom after we have started.

Before I can conduct a self-directed learning program, I must have a classroom library. Bricks and boards will do for bookshelves if I don't have enough, and books can be acquired from many sources. Every school has a book room which usually contains many books getting little use, so I rescue some of them from oblivion and put them on my shelves. While really old health and science books and most old social studies books should be left in oblivion, many reading and literature books, and some of the old math books, are perfectly usable. The readers often contain delightful stories. Similar usable books are available in most junior and senior high schools. Students will be involved in my classroom in rounding up books —this is an activity which pleases students. Paperback books from the student book clubs and other books lent or donated to the class will augment the library. Public libraries may lend books to classrooms for longer than the normal lending period. Students will also plan rules and procedures so that our library will serve our needs as well as possible. Pupils in a free learning environment value books, so our books get lots of use and also excellent care.

I will also have made up a list of sources for materials that I may need, especially those from which pupils can order, such as free materials from the Iron and Steel Institute, the Dairy Council, and the like. I will have many materials on hand before I start.

Years ago I read about Edgar Dale's "cone of experience": a succession of ways of finding out about something, beginning with the real experience. If the subject to be learned is contour plowing, the best way to get experience is by plowing a sloping field—presumably with initial guidance from an experienced plowman. If this isn't possible, the person wishing to learn may view a film or videotape, talk with a practitioner, or read about contour plowing—although each step gets a little further away from actual plowing. The same progression applies when preparing to teach by an unfamiliar but desired method: I'll learn best by doing it, but I can do other things to help me get ready. Try to observe a teacher who has self-directed learning in his class. If this isn't possible, see the film "They Can Do It" or a videotape of a teacher who utilizes self-direction. Less ideal ways to prepare include talking with a practitioner or reading about self-directed learning.

But this is nibbling at the edges. "Getting me ready" refers primarily to my psychological readiness. With a self-directed learning program, even a partial program, I will play different roles in the classroom than those to which I am accustomed. I need to understand those roles and the psychological differences between playing them and playing the conventional teacher roles. How can I get ready to restrain my impulses to tell and test? How can I increase my readiness to listen, to let it happen, to take risks of short-run failures in order to allow for much greater long-run successes? Such readiness is obviously an individual matter. I know teachers who have started out with SDL in their first year of teaching and others who have gradually evolved their own SDL pattern. And teachers in both situations have used SDL without going through any special training or therapy. My life is my adventure; your life is your adventure. For many teachers, perhaps most, the basic need is to prepare oneself by exploring and dealing with one's own feelings. In part this will involve trying out at least some aspects of SDL and seeing how I react, how it makes me feel. There is no substitute for experience.

However, there are a number of books and avenues that have proven helpful to individuals readying themselves for a different life in the classroom. As my early chapters reveal, I have worked with several people in TA, none of them doctrinaire but all eclectic. Bob and Mary Goulding and their associates use a lot of gestalt ideas and techniques, for example. Muriel James and Dorothy Jongeward (1971) write that the goal of gestalt therapy (more closely identified with Fritz Perls than with any other individual) is "to help the person become whole—to help the person become aware of, admit to, reclaim, and integrate his fragmented parts. Integration helps a person make the transition from dependency to self-sufficiency; from authoritarian outer support to authentic inner support." A comprehensive collection of activities to help expand awareness—for one individual alone to do, for pairs, or groups—is found in John O. Stevens' book *Awareness* (1971).

Another substantial contribution has been made since the end of World War II by the T-group movement, which started at the National Training Laboratory at Bethel, Maine. T-group stands for *training group*, and T-groups are designed to help people solve concrete problems in schools, social work agencies, government, and business organizations. An enormous number of people have participated in T-groups, and the literature about them and their varied results is impressive.

Churches, school districts, and corporations have brought in leaders to provide sensitivity, T-group, gestalt, or other training to permanent staff members. This has led, in turn, to regular staff members taking leadership training and setting up groups within the organization, to increase the number of aware individuals who can better serve themselves as well as the organization. I have seen successful programs under varied leadership and with various names attached to them. The human qualities of the leader are generally of much greater importance than the exact orientation of the training—as is the case in teaching. I advise anyone thinking of joining a group to talk with the leader at length beforehand: What happens in group sessions? What does the leader seek to accomplish? Can you sit quietly and tune in in your own way, or will you be expected to participate before you feel ready? Some leaders will permit prospective members to observe a group in action before committing themselves to join. I believe in the kind of group in which each individual may participate in his own way and not be verbally assaulted for silence or a decision not to respond according to someone else's idea of how he ought to respond. Some types of encounter groups, for example, although oriented toward helping, may cause serious distress to group members without providing any kind of supportive help. Each person considering joining any group should certainly find out ahead of time what will happen in the group and how serious conflicts or emotional crises will be handled.

I want to emphasize that group or individual training or therapy is *not* a necessary part of getting ready for SDL. I'm not about to give you any injunctions as to what you should or should not do. Self-improvement is an intensely personal matter. Additional books and materials are listed in the Notes to Chapter 7.

PLANNING AND FINDING OUT

After initial exploration of the proposed program, I am ready to plan its implementation—maybe I'm ready. That's a good reason for allowing enough time in the finding-out stage and the planning stage to make sure I'm really ready. This may require a whole year; several of the really great teachers I've known spent years evolving their own ways of playing the roles of teacher. And they never stop growing.

Planning involves thinking through a pattern of behaviors that I intend to use in my roles as teacher. I consider the several roles I will play in the classroom, among which will be the following:

1. observer of the unfolding scene to see what will aid me in performing other services;
2. teacher of groups: skill-building groups, interest groups, project groups;
3. conferencer with individuals: listener, teacher, encourager, and recorder of data that will aid me in future service to the student;
4. dispenser of information and suggester of resources;
5. leader/resource person to the whole class;
6. interactor in many casual encounters with students; and
7. evaluator/planner.

Throughout this planning period, I search for unique patterns that are comfortable for me, so I can behave as myself and not try to be somebody else. I also search for authentic experience through which I gain assurance in serving various and sometimes conflicting human needs in a harmonious wholeness. I use my knowledge lovingly to liberate myself and to help my fellow learners in the class.

I also get myself ready by facing the facts of mystery, failure, and tragedy as part of my teaching experience. A fifth grade child dies because no kidney dialysis machine is available. I try many ways to get Steven to come out of his shell and none of them work. More frustrating, I never find a handle with which to get hold of Marian—she remains almost as much of a mystery in June as she was in September. Along with the successes of teaching, there are failures and unsolved mysteries and tragedies. I must be ready to live with them all. There is no way to solve all the mysteries or prevent all the tragedies, for they are part of our human experience.

How do you plan to get yourself ready for SDL?

INVOLVING STUDENTS IN THINKING AND PLANNING FOR SDL

Loving and learning are intimately related in orienting students to a new plan of operations for the classroom. Teacher attitudes play an important part in this—the teacher with confidence in himself, and in the teaching strategies he uses, can effectively assist in the pupil's understanding of a new program. By contrast, the parsimonious teacher will betray his own doubt and lack of personal commitment and will cause many students to be overly cautious in embracing new plans. Teachers may find that student journals and student use of cameras and typewriters and tape recorders will stimulate the quantity and quality of creative writing. But this is much more likely to happen if the teacher believes in the method used.

The teacher must inform the students of his intentions: what does he see the classroom interaction becoming and how does he see it evolving? If the teacher is to describe this to the students, he will need to have a succession of clear images of what he wants. In addition, the loving teacher / learner, desiring to be a participating member of a classroom group rather than the dictator, includes the children in as much discussion as necessary of ground rules for classroom management. Each child who joins in such discussion or who sees his peers doing so can feel the beginnings of self-directed learning, can begin to feel "I'm in charge of me." Very helpful questions for such discussions are suggested by Randolph and Howe (1966, pp. 119–120):

1. Who are we?
2. Where are we in space and time?
3. Why are we here?
4. What are our operational problems?
5. How can we solve our operational problems?
6. How can we help ourselves to grow?
7. How can we assess our growth?

The teacher will also introduce students to the experiences he believes they need in the new program. If working at activity/interest centers is to be a part of the program, the teacher will establish such a center and give small groups opportunities to work there before the change-over to the new program. Or he may ask a student committee to plan and set up such a center. Or the students may role-play an aspect of using the centers, such as sharing scarce materials. Students, too, will suggest ways they see of becoming familiar with a proposed new program. By involving the students in every aspect of the orientation process, the teacher shows loving respect for his students.

When the preparing, planning, and orienting phases have been carried out, the teacher can start the new program with much more confidence of its success. Many of the problems will have been encountered, and some will have been overcome or satisfactory alternatives will have been found. When this preliminary work has been satisfactory, the confidence of both teachers and students will be high—and students will join teachers in the struggles with other problems as they arise.

The high school or junior high teacher may choose to start with one of his classes, trying out the new modes and making adjustments dictated by both student feedback and teacher experience. The elementary teacher may start with one period of the school day, such as the math or reading period.

In the following chapters a variety of ways of introducing self-directed learning in your class or classes will be explored. All of the suggestions made in this chapter will apply, to a greater or lesser extent, to the proposals made in Chapters 11 through 15.

The teacher listens and observes to see how the evolution of a new program is being received by students. He builds into any such program the avenues for frequent and comprehensive feedback, so that the system remains responsive to the needs of the total community of learners, students *and* teacher. He also plans with the students a variety of ways of evaluating progress, knowledges, skills, and social interaction learnings that may be deemed important. Utilization of feedback and evaluation can lead to important revisions in a program and can help students to focus on loving and learning without being distracted by minor details.

The loving teacher risks in exploring, preparing, and embarking on a new program and in making improvements that are called for as the program evolves. He learns along with students about what will make self-directed learning a pleasant and fulfilling way of life in the classroom.

Not every start on SDL results in success. A student teacher I had several years ago became interested in SDL during student teaching. She ran her class skillfully but rather conventionally the first year of teaching. During the summer she attended a workshop on SDL run in conjunction with a demonstration summer school in which SDL was the prevailing system. The six-week session provided Doris with many suggestions about SDL practices, and she observed four model teachers in the demonstration school. In September, she began with a self-directed learning program utilizing learning centers and color-coded groups working at each center for a span of time. It didn't work well enough, she felt. And so she pulled back and once again taught with specified periods for each subject, although she kept the learning centers for use by students both during the regular periods and for use when they had additional time. At first she felt defeated, but gradually she recovered her optimism and looked forward to trying SDL another time. She experienced failure, and she also learned from failure.

Mr. Sanders had started as a conventional teacher five years earlier—desks in rows, every kid on page 62 of the same book at the same time. True, he liked kids, was friendly in his manner, and never sent a pupil to the office. But he made the decisions and the students conformed—and vegetated. He noticed during the second year the lackluster interest, even when he knew his lessons sparkled by school of education standards. He became more concerned when he checked the achievement test scores: only very modest gains in spite of his big input of effort. To see what was wrong, he began observing individual children more closely and making notes on their behavior. He also began talking with individuals, starting with those he knew liked him. Here are some comments they made:

> GIRL: It's not anything against you, Mr. Sanders, but school doesn't have anything to do with our lives.
>
> BOY: Last year my big sister had a baby and had to quit school. She wasn't married and everyone knew it, but when I talked about it in class my teacher had a fit. She stopped the discussion just when it was starting.
>
> GIRL: In six years all the boys will have to register for the draft and all of us will be voters if we want to be.
>
> BOY: My big brother is sixteen. He drives a car, smokes, and drinks beer too. I'll be sixteen in four years, so what good does it do to have health lessons on cleaning your teeth and taking a bath when some kids are on drugs and have VD?

Mr. Sanders began to change his teaching. Often, he asked the students what they wanted to study or how they felt a topic should be approached. They told him, at first hesitantly, but soon firmly when they saw he meant business and often followed their suggestions. Once a week the class had a gripe session. At first these sessions dealt with petty complaints against the teacher or against a fellow student. But later the sessions were used to consider significant points about freedom, choices, choice-making, dealing with parents, and getting along with other teachers. Mr. Sanders learned along with the kids. At the end of his fifth teaching year, Jim Sanders was functioning very differently than he had the first and second years. He still felt he had a long way to go, and so he enrolled in a workshop on self-directed learning. He had a partial awareness that he still heeded injunctions from his parents and teachers stretching back into his early childhood.

The workshop was an equivalent credit course run by the school district. It was taught by a district teacher, and those who passed got the equivalent of college credit for advancement on the salary schedule. This class focused on self-directed learning in its fifteen weekly sessions. The instructor, Ms. McGee, told of her method of starting self-directed learning soon after the beginning of the year in a fourth grade class. On the first day, she asked each child to write for himself a plan for his learning activities for the social studies period, indicating a goal or goals and activities to be undertaken to reach the goal. After a few minutes of general discussion, the children settled down to planning and Ms. McGee moved around the room helping individuals. Most had finished in five minutes and began carrying out their own plans. On the second day, Ms. McGee held a meeting of a group of six pupils who were still having difficulty choosing ways to spend their time. By the end of the second week most kids were writing their own plans for the entire day quickly. Some were doing them one afternoon for the next day, and some were doing them at home so they could get a fast start the next day. She noticed that students began to bring books, hobbies, small pets, and games from home—not to play with at recess but to incorporate as part of their own curriculum. She got more requests from individuals for audiovisual materials, books, and field trips than she had in previous years. At back-to-school night, all but one family was represented, and parents expressed enthusiasm for the ways their children were tackling school work. One parent asked why her daughter never had homework and was satisfied when she was told that the child completed all her work at school and so didn't need to do additional work at home. Several parents volunteered to visit the class and demonstrate their expertise in various skills. Others agreed to be aides or to lead field trips involving small groups of students who wished to go to such places as the aquarium, the county farm advisor's office, the county jail, and a nursing home.

Mr. Sanders picked up a number of such ideas during the semester and applied some of them in his class. Others he held in abeyance, waiting until he could evaluate their usefulness or find ways of applying them that appeared to fit in with his program. Through your district or through a local college, are you able to have in-service training of this kind?

SUMMARY

If you were going on a three-month trip, you would do a number of things to prepare for it. If you are going to teach differently, you'll need to do a number of things to get ready. The most important of these is getting yourself ready. When I'm ready, many different things will happen in the classroom. Among them will be new awarenesses and ways of loving and learning.

NOTES TO CHAPTER 10

A major strand in the teaching experience and literature supporting SDL comes from the language experience approach to reading, led by R. V. Allen and Dorris M. Lee. In 1963, Lee and Allen revised a 1943 book on language experience called *Learning to Read Through Experience*. This contains a rationale and much needed material on the application of this method in the classroom. Later, R. V. and Claryce Allen prepared *An Introduction to a Language Experience Approach (1966)*, a series of teacher binders (K–3) published by Encyclopedia Britannica. These are invaluable. There are also accompanying pupil books utterly unlike the usual workbooks. The Allen pupil books are open-end and encourage venturing by the child. Yet the teacher binders can be used without any of the pupil books. Another valuable book on this subject is Russell Stauffer's *The Language-Experience Approach to the Teaching of Reading (1970)*.

Another important book on individualized reading is Walter B. Barbe's *Educator's Guide to Personalized Reading Instruction (1961)*. I also frequently return to Sylvia Ashton-Warner's *Teacher* (1963) for reminders of the necessity of starting with the student where he is. Her idea of "organic" vocabulary is basic: each child desires to know words in his language in his own unique order for his own purposes. By giving him the words in this order, the teacher contributes to the child's natural evolution. Similarly, the experience stories (or charts) used by many primary teachers build vocabulary and confidence which promotes individual venturing in the world of ideas and feelings.

An excellent film portraying SDL is *They Can Do It*, available from Early Childhood Study in Newton, Massachusetts. It shows Lovey Glen's first grade class in a Philadelphia ghetto area and is one of the most unrehearsed and frank films on the classroom that I've ever seen. Lovey's failures as well as her successes are amply illustrated. At the beginning and end, her philosophy is expressed very effectively.

Another scholar who has performed a valuable service is Patrick Groff, who has collected articles on studies which compare individualized reading with basal reading. One article has appeared in *Elementary English* (Groff, 1963) and one is reprinted in Virgil Howes' book, *Individualized Instruction in Reading and Social Studies* (1970).

Secondary teachers will find suggestions in Thomas R. Giblin's *Popular Media and the Teaching of English* (1972). Featuring contributions from a wide range of teachers, this volume has sections on the nature of the media opportunities today, McLuhan, literature, paperback books, news, television, and film. Students at all levels are learning to make films. A high school television station is likely to be a reality in the near future. The reality is that students *can* do it!

A child needs to know what he can do, not what he cannot do.

Ned O'Gorman (1970)

Eleven

STARTING
SELF-DIRECTED LEARNING:
Six Pathways

Perhaps O'Gorman's statement applies to teachers as well as students. I think it does. A real teacher is one who interacts with the people and things of our universe, seeking the questions that need answers, rather than waiting to accept the questions others ask us to answer.

The teacher seeking questions to answer, questions that have a probability of vitality tomorrow as well as today, may move with his students in the direction of self-directed learning by any one of six pathways:

1. via small group work;
2. via whole class activities;
3. via a color-coded group activity program using learning centers;
4. via self-directed work along with teacher-directed work;
5. via the contract plan; or
6. via a combination of features of one or more of the previous five paths.

PATH 1 is by way of planned group activities. Small group experiences may be used for orienting children to the proposed SDL program. For many teachers, it may be easier to move from small group activities to individual activities. Small group work has its own intrinsic worth, because it affords opportunities for a great deal of social learning and for individual expression within the often friendly atmosphere of the group. A number of students who are reluctant to speak out in a large class will speak in the sympathetic milieu of a group.

You might start with the following as a problem for groups to discuss. This problem was designed for a senior high school class by the Education for Human Concerns program (Philadelphia, 1968):

> Pretend that a bomb has been dropped and ten people are left in a bomb shelter. There is only enough food and oxygen to accommodate seven of the people until the fallout has reached a safe level. These seven will have to create a new society. Your group must reach a unanimous decision on which three people must go. You have thirty minutes to reach a unamimous decision on this problem:
>
> 1. a 70 year old minister
> 2. a pregnant woman, hysterical
> 3. her husband
> 4. a laboratory scientist
> 5. an electrician
> 6. a famous writer
> 7. a female vocalist
> 8. a professional athlete
> 9. an armed policeman
> 10. a high school girl

If you teach a junior high or fifth or sixth grade, the above topic may be suitable. For a lower grade, try this one:

> The boys started a kickball game. Vince, the new boy, asked to play, but one boy said, "We don't want you on our team," and nobody on the other team said anything. What do you think should be done about this?

To make a discussion of such a topic work, reasonable preparation includes selecting and training group leaders, orienting the class, and dividing the class into groups.

Asking the students to answer a questionnaire is one way of getting information to use in selecting initial discussion leaders. The following question, borrowed from Fox, Luszki, and Schmuck (1966, p. 27), may augment what the teacher already knows and give adequate basis for choices: "Which three persons in this class are most often able to get other pupils to do things?" As with other sociometric devices, there will tend to be significant agreement among members of a class about which of their peers get others to do things. The teacher may select those students as initial group leaders. Leaders who do not excel in a first or second experience as leaders may be replaced by others. Characteristically, though, when the learning environment focuses on individual achievement, many more students emerge as able part-time leaders than in the conventional situation found in most classrooms—in which the regular stars tend to maintain their position, often throughout an entire year.

Through discussion among the chosen leaders or in the class as a whole, acceptable ground rules can be made for group discussion. Here is a list adopted by one class:

1. Each of us will pay attention to the discussion.
2. Each will listen to what others have to say.
3. Each needs to feel a part of what's happening, so we'll try to include everybody in discussion.
4. Each will take part in any decisions we make.

Group leaders need to understand the role of the democratic leader as a traffic cop and as one who encourages contributions from all members of the group in order to bring out various points of view. He should refrain from pressing reluctant peers into talking. And, although he should contribute to the discussion, he must not push his own point of view too strenuously. The tape recorder may serve as a valuable tool in giving neophyte leaders insight into what is expected of them. I have also seen good use made of the interaction recorder—a student who does not talk at all during the discussion but notes who talks how often and with what manner toward others. At the end of a discussion period, the recorder gives the group his impression of their patterns of talking and of nontalking. (This was described in the story of Mr. McVickers in Chapter 8.)

Leaders may receive sufficient training during a thirty-minute session while the rest of the class reads self-selected materials. However, the teacher will find that devoting adequate time to this important early step will give much greater assurance of the success of early discussions. And —as I have seen so often—if the early experiences are positive, the students invest more of themselves in subsequent discussions.

When the group leaders are ready, the teacher may use one of several ways to divide the class into groups. The first time, the teacher may feel safer if he assigns students to groups. Later the leaders may choose their group members, the class may decide who goes where, or the leaders may be joined by those who choose to work in their groups. A more private way to decide is by a sociometric device: "I'd choose to be in Alice's group. My second choice would be John's group."

During the discussion periods, the teacher spends his time visiting groups, listening, intruding as little as possible, gathering information that may help in making improvements in the discussion program. Needed improvements may have to do with the topics discussed, the leaders, the levels of participation, the makeup of the groups, or the results of the discussions, considered in both content and process terms. Students as well as their teachers should have opportunities to contribute to evaluation and adjustment sessions designed to improve the system.

After the class has used such group discussions for a period of weeks or months, considerable progress may have been made toward the goal of individual self-directed work. The teacher will usually be able to perceive when the students are ready to move to working in pairs or as individuals. More students will show initiative, more will be asking questions and proposing solutions to problems. Fewer will be sitting on the sidelines.

LUKE:	You're all against me! I hate this class!
CARL:	I'm not against you. (Others murmur assent.)
LUKE:	Well, you make me feel you don't like me ... I guess it's because I'm fat.
JAN:	That doesn't have anything to do with it.
MAY:	I don't like some of the cracks you make about others ... like today you said Terry was a creep. Didja stop to think how that made Terry feel?
TED:	He *is* a creep.
TERRY:	Ms. Brown, will you make them stop?
MS. BROWN:	Do their words threaten you that much? (Terry shrugs.)
ALICE:	Let's stick to the main subject.
JIM:	What's that, smarty?
ALICE:	It's how we feel about Luke and how he feels about the rest of us.
JIM:	Well, I don't like him, he's always knocking other people.
LUKE:	Only the ones who're mean to me!
JAN:	Mean to you?
LUKE:	Yes, who call my mother a "nigger"!
JAN:	I've never said that.
LUKE:	But David has! And Ernie!
ERNIE:	Yeah, I. ...
LUKE:	But it's the hate, it's the way you say it. ...
MAY:	OK, so Luke's mother is black, does that make it OK for David and Ernie to use such a word?
LUKE:	Yeah, that's right. I mean, they shouldn't of said it.

Such group discussion can sometimes lead to real breakthroughs to understanding and acceptance. But in many more cases, honest discussion provides each individual participant with feedback as to how others see him and how others see the problem situation. With such additional data, others may find their way toward better answers as they think later about the discussion. As Clark Moustakas (1972, p. 72) says, "All true and lasting education is self-education."

PATH 2 is through whole-class activities. Psychologically, everyone needs to be in on the action, so don't be surprised if all the students want to be involved in a whole-class consideration of planned changes to a new program for them. Interaction within the large group may yield greater appreciation of individuals by individuals. I have seen class meetings, for example, in which great gains were made in understanding among students. Also, the class as a whole has a dynamic being which differs, sometimes markedly, from the subgroups—even very stable subgroups—which are parts of the whole.

Among the people who have written of practices which can yield fruitful class meetings is William Glasser, whose *Schools Without Failure* (1965) suggests problem-focusing and problem-solving techniques which can also serve to raise class morale and bring students to feel better about themselves and their class. Considerable usage in varied school settings, including California Youth Authority institutions, testifies to the viability of the Glasser methods. Other appropriate methods have been advanced by Ronald Lippitt and his associates. The Lippitt group's ideas are described in *Diagnosing Classroom Learning Environments* by Fox, Luszki, and Schmuck (1966), and in *Problem Solving to Improve Classroom Learning* by Schmuck, Chesler, and Lippitt (1966). The former book gives excellent examples of diagnosis of classroom climate. The latter lists student government as one way of involving the whole class in its own management and has a chapter on adapting various plans to a particular classroom.

The experiences of Aaron Hillman, a high school teacher, and of first-grade teacher Gloria Castillo, illuminate the work of outstanding teachers who use the whole-class approach, as well as other techniques, to get students to move toward self-direction. Their stories are told in Brown's *Human Teaching for Human Learning* (1971). Harold Lyon (1971) brings together a great variety of examples of learning experiences with all age groups. Included are experiences initiated by films, the use of music, role-playing, and nonverbal communication.

An eighth grade teacher made a list of topics he thought would be useful in introducing a class to the potentialities of SDL. Here are his notes and some comments on them.

"How does a person learn? How do you as an individual learn?" Pretty surely, the ensuing discussion will bring out some of the variety of ways people learn and the fact that many of the most interesting and vital questions that men ask have complex answers.

"How do you think we should organize this class so that you get the most out of it? List as many ways as you can think of."

"What is it you want out of school anyway? Not what your parents want for you, but what you really want." If I give this discussion time to become free, I'll begin to hear feelings, wishes, desires, hopes—all feelings have to do with becoming, with self-image, and with relationships with significant others each individual sees. Pupils want freedom to express and explore those feelings. They'll get that freedom in a self-directed learning classroom.

"Have students list their wishes about a learning environment: 'If I had my druthers, I'd ...'" Later discussion may divide the topic into (1) what we wish to do, and (2) how we'd like to go about it.

Each teacher will necessarily consider himself, his environment, and his students in deciding how to arrange a succession of learning opportunities which can lead the individual students toward more self-direction. As a loving leader, he will build into his plans avenues for feedback and ways of amending the plan. Then students will readily find that their wishes, so often frustrated in conventional classrooms, will be acted upon on a day-by-day basis. Putting a curriculum into gear means connecting it to the here-and-now interests of students and teacher and helping everyone to see that in a tangible sense it's *his* curriculum. Then he can invest his intellectual and emotional energy in it.

Although there is no foolproof method of deciding when students are ready to move further into SDL, there are clues. More students will hold positive self-images as revealed in their written and oral expression. If students write in journals, the teacher will note more self-acceptance and more venturing in content and style. A child who has never done so may try to write poetry. Other written work will show greater variety and greater confidence. Orally, students will express themselves more openly and more positively. Similarly, students will show more sophistication in relating to others—not always being exquisitely thoughtful, for sometimes the blunt words do more good than silence or beating around the bush. I always remember that, mysterious as it may be, students will accept advice and reproof from peers that they may ignore from me. If self-regard and friendly relations with peers are definitely on the upswing, I believe this shows students are ready for more SDL.

PATH 3 takes the student on two courses that will help him to become self-directed. By going through a series of directed activities in a sequence, he may catch on to the idea of sequencing his own work when he is given the opportunity to do so. By sharing materials and working space with others, he may learn to share more congenially in the future. Path 3 requires dividing the class into color-named groups and having each group work at each of several activity/learning centers according to a schedule. For elementary students, the schedule may involve daily visits to each learning center. For junior and senior high students, the schedule may involve visiting each center once a week. As an example of the latter, an eighth grade English class which meets five times a week can be organized so that each group (and hence each student) works at the reading center, the spelling center, the grammar center, the paragraph-building center, and the creative writing center once each week.

Learning occurs in many ways. We tend to think that peace and quiet promotes learning and that conflicting situations result in the disorganization of learning. But this is not always so, as the following anecdote shows (see Lederman, 1969, pp. 30–32).

Richard and Kenny squared off in angry confrontation, throwing such verbal blows as "You're a baby!" and "I can beat you up" at each other. Circling, pushing, finally striking out, letting off steam. When she senses it may be time, the teacher asks, "Richard, what do you want to do now?" and each boy elects to do the same thing. The former opponents combine their talents in building a complex structure with blocks, and they become better friends as they do it. The loving teacher recognizes the need for each student to assert himself, even in hostile ways, and the importance of permitting kids to work things out for themselves—although the teacher must protect students from injury. Somehow, most students most times know how to fight without injuring or being injured. The damage done by frustrating the true feelings of the kids may do far more harm than a black eye or bruised ribs. Also, the onlookers may learn a great deal from the encounter, including ways to settle differences short of physical violence.

Ms. Moon has thirty-one first graders. Knowing that she would be using SDL, she prepared a substantial quantity of games and activities to add to the available learning resources for the children. She brought an old upholstered chair, a five by eight foot rug, and a couple of large pillows with rugged covers, and with these things she set up a reading center. Children can sit in the chair or on the rug or on one of the pillows. One table has been set up as an arithmetic center, another as a health center, and another as a creative writing center (which incorporates spelling and handwriting). Counter space and bulletin board space serve as focii for social studies and science programs. Ms. Moon, with help from her principal, has recruited helpers. Several sixth grade students come for one hour per day, a ninth grader from the local high school also comes daily, and several mothers come for one morning each week. One grandmother also comes. This means that help is plentiful; a pupil will seldom have long to wait before getting help.

The morning is divided into five blocks of thirty minutes each, including physical education. Each pupil is assigned to a color-named group; each group is assigned to an activity for each period of the morning, as illustrated in Figure 6. For example, on a given morning the blue group starts at the reading center, green goes to health and science, orange to creative writing, and brown to arithmetic. The next period each group moves to a different center. If a child finishes a bit of work at one center and is motivated to work in another, he may move to another, provided he does not disturb other pupils and that his arrival does not overcrowd the center. There are two additional activity centers, one with skill-building games and puzzles and the other an art center. Pupils have access to these during any period, as long as they spend part of their time in one of the more formal skill-building centers.

The pupils are making good progress in selecting work to be done and tackling it. Thanks to the rich resources available in the room and the helpers available to the pupils, Ms. Moon spends a large percentage of her time in individual conferences with pupils. She stimulates, diagnoses, teaches, and strokes each child in turn, and then records necessary information immediately. She also moves around the room from time to time, helps the helpers, and enjoys her opportunities for interaction with the warm and

Figure 6. Color-Coded Group Program for SDL[a]

	Activity Center			
Time[b]	Reading	Health and Science	Creative Writing	Arithmetic
8:50-9:20	BLUE	GREEN	ORANGE	BROWN
		Recess		
9:30-10:00	GREEN	ORANGE	BROWN	BLUE
		Recess		
10:10-10:40	ORANGE	BROWN	BLUE	GREEN
10:40-11:10		Physical Education		
11:10-11:40	BROWN	BLUE	GREEN	ORANGE
		Lunch		

[a]Note that this schedule can be changed for any day of the week. Also, when there are special events—such as a folk dance lesson, a music event, or a film—one of the four blocks of time can be shifted to the afternoon. For a variation on the activity center plan, see Lorraine Peterson (pp. 181-189).

[b]In the above example, periods are thirty minutes in length. This works well in many primary classrooms. In intermediate classrooms, forty minute periods may be preferable. In junior or senior high classes, the standard class period of forty to forty-five or fifty minutes could serve as the period for which students would work at various interest centers within the room.

appreciative students. They realize they are fortunate and their faces glow with pleasure. This class learns basic skills, yes, but also much more that contributes to success in future learning endeavors. They are learning how to learn and loving it. They are learning how to love and delighting in this too.

Two pairs of teachers I know are using this interest center program in team teaching. Each class has approximately sixty students for the two teachers and also has double the normal classroom space. Each teacher plays to her strength for part of each school day, specializing in social studies, math, or science. Each has half the students on her list for weekly or more frequent conferences. Both spend time leading the whole class, aiding groups, visiting the centers around the room, and helping individuals.

When the students have become accustomed to working at the centers and show sufficient ability to work independently and to share materials and work space, the teacher may remove the requirement that each group work at each center according to a schedule, merely saying "you must accomplish a definite task at each center each day." A final stage, reached in some rooms, is the removal of all arbitrary time or task requirements: each student works wherever he wishes and on whatever he wishes for as long as he wishes, providing he doesn't deprive others of access to materials or equipment. In this stage, most students have become truly self-directed learners. In this stage, too, each has a vested interest in the continuation of the system which affords him such a wide area of freedom. Thus, most students remind their peers when they abuse any of the accepted rules and procedures, and the teacher is seldom required to be a cop.

This same pattern can be used in junior or senior high classes. A teacher may use interest centers and color-coded groups on certain days of the week—such as Tuesday, Thursday, and Friday—reserving the other days for lectures, films, or whole-class or group discussions. A teacher who was interested in experimenting first tried this pattern with her fifth period world geography class. Based on what she learned from the try-out, she later extended the program to her second period economics class. The following year she used it in all five of her classes throughout most of the year.

What is a learning center? Some teachers have always set aside spaces for specific types of student work, stocking them with appropriate materials. An example would be a science corner with an aquarium or terrarium, cords, pulleys and weights, slides and a viewer, and booklets on various science topics. At a given time, the corner might feature one single science topic such as atoms and molecules, the eye and vision, butterflies, energy, or the telephone. This is called an *informational learning center*, because it provides materials and opportunities for student work but often lacks a more specific instructional mission. I've known teachers who used such centers as ways to provide for individual differences: the faster or more able students were encouraged to work at them when they had finished basic assignments in social studies, spelling, language, and so on. Such centers have a place in an educational program, although they tend to be used largely by the students who play the academic game more successfully than the majority of their peers.

However, the *instructional learning center* has a more comprehensive purpose and more varied usage. Its purpose is to give students a number of preplanned, success-oriented, self-directing, and (often) self-correcting activities. The teacher will consider his needs before constructing such a center: objectives to be sought, activities and materials—all in terms of the student population with which he works. He will gather materials and ideas over a period of time—possibly several months—so that when he does set the center up, he'll have enough materials and activities to sustain the program for several weeks or longer. Teachers will find that, once a center has been in operation for a few weeks, the students will begin to contribute to it by bringing in materials and also by suggesting learning experiences to be tried at the center.

The teacher will set up a center when he's ready. The center should have a sign to identify it and some pictures or posters to make it attractive to students. Once set up, it should be tried out with one group of students, preferably the same group on several consecutive days. A rap session with the group after three or four days can give the teacher feedback to use in modifying the center for future use. Once operative for the class to use, the center may be visited by groups according to the color-code system or according to an alternative. For example, a student may visit the center as long as there is a pocket for his name card at the center. The teacher will have put up a number of pockets in accordance with the estimated capacity of the center. When one student leaves, he takes his name card from the pocket, thus creating a vacancy which can be taken by another student. This is one means of limiting the number of students at a center at one time.

When the student arrives at the center, how does he know what to do? The best way to answer this is to go back to the beginning of the school day. I'd have a class meeting then, at which announcements can be made, problems settled (or a plan for settlement agreed upon), events calendared, and an introduction given to the learning center activities for the day—or the week in the case of senior high students.

> *MR. OLSON:*　Today at the language center there are two new things. The first is this sheet—it gives you a paragraph starter and you are to finish the paragraph. The second is a tape to which you can listen with the headphones. The tape will tell you what to do.
>
> *LINDA:*　What's the paragraph about?
>
> *MR. OLSON:*　The starter says, "As I see it, the biggest problem we face in Oakville is a shortage of water." That is the subject, and you are to see how you can develop that idea. We've talked about it, you've read, some of you have, the material in the county grand jury report for the year, and Mr. Kieffer from the water board showed us the slides—remember? So you have some stuff about it.
>
> *LINDA:*　Well, how're we supposed to do it?
>
> *MR. OLSON:*　I hear you saying you want someone to help you.
>
> *LINDA:*　OK, OK, I'll try.
>
> *MR. OLSON:*　After you finish the paragraph and the tape, you may work with Making It Strange or the Productive Thinking program. Any other questions?

Another method, or one that supplements the introduction at the class meeting, is to use direction cards at the center. A direction card contains the kind of data Mr. Olson gave at the class meeting; it tells the student the nature of the assignment and the steps to be taken. Figure 7 shows a sample direction card and accompanying activity cards. "Job Sheet Fractions" (Figure 8) is another type of direction card which covers a series of related tasks and which refers the student to a series of activity or problem cards.

Figure 7.

Direction Card 1

From the deck of activity cards (also called job cards), select one you haven't done or one you wish to do over again. Pick out the necessary materials, follow directions on the activity card, complete the task, replace the materials, and if necessary set up the equipment for the next user. For example, turn the tape recorder back to the beginning, or put the transparencies in proper sequence. Replace the activity card in the deck.

Activity Card 1   (Showing two versions, *open* and *closed*. You may wish to have some of each type.)

Closed. Count out 3 red beads and 5 green beads. How many beads have you altogether? Take away 4 beads. How many are left?
Open. Count out 8 beads. Arrange these in as many patterns as you can think of. Compare your patterns with those of your partner.

Activity Card 2

Closed. Find the circumference and diameter of these balls. By this terminology we mean the circumference and diameter of a great circle of the sphere or ball. Use your graph to find the diameter of a ball with a circumference of one yard.
Open. In how many ways can you measure a ball? Can you find relationships between any of the variables you mention?

Students usually suggest: Find how high it bounces; weigh it; or find its volume, circumference, or diameter. They frequently try to find relationships between weight and bounce, volume and weight, volume and circumference. Some try to find its area.

Activity Card 3

Closed. Find the time it takes for twenty swings of pendulums of lengths 48 inches, 42 inches, 36 inches, and so on down to 6 inches. Draw a graph of your results.
Open. How can you vary the length of the swing of a pendulum? Comment on the results you obtain.

Activity Card 4   (Using the geo-board)

(a)   On your geo-board, make all the faces and base of a triangular prism.
(b)   Some of the faces are alike. What shape do they have?
(c)   Count the number of sides on one triangle.
(d)   How many sides do you have on a rectangle?

SOURCE: Activity Cards 1, 2, 3, and 4 are adapted from Edith E. Biggs and James R. MacLean, *Freedom to Learn*, p. 15.

Figure 8. Job Sheet Fractions

Check When Completed	Job No.	Materials Needed	Instructions
	1	Attribute blocks Problem cards F-1, F-2, F-3, F-4, and F-5	Use the attribute blocks to solve the problems on the cards. Check with answer keys.
	2	Small flannel board Envelope of felt pieces Problem cards F-11, F-12, F-13, F-14, and F-15	Use the flannel board and felt pieces to follow directions given on the problem cards. Check with answer keys.
	3	Drawing paper Crayons Problem cards F-21, F-22, F-23, F-24, and F-25	Follow directions on the problem cards. Give your work to the teacher.
	4		See the teacher for instructions.
	5	Math-in-acetate Worksheet F-1	Write answers on your own paper. Check with answer key.

SOURCE: Dona Kofod Stahl and Patricia Anzalone, *Individualized Teaching in Elementary Schools*, p. 197.

The use of contracts may also be involved. A student's weekly contract in social studies may require him to complete the work on Job Cards 11, 15, 17 and 21.

Each teacher who uses learning centers will want to make sure that he includes a range of materials and tasks at each center to provide for the range of differences in his class or classes. He will also need to hold some materials and job cards in reserve, so that a month or two after starting he can add new ones to rekindle or sustain pupil interest. However, student help should be enlisted in keeping the center alive and challenging, as well as for maintaining its attractiveness and usability. For example, students can write new job cards or make additions to existing ones.

Some teachers find that the use of learning centers and a color-code plan for visiting them lasts a whole year. The centers may be very successful in giving most of the children a taste of freedom, especially in self-pacing, and also guidance in going through basic subject matter in a general sequential way. A comprehensive curriculum can be presented by varying the materials at the centers, by having different centers open at different times of the year, and by having such whole-class activities as films, class meetings, and rap sessions.

Other teachers will find that, after four weeks or three months of the color-code plan, students are ready to use the centers and other learning activities more freely. The learning center and color-code plan provides an excellent halfway house on the road to greater freedom. A thorough description of learning centers and ways to utilize them is provided by Bernard T. Cote and Barbara Gurske in *Learning Center Guide* (1970).

In what ways do you use learning centers in your classroom?

PATH 4 to SDL goes via having self-directed activities as part of the school day or for some of the subjects in an elementary school curriculum.

The easiest way for the elementary teacher to begin SDL is by individualizing his reading program. There are several sound reasons for this suggestion. It is usually easier to round up quantities of reading books than it is to get sufficient quantities of books for social studies or science. There is more how-to-do-it material on individualizing reading than on any other aspect of SDL, so it's easier to get explanatory material to follow. It is also easier to introduce kids to the idea. However, Path 4 does not have to start with reading: the teacher can play to his strength, which may be in social studies or science or math. Similarly, the secondary teacher, whose special preference is for biology, can try out SDL with one biology class and only much later try it out with a chemistry or general science class.

It is reading period in Ms. Weldon's room. Aaron and Laurie have been picked as helpers for the day. Any student who has trouble with a word or other reading problem goes to one of the helpers or raises his hand so that one of them comes to him. Various children read magazines or books or work in workbooks on specific skills they need to master. When a child needs a new book, he goes to the shelf and browses among books until he finds one he wants. One girl gets a book from another; she's been waiting for it. Several are writing poems, stories, or reports growing out of their reading.

The teacher starts out the period by working with four pupils who need help with root words, prefixes, and suffixes. Once she has started them off with an explanation and some examples of how to do it, they work without her help. She then reads her records on three students and invites them for conferences. Two others ask her to confer with them and she does, following her other three conferences. Aaron and Laurie refer four others to her for brief help with problems they are unable to handle.

I suggest that the teacher continue with individualized reading until it is well organized and running smoothly. Meanwhile, plan your next step: self-pacing in math or spelling, or both.

Self-pacing in spelling or math means each student is placed in the book or workbook at his achievement level and is permitted to work at his own speed. Thus in Miss Weldon's fourth grade, eighteen students are in the fourth grade speller, three are in the fifth grade speller, nine are in the third grade speller, and two are in the second grade speller. Each student works on his lesson, although he may ask another to try him out on his words. At the end of the year, the spread will have increased: the best spellers will be even further ahead of the poorest spellers.

Self-pacing permits the student to respect himself. He lives his own rhythm, appreciates his own tempo. This does not mean that he is impervious to the different speeds of others around him. But official permission to move at his own speed validates that speed and himself with it. This attitude in a classroom encourages healthy and fair comparisons and discourages those negative comments so often associated with the usual classroom atmosphere. Name-calling ("slowpoke") may be replaced by quiet appreciation of the idiosyncracy of each person and a willingness to listen, to share, and to learn within a mutually respecting band of learners. The teacher who permits self-pacing demonstrates loving respect for individuals, himself among them.

Each pupil comes to school with a self-concept, a degree of self-esteem based on his previous life experiences. He has a vested interest in living up to his image of himself. As a teacher, I want him to have a positive self-concept. This tends to be easier for pupils from middle-class homes: they feel more at home in most schools. However, for children of lower classes and most especially those who are members of highly visible minority groups, such as the Chicanos, Puerto Ricans, and blacks, the middle-class school is a place in which the child's self-fulfilling prophecy is likely to be "I will fail." Early learning experiences in the middle-class school tend to be confusing for these children, and they tend to form early convictions about the difficulty of achieving in traditional academic work. For all children with such expectations, SDL provides a better learning environment, because it says to each child, "Your uniqueness is recognized and treasured, you start where you are and work at your own rate, and you will be given help in accordance with your own unique needs." My injunctions to him are, "Be yourself," and "Be the best you can be."

When the self-pacing has been adopted by pupils, when they've become used to it, then you can plan ways of allowing individual selection of topics and materials in science, social studies, and health.

Ms. Orton, following district curriculum policy, says: "Alaska is our next unit. We'll work on it for about three weeks." Students select, individually or in pairs or in committees, the aspects of the geography/history/-culture of Alaska they wish to work on. Two boys ask to make a flour and salt relief map of Alaska, one boy studies Alaskan schools, three study industries, three girls study the foods, two boys plan to trace the growth of the state since World War II. With teacher help, individuals and groups decide on ways to go about their investigations. Group and individual project time will be allowed, with wide differences permitted. Some will find there is very little material available on their topic and drift. Not all kids are highly motivated all the time. A catalog of the Riverwood School (Decatur, Georgia) observes, "Some of the older kids undergo a just-sit-and-do-nothing period that may last for weeks. (We have no television). But when they finally realize something to study, something to learn, something to *do* is theirs to discover, they seem to come alive at a bound and after that twenty-four hours a day is just not enough time to do everything." When students have many opportunities to write their own contract, to plan and carry out their own projects, more will find that the motivation is inside their own skin. When there's always encouragement to try and an absence of the usual concept of failure, more students will be able to focus on learning. They can forget their fears. They will grow in their love of learning.

Student reports, displays, and art work, will enrich everyone's understanding of Alaska. There may be one or more culminating activities to which other classes or parents may be invited, such as a play on the Alaskan earthquake of 1967. I encourage teachers not to end any unit of this kind abruptly. Yes, you may want to move on to a new unit, with most of the class embarking on new projects to investigate it. But some kids may get hooked on Alaska and wish to spend more time on it. If some boys get excited about the salmon industry, they may spend time off and on throughout the year finding out more about it, continuing to report to the class, and enriching the whole curriculum by so doing.

What I've just said illustrates an important principle of the loving/learning environment: I encourage students to do *well* the work they do. Someone who learns a great deal about Alaska or about the salmon industry may actually learn more overall than someone who gets small bits of four or five other major topics.

As your year goes along, evaluate how it's going, and involve the pupils in evaluating. Feedback from them may help a great deal in getting the kinks worked out of the system. And feedback will give you guidance in how to proceed in amending or adding to the self-direction in your room.

After the reading, spelling, arithmetic, and science/social studies/-health programs are progressing well, my next suggestion is to integrate your language arts into one program: listening, reading, writing, composition, and spelling—with emphasis on enjoyment and productivity. Along with this, establish remedial groups as needed, or provide individual help in spelling, handwriting, and composition.

Eventually, if you follow the additive procedure I have outlined, your entire school day will be SDL. However, I know many teachers who maintain a hybrid program: partly SDL, partly conventional. For example, some teachers have individualized reading and self-pacing in math and spelling but run their health, social studies, grammar, and science in conventional ways—teacher assignments, worksheets, tests, and so on. Students accept this seemingly schizoid system quite readily. They will follow teacher leadership even when it is thus inconsistent. But do not be surprised if they treat the conventional part of the curriculum like spinach and hurry through it so they can get to their dessert—the SDL part.

A third grade boy, given completely free choice in his reading period, selected a volume of the encyclopedia to read. Each day at reading time, he continued to read from this one volume. This went on for three weeks, at the end of which time he put the book back on the shelf, telling the teacher he thought he'd read enough of it. The teacher talked with him about it, discovered that he'd learned a lot—not about the content but about reading and kinds of reading. He'd found out that encyclopedias contain lots of information, that the print is usually fairly small and the density of material is high, and hence reading goes slowly as compared with a novel. The teacher could have interfered in any of several ways: bugging him about what he was reading, even ordering him to select some other book. She wisely allowed him to follow his own wish—until it ran its course. I can hear some teachers objecting that three weeks is a long time, that he could have done "so much" in those fifteen hours that were "wasted." His urge pushed/pulled him to the encyclopedia, and in the three weeks he learned a lot about the content, format, and utility of reference books. He also learned more about himself and his feelings, including loving feelings. He can love a teacher who permits him to follow, within reason, his own unique impulses.

Have you ever observed individualized (self-selected) reading? Are there teachers in your district who give students this freedom?

PATH 5 is the contract plan, a system of agreements between the teacher and pupils about work to be done, the way it's to be done, and due dates or times. Each pupil should have some choice as to what he does and how he goes about doing it. Once he makes his choices and agrees with you on them, a contract has been made, one which you can write down for your convenience and as a reminder to both parties. By implication, a contract is between two parties, and there should be obligations on both sides. I see many contract plans which are only a system of making assignments; the teacher has not obligated himself to any responsible part in the learning process. The teacher's responsibility is to be an available resource

to each pupil. This means being available to assist the pupil in understanding and carrying out or re-negotiating the contract.

SARA:	What I'd like to do is to continue with the poetry, if that's OK. I'm beginning to understand Rilke and there are several others I like, at least I like the little I've read. Will that be all right?
MS. COOPER:	Yes, Sara, the poetry will be fine. Some of the class will be going on to essays and literary criticism, but two or three others are going to continue poetry. What do you plan to do with the poems?
SARA, hesitating:	Well . . . I want to write some of my own, you know, to see if I can. I wrote some lines last night, but I don't think they're very good. But I want to keep trying, and the poets I read do encourage me.

The next contract Sara makes with Ms. Cooper may differ greatly
from the one just described. It may involve, for example, a very specific
writing exercise requiring practice in one or more specific grammar skills.

Ideally, a contract will be an individual and private affair between
teacher and pupil. Pupils appreciate each other's individuality—their
strengths, weaknesses, and also their yearnings. Pupils also appreciate the
values of privacy and intimacy possible in many aspects of the teacher–
pupil relationship. This is possible when pupils respect each other, and
privacy is possible with two chairs apart from the rest.

Grading tends to cast a shadow over the pleasantness of pupil–teacher
relationships—as it does over the supervisor–worker relationship in industry. The pupil who is anxious about his grade will avoid exposing his
ignorance; in fact, he may be very parsimonious about revealing anything
he considers important. Pupils graded by a joint cooperative method, in
conference with the teacher, learn as much as pupils graded by the usual
competitive method.

Another alternative for the junior or senior high teacher or the college teacher is to go all the way to a self-selection and self-pacing program.
I allow students in education classes to select projects, to work where they
choose, to work at their own pace, and to report to me or to the class in
any way they wish, if and when they choose to do so. Many students go
to an elementary school to tutor young students. Others do research in the
library. Some take time to sit and think. Reports have included a play, an
anecdotal record on a student, poems, and slides with an accompanying
tape. Many of the finest reports have been conversations in which individuals came in to share their feelings with me. They often bring me love. I too
need nourishment. I grow as the individual student grows with love.

Students really want to be involved in the life of their communities.
A group of high school students, interested in the history of their community, hit upon the idea of interviewing older people who had lived there

for forty years or longer. Each student contracted to interview four or more such people. One of the favorable outcomes was the compiling of an extensive list of senior citizens willing to be resource people to high school classes on a wide variety of topics including foreign cultures and languages, foods and cooking, and arts and crafts. Adolescents in another community repaired old houses and took care of children and infirm adults. Why can't such projects be given high school or college credit? They are. California State College, Sonoma, for example, gives credit for community involvement projects, such as tutoring younger students and working in hospitals. In effect the student makes a contract to perform certain work during the semester. He learns and he makes a contribution to the community. Most community responses to such programs are very favorable. They help the citizens to respect the school as a collection of people concerned with the nature and welfare of the commmunity as well as absorbed in conventional scholarship. Mutual respect leads to improvement in school programs and improvements in the lives of the communities in which schools live.

What clues can I get, from the contract system in action, that my students are becoming more self-directed? The clues I'd look for would be in the ways students approach contract-making, the content of their contracts, and their evaluation of their achievement. When students begin to show some impatience and ask for different topics, for more open-end questions, and for problems to explore, I figure they're growing toward self-direction. When they move away from a page-by-page approach to the study of physics or math, then I guess they're exploring uses of freedom. When they evaluate themselves less in terms of how many right answers and more in terms of broader commitment to long-term self-improvement, I believe they are advancing toward the point at which they can benefit from even more opportunities to choose and decide for themselves.

PATH 6 involves some combination of the other plans. Ms. Petrocelli used a combination of methods in her seventh grade class. Each day started with individualized reading. She worked with groups of students with common difficulties and held individual conferences during this hour. In science, health, and social studies, she often made—or had a student make—a short presentation using the overhead projector or frames from a filmstrip as illustrative material. Following this, students worked in small groups as described in Path 1. Ms. Petrocelli made contracts with certain students, especially in arithmetic. She held whole-class sessions once a week on current events, and she also held gripe sessions to give students opportunities to criticize the program and suggest ways to improve it. For Ms. Petrocelli this system worked well, and she found that each year more students figured out ways to become more self-directed. At the same time she encountered a number of students each year who had real difficulty becoming self-directed. No teacher will be able to deal with all the problems, to persuade all students to utilize the freedom that's theirs for the using.

A NOTE ON PATHS

I always remember that my goal is self-management by each student. I take a path which seems to lead in that direction and at the same time to be in line with my evolving approach to myself and my teaching. It won't work in the abstract, it will only work *with me* as a part of it. As I learn to be less of a demander and more of an encourager, less of a teller and more of a listener, students will come out into the arena of action and take more initiative. Each will begin to take more active command of his own learning and living.

Back in Chapter 3, I asked you to write down what you'd like to change about your own teaching. At this point, read what you wrote. In the light of suggestions made here in Chapter 11, which direction do you plan to take now?

CONCLUSION

Authur W. Combs asked a group of his college sophomores in an education course why they weren't committed to the educational venture in which they now spent so much time and in which they planned to spend their working lives. Because, they said, the things worth committing ourselves to don't get you ahead in school. Combs and others have dealt with this problem by allowing students great latitude in selecting work and in pursuing it in their own manner. I committed myself to learning and loving for myself, not in a purely selfish way, but in a continuing open invitation to others to share the vast amount we have in common, our humanness and our potential for much greater humaneness in the global village we inhabit.

NOTES TO CHAPTER 11

Different how-to-do-it books will suit different readers. I have followed the policy of mentioning many which I have used, hoping that some of those that you can find will prove useful.

A number of articles and books have come from studies funded by the government, by a consortium of school districts, or by a foundation. Among these is *Toward Humanistic Education*, by Gerald Weinstein and Mario D. Fantini (1970). This study, like that of Richard M. Jones (1968) in *Fantasy and Feeling in Education*, George I. Brown, (1971) in *Human Teaching for Human Learning*, and Harold C. Lyon, Jr. (1971) in *Learning to Feel, Feeling to Learn*, attempts to redress the balance between cognitive and affective elements in education, both as content and as process. The teachers in the study found numerous ways to involve student emotions in the process of learning. Instead of being sideline-sitters, many students committed themselves. My responsibility is not to make sure the student knows specific facts but to see that he becomes *involved* in the life of the mind and the spirit. Yesterday's facts are often less useful than yesterday's leftover mashed potatoes.

Edith E. Biggs and James R. MacLean (1969) stress math in their *Freedom to Learn*, yet many of their quietly explained techniques apply to other parts of the curriculum. *Independent Activities for Creative Learning*, by Helen Darrow and R. Van Allen (1961) offers numerous experiences designed to go beyond the normal drill and other repetitive activities. Alfred Gorman collects a number of well-tried techniques in *Teachers and Learners: The Interactive Process of Education* (1969).

Hunters Point Redeveloped is a report of a year-long field and classroom study by a sixth grade class in Hunters Point, San Francisco. It is edited by Robert R. Leeper (1970). Byron G. Massialas and Jack Zevin (1967) compiled the examples of classroom learning in *Creative Encounters in the Classroom*, an especially valuable book for junior and senior high teachers. For teachers of young children, Kenneth D. Wann, Miriam S. Dorn, and Elizabeth A. Liddle (1962) have done *Fostering Intellectual Development in Young Children*. An excellent magazine which I often use is *The Reading Teacher*.

There are many approaches to curriculum and curriculum change. A brief but very helpful book is *The Process of Curriculum Change* by Dorothy Skeel and Owen Hagen (1971). The authors describe a hypothetical school district in which parents, students, university personnel, teachers, and administrators work together to bring about curriculum revision. The feelings, thoughts, and aspirations of all involved are presented so that both affective and cognitive considerations are seen interacting.

Support for the SDL practices I advocate will be found in the following sources: Gerald T. Gleason (1970); William Nolen (1971); Caleb Gattegno (1970); Charles Silberman (1970); Lawrence K. Frank (1963, pp. 11–37); Clark Moustakas (1967); Ronald Lippitt (1972); Paulo Freire (1961, pp. 65–73), Richard DeCharms (1971), Frank E. Nardine (1971), Duane Manning (1971); Vincent Rogers (1970); Kevin Ryan and James Cooper (1971, pp. 182–215); Robert S. Soar (1972); and Robert Biehler (1971, pp. 319–330, 501–523).

Kaplan and her associates (1973) have written a detailed description of learning centers and their uses. This book is exceptionally clear in its explanations of the roles of teacher and pupil in relation to learning centers.

Teachers "*are the ones who touch students and interact with them; they are the ones who implement educational policy and curriculum content, scope and sequence; and—most important—they are the ones who establish the educational climate and who structure learning experiences. In short, they have almost complete power over the* process *that takes place in the classroom, and it is my contention that process is more important than content in education.*"

James J. Foley (1971)

Twelve

STARTING
SELF-DIRECTED LEARNING:
Different Strokes
for Different Folks

In this chapter I offer some additional suggestions about working toward self-directed learning in your classroom, specific suggestions to junior and senior high teachers, to first grade and kindergarten teachers, and additional suggestions to all teachers about starting out and about starting the school day.

WAYS SECONDARY SCHOOL AND COLLEGE TEACHERS CAN START THE USE OF SDL

First of all, be sure you are ready. Please refer back to the first part of Chapter 10. Second, start with one class, using the experiment with this class as a learning experience for you and the students.

If you teach math, science, industrial/vocational or homemaking arts, art, physical education, or foreign language, you may choose to begin by introducing self-pacing. The work to be done by a particular class may be quite precisely prescribed, but the rate of progress may be left up to the individual. For example, in General Science, I could give each pupil an outline of the required work and specify that it's to be done in the order in which it appears on the sheet: "Geology, the makeup of the earth's crust," followed by appropriate subheadings and specific assignments. This sheet can list what is to be done under each heading: text and supplementary reading, filmstrips to view, experiments, worksheets, reports to be completed, and tests to be passed. These days, with individual study carrels often available, a student can view a filmstrip alone when he's ready, can get other information from a tape, and can take an exam which the teacher will have prepared as a tape or in mimeographed form.

At the end of the quarter or semester, some students will have completed the whole amount prescribed, while some will have done less—but that's probably true of many of your classes now. I would avoid establishing a grading system based on the amount of work accomplished, because that shows only a primitive regard for the individuals in the class. If I grade a student down because of limited output, I tell him his rhythm of life and pace of work do not measure up to my standard. I prefer to confer with the student and remind him of standards he may face in the world of work. I will encourage him to learn to work at differing speeds in line with the requirements of the task or the taskmaster. Just as most of us increase our reading speed without hurting comprehension, so we can perform other tasks faster when there is a good reason for it. I always pay more attention to quality than to quantity as I seek ways to help students accept themselves and feel OK about their achievement.

A young swimming teacher seldom acknowledges a failure among his pupils, who are both adults and children. For some, he feels the person has achieved if he can overcome his fear of water and just get into it. And he communicates this feeling to the learner. How many children, though, hear from parents or teachers or others, "I can't understand why you can't do this (tie your shoe laces, solve a problem)—it's so easy."

The experiment in self-pacing with one class may lead in several directions. If there are bugs in the system, facing them honestly in discussion is likely to yield valuable insights into student morale and motivation as well as practical possibilities for making the class function better. Some students have difficulty selecting a piece or part of a task to work on, others have problems retaining information until it is needed for a test or performance hurdle. These are genuine instructional problems deserving of careful consideration. Bringing them out into the open helps everyone realize that he is not alone in having difficulty, that everyone does. In the usual high school, the very bright student may make some effort to disguise his brightness rather than face the derision or envy of his peers. In a self-directed learning classroom, each can be accepted and honored for his unique talents—whatever their nature. Working at one's own pace reassures the individual that he is being accepted for himself rather than being consistently compared to some arbitrary standard. The teacher who encourages self-pacing demonstrates his loving responsibility toward each unique student that he is privileged to have in his classes.

If the self-pacing works well, a particular teacher may have gone as far as he can comfortably go. And that is a great step in the right direction. Another teacher will see beyond self-pacing to self-selection, where the teacher displays an even more comprehensive loving respect for the integrity of the individual student. Or the teacher may use self-pacing all the time and permit self-selection when the student has gone beyond each basic assignment. For example, in biology the teacher may set up minimum material to be covered on vertebrates and then permit the student freedom to choose what to do beyond that minimum. To be consistent, this means permitting the student to go beyond the field of vertebrates entirely. Two or three days or weeks later, all students may again be required to start on a minimum assignment designed to start students toward acquaintance with another major topic. I encourage each teacher to think big about possible ways of working that promise learning and growing by students. And then try out new ways. Loving and teaching always involve risk.

SPECIAL NOTE TO FIRST GRADE AND KINDERGARTEN TEACHERS

Most first grade teachers, because of the traditional burden of "getting kids off to a good start in reading," cling to the tried and true basal readers. They believe that such a carefully prepared system, proved in classroom usage, must be the right way, must give them the biggest insurance policy for success. This may be so, if you accept all the questionable hypotheses on which the basal reader system is based—especially the idea that we, because we are adults, always know what is best for the child, or the idea that there is one best sequence of teaching skills in reading. Both of these ideas I reject.

For too many teachers, the basal reader program is a security blanket. Now they can discard it, because there's a program that is complete, thorough, beautifully outlined, and carefully classroom tested, a program you can use with beginning readers. It is the individualized reading program described by Jeannette Veatch (1966) in *Reading in the Elementary School*. Also refer to two chapters by Veatch in (1963) *Curriculum for Today's Boys and Girls*.

Another program I recommend is the language experience approach to reading. It brings together in a natural way all the language arts: speaking, listening, reading, and writing. A very comprehensive how-to-do-it is found in R. V. Allen and Claryce Allen (1966), *Language Experiences in Reading*, a series of binders for kindergarten and grades one, two, and three.

Kindergarten teachers who want to give pupils a big boost on their way to success in reading *and* all the other language arts in first grade can adapt ideas from Jeannette Veatch's (1966, pp. 207-235) *Reading in the Elementary School*. Many of these procedures can be used very easily in most kindergarten classes with many of the pupils, and that's the way such techniques should be used—that is, with those who can profit from them. As an alternative to the Veatch plan, use the *Language Experiences in Reading* kindergarten binder, referred to above.

ALTERNATIVE WAYS TO START

You can introduce SDL to a few of your students at a time. Start with a group that you believe will catch on quickly, will stick with it, will be able to take the freedom, and will be able to work independently without bugging the other kids in the room. Avoid starting with a group composed exclusively of your "good" or "bright" students. They have been favored by the conventional system, and their selection will be seen as confirmation of the unfairness of the system—and thus SDL may be seen as unfair by those who are left out. If students look at SDL unfavorably, it will be difficult to start it. There is one disadvantage to this plan: other students will soon ask why "those lucky guys get to do it and we don't." But you can term your trial an experiment, explaining that you must wait and see how it turns out. Most students and parents accept an experiment as justifiable and hope it succeeds.

A second alternative is to try out SDL, or some aspects of it, in summer school. This may give you an adequate opportunity to try out your skills and to prepare yourself psychologically and experientially for teaching this way in the regular school year. Once again, you start with your own OK-ness and your own readiness to behave differently.

However I may try things out, I keep my eye on the ball: I want to improve the learning environment for the whole collection of learners, including myself.

MULTIGRADED CLASSES

A number of teachers who prefer SDL also prefer multigraded classes. Why should we segregate all seven year olds into grade two or all fifteen year olds into grade ten? We acknowledge the fact that any class at any age will have a substantial range of individual differences in interests, tastes, and abilities, and that most efforts to limit such ranges are futile. Why not go in the other direction, celebrating the differences and utilizing them to create a richer human environment for the students to encounter? Nine year old Jeff may be the best chess player in a grade two-through-six class, and he may teach others to play or to play better. Eleven year old Jenny will help with guitar and vocabulary building, while ten year old Arthur uses his strengths in math and in art activities, such as batik and tie-dying, to help other students. Such multigrade classes help students get over hang-ups due to the normal age-grade progression. It helps teachers remember the realities of individual differences that exist and their varied responsibilities in dealing with the individual needs.

STARTING THE SCHOOL DAY

How about the start of the individual school day? Are there ways to begin a day which will increase the probability of productivity? Indeed there are. They depend in large measure on my being me, genuine, open, willing to listen and to respond to feelings. Toni, a third grade teacher, senses the feelings of children as they come into the room. She watches and listens, noting significant smiles or frowns that give her clues as to the mood of the class. She starts the day by informally conversing with the students about what concerns them. None of us is wholly immune to the world around us. When we feared the Apollo 14 astronauts might not return safely to earth, each of us felt some pang of human concern. When a black or Puerto Rican man reports being arrested and beaten by police, his immediate neighborhood will be resentful. As a teacher, I can conduct discussion about such a painful topic first thing in the morning, acknowledging the close relationship between the school and the outside world. This serves to allay fears, to confirm the importance of the school as an avenue to responsible adulthood, and to deal with first things first so that the students can then go on with their work. This is not to minimize the importance of these community or world events or to suggest sweeping them under the rug. It is rather to face them squarely and openly and to relate them to our lives here and now. In that way some of the worry, some of the uncertainty will diminish, and students can see the people and events in their world in better perspective. As a loving teacher I can seek no less. To make education relevant, we must deal with contemporary problems, so that individual students know school considers their concerns important. Then they can afford to invest themselves in school learning. They can also more easily recognize their own OK-ness, their own lovableness, and they can appreciate and maximize opportunities to love other people.

APPENDIX TO CHAPTER 12

When individualized reading is compared with the more usual basal reading method, readers in individualized reading (IR) do as well as or better than readers in basal reading (BR). A number of research studies substantiate this. For example, Acinapuro (1959) compared the reading skills of fourth, fifth, and sixth grade students at the end of a year. The IR students exceeded the BR students in silent reading, comprehension, oral reading, and total silent reading; on vocabulary the difference was not significant. Other studies show similar results. However, a number of studies show no significant differences between the two. Those studies which show BR achievement superior to IR achievement generally have one or more serious flaws. For example, in one study the class sizes in the BR classes were considerably smaller than in the IR classes. In another study, the period of time spent on each of the two methods was scarcely long enough for the students to catch on to IR.

The language experience approach to reading has similar psychological benefits to SDL. When LE is compared with BR, the results are similar; generally, LE does as well as or better than BR.

NOTES TO CHAPTER 12

During the writing of this book I became acquainted with *The Diary of Anais Nin* (1966, 1967, 1969, 1971). As of now there are four volumes available in hardback and paperback and more sure to come out soon. Anais Nin has stood for human liberation, not just women's liberation, for several decades. Her comments on literature, the arts, people she has known, and most of all about *living*, are constantly interesting.

The Metropolitan School Study Council has done many valuable investigations. In the *MSSC Exchange* (January 1971), Martin N. Olson reports on the use of Indicators of Quality, a means of evaluating secondary and elementary classroom teaching. The survey of over eighteen thousand classrooms found that small group work, individual work, discussion, laboratory work, pupil report, and demonstration rate high on the scale. This supports my contention that students really respond to environments in which their *activity* is encouraged.

The Lincoln Filene Center for Citizenship and Public Affairs at Tufts University has produced a program for intergroup relations. John S. Gibson (1969) authored *A Program for Elementary School Education*. The framework is based on the governing process, showing the relationships of the people, the officials, the political process, the structure of government, decision-making, and policy. Many very specific lessons are presented on likenesses and differences of people, and on various ethnic and racial groups in American society. Many of the materials are readily adaptable to various grade levels. A substantial bibliography is included.

I am very aware of the controversy about speed reading. Ronald P. Carver made a study of the subject and reports his findings in *Psychology Today* (August 1972).

"*One of the most important beliefs the schools must teach children is the self-descriptive statement, 'I am able to think autonomously.'*"

Jerome Kagan (1966)

Thirteen

CLASS MEETINGS SEEK INDIVIDUAL AND GROUP ACCOMPLISHMENTS

Self-directed learning stresses individual and pair and small group activities. Total class activities also have a place in a loving learning environment. They provide additional opportunities for significant self-realization by individuals.

Population growth and advancing urbanization increase the likelihood that students who today are six or sixteen will, as adults, be involved in large group meetings—perhaps neighborhood, block, or apartment house meetings in addition to such traditional gatherings as PTA or the city council. The trend toward confrontation in the handling of public business puts a premium on the individual's capacity to handle himself and to live with upset feelings. The "together" individuals will be the ones who are able to make confrontation profitable in terms of humane solutions to human problems, or who will agree to go home and give it some more thought or some more research.

Confrontation naturally occurs in groups of students—unless adults suppress it, and even then it only goes underground. A student resents being pushed by another, even accidentally. The child whose lunch is stolen is angry. Students who need to use the same instructional materials or work area cannot always find a compromise they can live with without harboring ill will. It makes sense to establish a daily forum in which potential bad feelings and misunderstandings can be discussed openly. Such a meeting helps to prevent the spread of foolish and often cruel rumors and helps students and teachers to focus on facing problems and on the honest attempt at a solution. It helps to make life in a classroom more enjoyable as well as more exciting.

Mr. Kline always has space for two agendas on the blackboard. One is his agenda, and one is headed "Your Agenda." The latter is an open invitation to any individual, group, or committee within the class to write down an item considered by him or them to need the attention of the whole class. On Tuesday Amy writes, "Can we have a picnic on Angel Island?" It is duly considered. On Wednesday, the committee which is putting on the Eskimo play asks for time in which to explain needs they have for props. They get some promises of help.

The class meeting may occur at any time during the school day, or, in the case of a secondary class, any time during the week. Ms. Anderson and Ms. Castleberry, team teaching for a summer session, usually held class meetings first thing in the morning and sometimes again just before the students went home. Ms. McKenzie and Mr. Kline held meetings at various times during the school day, occasionally calling together their fifty students for an impromptu bull session right in the middle of whatever variety of activities was occurring. The main thing is to allow for consideration of questions felt to be important by both teachers and students. The class meeting should not be primarily a teacher lecture or a forum for student complaints, but a problem-facing and problem-solving time.

Class meetings are held for various reasons. Ms. McKenzie uses hers at the beginning of the day to introduce materials and processes that will be found at the learning centers that day. On a Thursday she might say, "The new activity at the science center is meal worms." Mr. Solie uses part of some class meetings to maintain continuity. On a Tuesday he might say, "The poetry magazine has a number of contributions—five to be exact. Do you want to continue?" Guidance occupies part of the meetings in Mr. Ponzio's room. On a Wednesday he might say, "Yesterday our team played against Laurel. The Laurel teachers said after the game that they thought our sportsmanship could be better. What do you think about that?"

The teacher has the responsibility for seeing that the class meeting accomplishes its purposes—or works toward that end. In Mr. Kline's class, students talk freely, argue, sometimes do not pay attention. Mr. Kline uses a great deal of patience along with his lively sense of humor and a variety of approaches to keep everyone in the meeting and participating. Occasionally he finds that a student's behavior can no longer be allowed to disrupt and banishes the student to do some work while the class meets. As students become accustomed to the accomplishments and the good feelings that come out of class meetings, banishment will rarely be needed.

While on a field trip in the school bus, Mr. Casteneda's class passed two people hitchhiking. The young man had a full beard and shaggy hair, and the young woman's dress dragged the ground. They carried a variety of gear—sleeping bags and pots and food. Mr. Casteneda heard comments from the students, mostly derogatory. That evening he decided to include this incident in the evaluation of the field trip. When he brought it up next day, the students talked of the hitchhikers as "weird," "stupid," "kooks," "lazy," and "dirty." It was the consensus that these young people were "outsiders." The teacher decided that, rather than counter such expressions himself, he would try an experiment. He asked the thirty students to form into groups of five members each for further discussion. Quickly each student sought to get into a group with his friends. Mr. Casteneda then said that groups of five were too big and that they would have to reform into groups of four. The groups responded in several different ways: by drawing straws, by a volunteer dropping out, or by a self-appointed leader pushing one out. The teacher then asked for discussion of feelings about what had just happened: how did you feel? It turned out that the order to reduce group size from five to four had created instant anxiety: "I sure don't want to get kicked out." Those who stayed in their original group felt "safe" and "happy" when the cut had spared them. Those rejected either said they didn't care or didn't like the group anyway or admitted their disappointment and self-doubt: "What's wrong with me?" Afterward, a student said, without being asked by the teacher, "I guess I know how those hippies feel sometimes." A number of other accepting remarks were made about the young couple. In such ways as this, a class meeting can consider controversial issues and troublesome feelings and can reach, sometimes, a higher level of acceptance of human variability in life style.

In the first grade, a class meeting deals with proposals for rearranging the furniture. A ninth grade class faces the fact that the students and the teacher expect very different things from each other; while the students are looking for a boss, the teacher keeps hoping for independent learning effort from them. In a fifth grade, students use the class meeting to argue persuasively that present class rules interfere with legitimate and praiseworthy learning activities. A tenth grade science class used each Friday as the reporting/sharing period. In a class meeting, the students demanded and got a thorough examination of standards appropriate for reporting, and the discussion resulted in a marked improvement in the reports that followed.

Big Ben, we called him. Always one of the last to arrive, the last to settle down, the least attentive yet the most expressive. A healthy, sturdy boy often adorned with a smile, Ben was quick, impulsive, likely to be off on a new tangent before you caught up with where he no longer was. His presence complicated any class meeting, as it complicated any learning endeavor to which he directed his considerable energy. He exasperated the two teachers in the team teaching arrangement, occasionally socking the male teacher and frequently challenging each teacher verbally. Frequently other students complained about Ben's behavior. Yet his presence enlivened the scene—he was a walking foe of apathy and boredom. During the four weeks of this summer school, the fifty students in grades one-through five in the class came to appreciate Ben and to respect his individuality. Ben, on his side, sometimes moderated his behavior toward others. The class meetings offered chances to explore the complexity of Ben's relationship to others, teachers as well as students. I don't wish to convey the impression that the class tamed Ben or that the meetings offered therapy, so everyone felt better about Ben and Ben felt better about himself. But learning occurred in the rough and tumble of verbal and sometimes physical exchange, and it was a healthy way for people of different ages to become acquainted.

The teacher's role in such meetings varies. He must at times demand and wait for attention, make announcements, give reminders, or issue orders when safety or some problem (such as the rapid shrinkage of a needed supply) threatens to shut down a worthwhile instructional adventure. At other times he may lead a discussion, and at still others he may be a relatively quiet yet available resource to the students. Does this seem confusing? It reflects the loving teacher's ability, frequently, to imagine ways of behaving that will facilitate the becoming of others. This necessitates changes in role from time to time. When we seek independent adults who can serve their own individual as well as group ends we recognize that such independence does not happen when an eighteenth birthday is celebrated. It happens, if it happens, because of multiple opportunities over a period of years for the fledgling to spread and test his wings and to be present when others do the same. Thus, the future PTA or union president needs many experiences as a group chairman, as a reporter, as a debater, and a listener, so that he can develop a frame of reference within which he can operate more and more successfully in latter years. The teacher may appoint a student as chairman or students may elect one. The chairman strives to succeed in the here and now, foreshadowing later life experiences. The process starts with preschool, nursery school, kindergarten, and grade one, and it may progress to the executive offices of a large corporation, a college faculty, or the state senate. So the teacher, instead of monopolizing the leadership of the class meetings, shares this with his students. A chairman may be elected for the week or even for the day. If the teacher sits back to listen thoughtfully, he may later figure out ways of working with individuals and small groups that he would not have thought of so quickly except for the class meeting. Meanwhile, he's on hand to answer a question, ask a question which may help students to refocus, or reassert his leadership if this should become necessary.

When teachers take the risks inherent in such shared leadership, they harvest a wealth of understanding and love over a period of time. Not every New England town meeting is a success, but the potential for success grows with participation—especially when respect is shown for each individual, whether he is highly verbal or relatively reticent. There is so much to gain from venturing out into the excitement of real interchange. The marketplace of ideas and feelings is never dull.

NOTES TO CHAPTER 13

I am departing from the format used in previous chapter notes because I feel there may be greater feelings of insecurity about the class meetings than about some of the other practices. This time I want to give you a list of articles and books, some mentioned before, which support two points: (1) that students are generally more competent than we as teachers recognize; and (2) that students can manage to make complex learning environments, such as class meetings, work, and work well.

Eli M. Bower and William G. Hollister, *Behavioral Science Frontiers in Education* (1967).

George I. Brown, *Human Teaching for Human Learning* (1971).

Albert Cullum, *Push Back the Desks* (1967).

William Glasser, *Schools Without Failure* (1965).

Glen Hass, *et al.*, eds., *Readings in Elementary Teaching* (1971). See especially articles by Louis S. Levine and Joseph Luft, pp. 238–246.

Robert R. Leeper, ed., *Hunters Point Redeveloped* (1970).

Duane Manning, *Toward a Humanistic Curriculum* (1971). See, for example, chaps. 9 and 10.

Richard Schmuck, *et al* (1966), *Problem Solving to Improve Classroom Learning.* See especially pp. 39–62.

As you will see, each of these references also has a great deal to say in addition to ideas about class meetings.

Robert Sande has made two other guidance films, *"Self Esteem"* and *"Who's Responsible?"* The "who" is me, in case you hadn't guessed. One member of a summer workshop on SDL was so enthused about Sande's BFA films that she took all three of them home and she and her husband and three children viewed them together.

Educational Implications of Self-Concept Theory by Wallace LaBenne and Bert Green (1969) argues for enlightened dealing with students. Honesty, suspended judgment, and the meeting of individual differences are all essential in achieving a healthy learning environment. The book has a relationship to Stanley Coppersmith's *The Antecedents of Self-Esteem (1967).*

Our schools must be prototypes of our culture, posing real obstacles, real threats, and real conflicts. The overwhelming advantage of school is that the child can, under the sensitive ministrations of his teachers, survive his failures. He can have a second, third, and if he needs it, a tenth chance.

Bruno Bettelheim (1969)

Fourteen

FACING PROBLEMS
IN SELF-DIRECTED LEARNING:
Debugging the System

DISCIPLINE IN SDL

Any good educational program stresses enjoyable learning experiences for those involved. When you visit a room in which most of the students are enjoying learning, you see few discipline problems. Students are busy doing meaningful things, and there is no contest between teacher and students—all are regarded as learners benefiting from the environment.

The loving teacher creates an environment in which each free individual can seek and find. There will be fairly frequent psychological payoff for each, especially the intrinsic reward of achieving something he sought to achieve, but also the extrinsic rewards of teacher and peer approval. I always involve parents, and their approval acts as an additional reinforcement. Such rewards are a bigger payoff than the child gets from raising hell in the classroom.

I am going to set up a self-directed learning system, either for a self-contained classroom, or for several classes of students. I imagine rules and procedures needed to permit us to work in harmony. I introduce this as a subject of discussion, as I would any other feature of SDL: "What rules and procedures will help us work?" My bet is that, while students may suggest many rules, they will end up by adopting relatively few—because there's no sense in having rules about every conceivable occurrence—such as "Don't put beans in your ears." Agreement to talk in a quiet voice, to move around the room quietly, to share materials, to clean up one's own mess, and to leave in peace anyone who is concentrating on his work—these should suffice. I help in discussing and clarifying the proposed rules. I make clear to the students at what point I will take over direct control of the class if the rules system breaks down.

There are two very strong reasons why this system will work. When children make up the rules, they have a personal interest in seeing that those rules are followed. And in an open structure learning environment, every member has an interest—a daily and hourly interest—in defending *his own* freedom, which means he must *also* defend the equal freedom of others. I have watched this in many SDL classrooms: students show respect and love for each other by allowing each person to work undisturbed. This does not mean that no one ever interrupts or kibbitzes. Ted may go over to where Barry and Nick are building their telescope and observe, ask questions, and interrupt their work because of his own interest. Because Barry and Nick like what they're doing, they enjoy bringing Ted up to date on their progress. In the same way, many students will observe the hydroponics experiment or the making of a boomerang to see what is happening during the day. But when someone intrudes on the work of another in irritating ways, he is "told off"—quickly and directly—by the people whose work is being disturbed.

In part, learning and loving in the classroom depend—as they always do—on faith in human beings. Time and time again, when I show faith, pupils respond with faith. Faith is a two-way street. Each of us starts out with some expectation of the other or others. Because of degrading experiences they've had in kindergarten and first grade, many second grade pupils do not have faith in teachers as people who are willing to help them. In a way, each new teacher encountered by the child or young adult is one he must check out: Is this teacher one I can trust? When the teacher shows himself willing to enter into human relationships based on mutual trust and faith, the child will usually respond positively.

School is not an option for most children—attendance is compulsory. But we can never compel willing effort by students, only compliance. In a loving situation in which children are free to choose what interests them, each child has a stake in maintaining the integrity of the situation. That means every student has reasons for learning self-control and for exerting his share of peer pressure on others when they transgress.

If I had serious discipline problems after SDL had been in operation in my room for several weeks, I'd hypothesize one of two problems:

(a)   A fair number of students in the class don't understand SDL as I've explained it. I'd better back up and take time to help them see—as a group and especially as individuals—what its benefits are to them.

(b)   I don't in fact have SDL, but instead have some hybrid which confuses the students. For example, if they try to use the freedom they think they have only to be criticized or punished by me, then they react with hostility or apathy. A student may say, "Make up your mind, Teach, either we have freedom or we don't." If this is the situation, I need to go back and rethink what I now have as a learning environment and what I hope to have. Some students will adjust better to a gradual increase in freedom, while others may be able to make the jump to a wide area of freedom quickly and easily. (This was discussed in the case of Mr. Landon in Chapter 4.) A review of Chapter 12, which described paths to SDL, may be in order.

There is a third possibility: that my difficulties stem from some combination of the above two problems. As an example, perhaps I have an SDL program, but the rules and procedures need to be reviewed and clarified, or amended. In any case, observation and thinking by me, and possibly open consultation with another teacher or the principal, may lead to some successful remedies. But I cannot blame SDL because of some factor in the situation which would be there anyway and would influence what happens regardless of the system I employ. Nor can I use such problems, real or anticipated, as excuses for not trying SDL.

Each teacher faces problems related to pupil behavior vis-a-vis other students and himself. Do you feel threatened by students? Do you feel comfortable if students call you by your first name?

Rudolf Dreikurs (1971) asserts that pupil behavior is purposive. The child misbehaves for one of four reasons: (1) to attract attention, (2) to demonstrate that he has power as a person, (3) to get even for something he sees as a wrong against him, or (4) to avoid tasks at which he expects to fail. The teacher can do several things which may lead to a change in such behavior. He can observe to see what is really happening and sometimes will immediately see the cause of the pupil behavior: Mary is reminding me she is a person who needs to be stroked often. The teacher should also notice his own spontaneous reaction to the misbehavior—an impulsive reaction may add fuel to the fire. I practice reacting in a rational way even to a violent outburst—it helps the student regain his composure and helps the student and the class focus on the real problem: Nancy is mad because her best friend is becoming close friends with another girl. One way to respond calmly is to ask the student why he is behaving that way, and thus disclose his real goals: "What is it I really want?" So often the student wants to be stroked, and so I stroke him. If the situation is tense and no immediate discussion seems likely to be profitable, I agree to see the individual (or individuals) at the next recess or lunch period for a conference. As I have gained confidence, I have found loving ways to reassure upset students.

There are many ways to approach the kinds of pupil behavior described by Dreikurs (1971). Among the excellent ways that teachers have developed is the SEE, or Self-Enchancing Education program. One of the major goals of SEE is self-management by the child. Teachers need to see themselves as resources to students, rather than as bosses who impose on them. Pupils need to recognize the importance of self-management as a cluster of skills which evolve through childhood into adulthood.

One of the techniques featured in SEE is the use of cards which identify social needs/skills/behaviors which are needed at particular times for the benefit of the individual, the group, or the whole class. Each card identifies one such skill. Each pupil has a complete set of cards and is expected to display one when appropriate. The eleven cards the authors suggest as of greatest importance have the following words:

Getting myself in
Ready for work
Listening
Group discussion
Working with the teacher
Following Directions
Working alone
Working with a partner
Working in a small group
Self-freedom
Getting myself out

The teacher's responsibility is to help in case the individual or the group shows inability to self-manage. Suppose a number of pupils are goofing off and continue to do so. The teacher may announce that he gets the message from the group that they need him to take control temporarily, until the pupils can return to self-management. Alternatively, he may reflect the situation in the room as he sees it by a statement such as, "I am getting very frustrated and concerned because you are not responding to your social-skill card." It is very important that I as teacher make such statements in a form similar to that suggested. The sample statement deals with the situation and my feelings without criticizing an individual. It also appeals to the students to continue supporting a system which they had a hand in establishing.

Other ways of handling problems are also recommended by the authors of SEE. The child who has minor difficulty in controlling himself may be asked to be an "island" apart from the "continent" for a short time, until he is ready to return. Pupils with greater difficulties in self-management are asked to visit their own "office" (a study carrel), or to visit the guidance worker or the principal. Occasionally the principal takes a pupil home from school early, but always with a contact made with the parent and an encouragement to the pupil to return next day. It is of great importance to avoid giving the pupil or the parent the message " You're not OK," so the procedures used and the words used if a pupil is taken home must be carefully selected. There are many instances in which the parent regards the brought-home pupil as a candidate for automatic and possibly severe punishment. Or, if the family is disaffected, this may seem to be another proof that the school does not care about them or their child. The intention of Randolph and Howe, the authors of SEE, is to build bridges of friendship between school and home. They develop, in thoughtful ways, the procedures to be followed and the roles school personnel and the parent should play in order to enhance the pupil's feeling of OK-ness. Their ideas seem to me to fit in very well with the spirit of SDL, because they offer steady and supportive encouragement to the individual to learn the uses of freedom in the service of his own goals. An ounce of love is worth a pound of conventional discipline.

In many conventional classrooms, there is psychological warfare between teacher and students. Teachers are advised to start out tough and maybe ease up later, if the kids are docile. Later is often too late: the students have lapsed into apathy because they recognize the class is entirely the teacher's ball game. In SDL I regard each class, whether it is kindergarten or tenth grade or a class of college seniors, as a collection of learners with common interests and also different interests. Starting from this point, a class can build a set of agreements about behavior designed to enhance everyone's learning opportunities. Once these agreements are understood and accepted, each of us—teacher and student—can focus on learning and loving in an environment we created and which we can change if we need to. There will be breakdowns in the system and no amount of goodwill will prevent all of them. Teaching is oriented toward problem-solving, and some of the problems that arise from student behavior are tough ones. Students can always say the opposite: some of the problems arising from teacher behavior are tough ones. In the toughest profession in the world, how can it be otherwise?

PROBLEMS WITH SELF-SELECTION

The Child Who Won't Start

What if the child will not take initiative in his own learning? What if he simply sits and waits. Gene Darby tells of the first grade boy in her class who sat in his seat for weeks, silently refusing to read. Four weeks passed, then five, and by this time Gene was getting very uncomfortable, although other children were rolling along beautifully. One day in the sixth week, the boy got up and went to the bookshelf, picked out a book and sat down to read. The sit-in was over, and from that day on he read regularly. Gene had affirmed her position as an available, living resource to him and had shown her own freedom from the compulsion to manipulate another person. Positively, she showed loving respect for him as an individual with his own integrity and had fulfilled her loving responsibility to him as a person by being available to him throughout all those weeks.

An even longer period of nonparticipation occurred in the class taught for two years by Averil Anderson and Florence Moon. One girl played with water a large part of the year—she sat or stood at the sink playing with containers and utensils as though this were where she belonged. By the usual guidelines, this child accomplished almost nothing during her first grade year. The two teachers were concerned but avoided strenuous interference. Other children interacted with her, but generally in limited ways. At the beginning of her second grade year, she began to work at reading, math, spelling, and other subjects. By Christmas she had completed most first grade work and was approximately on grade level by the end of the year. She had obviously learned some important things by watching and listening during her first year. Most important, she had found out that her teachers would not force her to do anything. And so when she was ready to start conventional work, she started and went like a house afire. Who knows why? Who needs to know? As Alan Watts says, an overpowering urge to know and to control interferes with living—and learning and loving. How long have you waited for a student to settle down and produce?

There are two ways the loving teacher can approach the sit-in, directly or indirectly. Before deciding, I observe the pupil. Dreikurs asserts the pupil's behavior makes sense in his own eyes. Can *I* see what sense it makes to him? Sometimes I can. Mr. Horn noticed that Jimmy looked at Cheryl longingly and guessed that Jimmy considered himself in love with her. On the basis of such hunches, I can plan my behavior so as to go with the student rather than against him. For example, I avoid teasing a sixth grade boy because he's attracted to a girl. I may encourage, by contrast, in a group or an individual conference, a discussion of the feelings and responses of loving relationships between a man and a woman.

If I choose to approach the nonparticipant directly, I'll say to him in private: "Why aren't you reading?" I must feel secure before saying this, because he will know something of what I feel and may respond in a way that I am unprepared to handle: "None of your business," or words to that effect. As an authentic teacher, I reveal something of myself to students frequently. Part of what I reveal is: "I am here and I'm ready to talk with you about what you see as important now." Students often respond in kind, and the student may say in response to my direct question: "I don't feel like it right now. Is it OK if I do something else for a while?" To the extent that I can be my true contemporary feelings, I can grant the student the right to meet his contemporary needs.

If I choose to approach the nonparticipant indirectly, I can do so through materials, through activities, through another subject, through another person, or through stroking the nonparticipating student. I can add some interesting new books or magazines to the classroom library. Or I can bring in some new instructional materials or apparatus I think may be of interest to him, such as artifacts from an Indian reservation. I can involve him in some other activity. For example, I can ask him to be a subject in a nutrition experiment the class is running. I can ask another student to invite him to join in some meaningful project, such as the writing of the class newspaper. Or, again, I can stroke the nonparticipant.

I may approach this student directly, indirectly—or not at all. I'm not sure I could have waited as Florence and Averil did, but I recognize the way in which they respected the girl's integrity, convinced of their own OK-ness and her OK-ness, and convinced that she would work when she was good and ready. That way, *she* made the decision to start. She established her own integrity in the class: as a nonparticipant, she showed her own freedom to do or not do. And when she decided to read, this too was the act of a free person. A free person can more easily learn and invest love in his relationships with others.

Whether I approach the child directly or indirectly, I recognize the importance of avoiding the giving of an injunction which may cause him to retreat into himself. A question I may ask myself at a moment when I'm tempted to give or imply a command is: Will my feeling momentarily better be worth the probability of the student feeling put down?

The Child Who Always Makes "Bad" Selections

How about the child who picks only easy books, books which he can read with almost no effort? Shouldn't the teacher insist that he read some books which challenge him, which require expansion of his reading skills? I think first of the environment in which he finds himself. There should be four to six or more books per child so that at any given time he has a number from which to select. If no new books have been added to the collection for a long time—say seven or eight weeks—he may not find much stimulus from the ones available. So I round up some more books from the book room or the county library or get more from parent and pupil donations of Arrow books.

Even with a fine supply which includes new titles, some child will tend to pick easy ones. Is this a waste of his time? Well, all books, including easy ones, consist of words in the characteristic patterns of our language, so that even with easy books the pupil gets practice from his reading. We know very little about how pupils develop sureness about their fluency or how they develop speed, but we have reason to believe that practice is one of the key factors. So practice in easy books is still practice. Still, shouldn't the total environment in which the child functions challenge him sufficiently so that he will exert his highest learning powers? Yes, but not consistently at one level. If you have thirty minutes' free time, do you always pick up a professional book to read? I don't—I may pick up the *New Yorker, Saturday Review,* a novel, or a science fiction book rather than a professional book. Pupils make similar varied choices from time to time.

How about the pupil who selects books that are too difficult for him? If I say to Johnny, "That book is too difficult for you," I am behaving as a parental teacher, dominating him, doing "what is best for him." I don't believe I know in all cases or even most cases what is best for another person, even though he is much younger than I. The pupil may choose a hard book to gain status in his own eyes: "I know it's tough, but I can do it." So who's the loser if in fact he can't read it? No one. Like the boy who read the encyclopedia for three weeks, the pupil with the too-hard book will learn from his choice and will eventually make a new selection. Perhaps eventually will be five minutes from now.

Similar approaches seem advisable for pupils who read entirely on one topic (the girl who reads only Nancy Drew mysteries), the child who in your opinion shows poor taste over a period of time, or the child who refuses to tackle what you think he needs. In all cases, there is an element of opinion: for example, who knows what a pupil needs at a given moment? Probably this is knowable only by him and then the knowing may be unclear. To a very considerable extent we must rely on the child to choose sensibly for himself. When he becomes an adult, he will seldom have a parent or teacher to decide for him.

In a basic subject such as arithmetic, I would wait a reasonable time for the pupil to act on his own to start mastering what he seemed ready to do; if he does not start, I might assign it to him. But I would choose to make the assignment out of a different book or workbook, one new to him, preferably one with a different approach, one which has something which may intrigue him. But an assignment is an assignment, and I would not make them wholesale. If I do, the values of SDL will begin to evaporate, and kids will fall right back into the old rut of doing only what they're forced to do because you assign it. Rogers (1969, pp. 251–252) asserts that the

> *valuing process in the human being is effective in achieving self-enhancement to the degree that the individual is open to the experience which is going on within himself* .... One way of assisting the individual to move toward openness to experience is through a relationship in which he is prized as a separate person, in which the experiencing going on within him is empathically understood and valued, and in which he is given the freedom to experience his own feelings and those of others without being threatened in doing so.

Pupils of all ages show varying reactions to opportunities to interact with features of the environment. I have seen kindergartners and also third graders enjoying and also learning from play with Cuisenaire rods, play without teacher direction. Later, the same children may benefit greatly from structured lessons with the rods because of the earlier experience— they have a better frame of reference and an increased readiness to go further in understanding. Free experiences and controlled experiences can be profitably mingled.

Our economy and our political system function on the basis of choices made or not made by the various individuals and electorates; I can choose to get out on a rainy day to vote for members of the city council, or I can decide to stay at home. Adults cannot be expected to develop competent and sophisticated skills in choice-making without considerable experience as children and youth. In order for pupils to profit from choice-making, much of the opportunity afforded them must be genuine. That is, the kids must truly be allowed to make choices from an array of real possibilities. Student government, for example, should either allow pupils to select their own leaders and make some genuine choices about their class or school, or else it should not exist. Is there student government in your school? Your class? Is it real or fake?

PROBLEMS WITH SELF-PACING

What about the child who works too fast, rushes through, probably missing much of the important content? Without intensive checking, it is virtually impossible to tell whether this is a valid conclusion or only an impression based on observation of what I may happen to notice about the child's behavior.

Material differs enormously in its nature, all the way from "two plus three" to the reasons for Arab-Israeli conflict in the Middle East. No single set of evaluative criteria will be adequate to measure pupil success. If I want to understand the geography of Arab-Israeli conflict, only one of several important factors in the situation, I must gather background data and become acquainted with several maps, such as one showing population distribution. The fifth grader should be considering problems which approach the complexity of the Arab-Israeli conflict—such as the causes of the Civil War. It may be that the fifth grader who learns to listen to his fellow students and to consider what they say may be making more important progress than if he passed three multiple choice tests.

My observations must concern themselves with many possibilities. The process by which the pupil "gets" something is hard to pin down; it seems very probable that "messing about" with material and crossing the boundary between knowing and not knowing may occur many times before the child can be said—or the adult can be said—to have mastered the concept or relationships. The aware teacher sometimes knows what the pupil has accomplished. But many times he lives with mystery.

In my conference with the child who appears to read hastily, I would stress what he *did* get out of his reading, point out some of the things he may have missed. (I would talk with him about what he has read, or, if I am really concerned, I would read the book I notice him gulping.) During the discussion, see what ideas come out about his improving his reading; in many cases, he'll bring out the points I hope he'll get: by going a bit slower he'll get more understanding as well as more pleasure. The child who rushes through his math too quickly may be asked to correct his own paper as a matter of routine and then show it to the teacher. Praise his accurate work, and point out his errors. Give him specific instruction in the skill on which he's working. Ask him how he could improve. If he has a habit of careless, inaccurate work in math, it may be helpful to give him a specific assignment to follow up the one you've just gone over. Then, hopefully, you can note his improvement. If there is no improvement, perhaps he's working on something that is beyond his grasp at the moment. Often, encouraging the pupil to work on another skill in another chapter or even another book may be the way to avoid an impasse which will inhibit learning. A detour may help in the long run. A week later he may tackle the problem he was hung up on and master it readily, and happily.

What about the child who consistently works slowly, who never seems to finish? With due regard for his own pace and rhythm, you feel he's going too slow, getting too little accomplished. In subjects such as social studies, science, or health, possibly he's gotten in the habit of tackling assignments that are too long, so that he ends up dawdling. Suggest that he assign himself shorter amounts at a time, so that he will have more frequent endings. Avoid discussion which centers on "all that there is to be done" or that makes comparisons between him and any other student. After all, some plumbers, librarians, engineers, and short-order cooks are speedier than others. And he has a right to be a person of slow or medium tempo if that is his nature. Many people differ in the tempo with which they tackle different jobs; others alter their tempo at different times of the day —or at different times of their lives.

GROUPING PROBLEMS

I may have too many groups to handle at one time: if I meet with each group as often as I feel I should, there will be too little time for individual conferences or whole-class activities. Three approaches can be used to solve this problem. I take a look at the groups in operation and include the potential groups, the ones I have not yet called together but that I believe would benefit appreciably from group work. Which ones are of greatest importance right now? Those should be continued and worked into the schedule. Which ones are of less importance right now? These can be postponed to a later time, perhaps a week or two. By that time changes will have occurred in my class; some of the existing groups may have worked through to a fairly successful conclusion of their work; some of the groups that I thought should be started may no longer be needed, and other needed groups may have appeared on the horizon. Loving educational leadership by the teacher appraises needs and establishes priorities for action. This is an important aspect of loving responsibility to students.

Another acceptable way of handling groups is to have a student lead one of the groups that I feel has a high priority. I can also help children improve their work in groups. In an effective group, individuals become sensitive to the needs of other individuals. They learn to join in setting group goals and agreeing on ways to reach those goals. Free expression of feelings and opinions occurs more easily in a democratic than in an autocratic group, so students who are to serve as group leaders need orientation to their responsibilities. The individual who participates in a shared decision-making process is more likely to act on the decisions than one who is left out. Such participation is vital to fight apathy. All students can learn to participate more effectively in group work.

Another way to help make the program work is to economize in the use of my time in groups. I pinpoint what the group needs and teach that as directly and precisely as I can, or I teach one skill or subskill on a particular day to the group. This has two advantages. First, the kids spend relatively brief time in the group each day, and hence each student has more time to work on what excites him at the time. Students will not be so likely to build up a resentment against the group or its work. Second, because any group work is, in part, a shot in the dark in which I am operating on the hypothesis that all these kids need this skill now, I will be wasting less of my time and less of theirs. A reasonable amount of humility helps in the realization of the loving/learning environment.

Groups function better when they deal with real rather than fake problems. If I find students unable to get involved in discussion and hence not gaining much in cognitive information or process skills, I try giving them a paragraph such as the following (see Shapiro, 1970, p. 33) and asking them to react to it:

> Mrs. Inocencia Flores, a resident of New York's East Harlem, wrote in her diary in February 1964:
>
> "Wednesday, Feb. 5: I got up at 6:45. The first thing to do was light the oven. The boiler was broke so not getting the heat. . . . The children go to school and I clean the house and empty the pan in the bathroom that catches the water dripping from pipe in the big hole in the ceiling. You have to carry umbrella to the bathroom sometimes. I go to the laundry place this afternoon and I wash again on Saturday because I change my kids clothes every day because I don't want them dirty to attract the rats. . . ." (Shapiro, et al., 1970)

Students who have had practice dealing with such material can soon select topics they wish to discuss and can improve their information-gathering, hypothesizing, and decision-making through mastery of group work skills.

PROBLEMS THAT OCCUR WHEN STUDENTS SERVE AS TEACHERS

When students serve as teachers, a few problems usually arise. Here are suggestions for dealing with some of those problems.

The monopolist, the one who always wants to be teacher: Call on others often, call on him occasionally. Point out to all students the values of the student as teacher. Stroke the student when he does a good job as teacher. And encourage him in other learning endeavors, such as the news article he is writing.

The over-solicitous one: Encourage client feedback so he will come to see himself as others see him. This same plan may help with the know-it-all pupil who may tend to overpower less verbal members of the class. When loving peers "tell it like it is," everyone benefits, although the learning process is not always trouble-free. Similar benefits come from role-playing: both teachers and pupils gain insight.

The know-nothing student who is very reluctant about serving as teacher: Call on him only when he's ready. Meanwhile, in individual conferences build up his self-esteem. Encourage him to help another individual who very badly needs help—but make sure the helper is properly prepared to give that help.

The quiet child who shows no interest in being teacher: I have known a number of children who never served as teacher. Loving respect for the individual will help me to encourage him to try when and if he's ready. Only he knows when he's crossed the threshold and is ready. But I look for the signs that he may be getting ready.

Resentment and bad feeling engendered when a student serves as group leader: Remind students to allow time for open discussion of how the group is functioning—an important element in self-evaluation by the group. Encourage honesty. Encourage expression of the feelings and the several versions of the situation as perceived by members. And encourage pupil suggestions of solutions. In a free environment, pupils will benefit from practice in dealing with such problems.

PROBLEMS WITH REPORTING AND SHARING

Perhaps the greatest problem is the shortage of time. Is there ever enough time? Yes, if we can get over being bugged about time and enjoy what we do experience. In the vibrant classroom, there will always be active competition for the attention of all class members. In the film *They Can Do It*, a boy becomes excited about typing. Whenever he has an opportunity and the typewriter is free, he heads right over to it. Each of us has his own list of priorities. For a number of students, reporting and sharing get a high priority. Both teacher and students will learn to consider priorities and will act to protect time for the most prized work. When the reporting activities merit attention, they will get it.

The other main problem is poor preparation by those who wish to report. While self-nomination should be the main way to decide who reports when, the teacher always retains control over this. So he may wish to question the prospective reporter or reporting group, to see what they have in mind and how they plan to go about it. After a few pointed questions, the individual or group may agree that they need more preparation. In spite of this screening, there will be mediocre and even poor reports. Open and full discussion will go a long way to help build class standards that will raise the general level of reporting. In early evaluation sessions, pupils may offer only wishy-washy or harsh comments. But as they come to realize that everyone gains from honesty, a different type of comment will emerge—one that focuses on the objectives the report set out to reach and the methods employed to reach them. At the same time, frank give and take will lead to better listening to the reports that are given. Peer pressure will encourage higher quality reports and also higher involvement by the class in attending to them. Experience can lead to greater diversity of reports, as the active imaginations of all class members are enlisted in making learning fun. Is reporting a significant aspect of your curriculum? If not, why not?

COVERING THE CURRICULUM

"This notion of coverage is based on the assumption that what is taught is what is learned; what is presented is what is assimilated. I know of no assumption so obviously untrue. One does not need research to provide evidence that this is false. One needs only to talk with a few students (Rogers, 1969b).

I start with a question: Aren't we in fact covering much of the set content in math, social studies, and science, for example? Look over what the kids are doing and see if there is not a lot of coverage. This does not mean that every child will be covering identical material—to push for this ignores individual differences in rhythm, in ability, in interests, and in tempo. Identical coverage can only be achieved by destroying the freedom to teach and the freedom to learn. However, if my survey shows that I am not getting a good spread of coverage, adjustments in my work with individuals and groups is called for: helping both individuals and groups to set realistic goals for themselves and to honestly evaluate their successes and failures in attaining those goals.

Two other questions may assist me in facing this nagging problem and in discussing it with others, including my principal or curriculum supervisor. First, why cover what is specified? This is always a permissible question—in fact it should always be the first question we consider. Time marches on, and in another two years, the new math may be superseded by the new new math. A curriculum guide written only two years ago may already be about 50 percent useless. This is an additional reason why most textbooks are of only limited usefulness and why current materials such as magazines and newspapers may be more useful.

Second, am I not covering worthwhile alternatives to parts of the prescribed curriculum? Again, this may be hard to answer, but I give it a try. Conversations with my producers/consumers of knowledge will bring out a great deal of what is really happening. Serendipity must be widely recognized. A major research effort to find out what makes grass green did not answer the original question, but an impressive number of other valuable learnings resulted from the study. Many such learnings will occur in a self-directed learning classroom, for serendipity lives.

WAYS STUDENTS WORK

Through the spaces between his fingers Carl could see the tan desk top with its fake wood pattern. He knew it was fake because he had seen Flint, the custodian, repairing a desk by putting the lid back on. Carl had noticed that the top surface color and pattern differed from the rest of the desk top—he could see where the finish had been chipped away. He had asked Flint about it and Flint explained lamination, the process of putting several layers together or of putting a thin layer on the outside to serve as decoration as well as finish.

Carl thought of an art project. At home, he would take several pieces of wood, glue them together, and then use tools to shape the block into something, either a representation of an animal or some free form thing.

The film was over, the tag end of the film flapped as it went round and round on the take-up reel. Ed shut off the machine, the lights went on, and Mr. Horn began questioning the class about the film. Most of the questions focused on the content of the film, and really asked: "Did you watch, did you pay attention;" rather than, "Did you understand, and can you apply what you saw?" Marshall and Tamara fielded several of the questions, proving that they had watched. A number of students did not raise their hands when the questions were asked, Carl among them. He noticed Evan looking at Cheryl, looking curiously at her breasts. About three months ago one of the boys had noticed that her breasts had begun to push out her sweaters and blouses. One told another and soon all were informed and began looking at Cheryl differently.

Mr. Horn knew that, although some of the students hadn't paid attention to the film, it was a comparatively interesting instructional film. In effect, he thought, "I carry out my responsibility by providing the film which I know is good and by following up on it. You can lead a horse to water. . . ."

I look at my responsibility differently. Usually, I will ask students to suggest topics on which they would like to have films. Usually, I announce the showing of films a day or more in advance and allow those who do not wish to view the film to plan an alternative activity, in the library or elsewhere. This is possible in an elementary school as well as in college, when the teacher thinks first of the needs of individuals. Don Kline and Kay McKenzie set up a small permanent movie theater in one corner where films could be viewed by one to twelve students at a time.

Pupil interests wax and wane. The child who is delighted with snakes today may be equally excited about them a year from now or twenty years from now. If so, he was one of those who found his "thing" early, and he may spend a lifetime enjoying it. In most cases, though, one interest will wane as other interests claim the individual's attention. A girl will find out all she wants to know about horses and will move on to some other interest which may equally absorb her attenion and her effort. If a child gets a lot of math one year and very little the next, this may not be cause for deep concern. Most children over a period of years will even out their learning to some reasonable extent. We as teachers will probably "get more out of them" by encouraging and by respecting their integrity than by being insistent about long lists of arbitrary tasks to be done.

Even though all this is true, I may still counsel with the girl oblivious to things other than horses. I may spend time helping her become aware of the value of other subjects. One way to do this is to hitch a rider onto her interest in horses: ask her to do a social science project involving the uses of horses and the ways some of these uses have diminished. As her teacher, I still feel the responsibility to insist upon some minimum in basic subjects such as math or language. That doesn't mean I'll get it—because students can be very stubborn, and a contest of wills may result in everyone being the loser. But usually I can use the individual conference as a means of extending the child's horizons so he can better appreciate the relatedness of other subjects to his life. Parenthetically, I don't recommend withholding privileges as a means of forcing compliance: "You can't read until you turn in your geography report." I will be a true teacher by showing loving respect for each pupil's present interests.

CONFERENCES

A number of problems may arise in handling conferences. The closer we get to meeting the needs of the individual, the better we help him. Effective conferencing is a fundamental part of building that help. Here are suggested ways of handling problems.

Not enough time for conferences: My reply to the problem of shortages of time in the section on grouping will apply almost equally well here. First, each teacher should check his use of time by keeping a log of his time for two to four days, so he can see where the time goes. Thoughtful reading of the log may suggest appropriate shifts in use of time. As an example, an undue amount of time may be spent in share and tell, while waiting for individuals to conform to some arbitrary standard of behavior before leaving the room for recess, or when giving the whole class instructions about how to go to an assembly or participate in a fire drill. Or too much time may be spent in leading groups; some groups might function as well with student leadership, while others might be phased out.

With practice it will be possible to reduce the amount of time needed for conferences. I have held conferences in as little as two or three minutes that covered what needed to be covered; this left me more time for those conferences which required ten minutes. When a conference is urgently needed, consider stealing a few minutes from recess or lunch period or holding it after school. My professionalism isn't ruled by the clock.

Teacher uncertainty as to what to say: Each teacher learns by experience. Role-playing may help, too.

Pupil uncertainty as to what to say: If the teacher can get the conference off to a good start, this will put the pupil at ease. And then he will join in the conversation more readily.

The student who is too demanding: He wants many conferences, never wants to end a conference. I give him as much time as I can, but I tell him frankly that other students also need my help.

How to close a conference: see below.

For the last four problems, I have three suggestions. First, role-play the situation which creates a real (or anticipated) problem. A fellow teacher, a spouse, or one of your own children will be willing to role-play it with you. Honest trying out will yield both insight and an increase in feelings of confidence about handling the problem. Second, read what Jeannette Veatch has written on the subject—see her *Reading in the Elementary School* (1966, pp. 120–165). Third, learn by experience. So many of the how-to's can only be truly learned by becoming a part of your repertoire of competence through real experience.

Are you aware of any change in your teaching behavior since you started reading this book? In your feelings about how you teach?

Teacher behavior makes a difference in how the pupil feels about himself and his work and hence in how he behaves. When the teacher has calm, accepting transactions with students and gives individual instruction in private conferences, children tend to feel better about themselves. Pupil self-concepts are more positive in classrooms in which: (1) teachers communicate largely in private or semi-private ways with pupils; (2)   teachers openly facilitate task-oriented behavior; (3)   teachers show interest in divergent responses by pupils; (4)   teachers attend closely to individual pupil needs; (5)   teachers use control techniques involving humor; and (6) teachers use a relatively low amount of negative evaluation, a low amount of domination through threat, and a low amount of harsh taskmaster behavior. The positive behaviors listed tend to be associated with pupil gains in reading. These positive behaviors are exactly the ones I am recommending for teachers. They are also ones which, in many instances, will be the natural ones for the teacher who employs SDL in his classroom—they will flow out of the love the teacher comes to feel for himself and for his pupils as he and they interact in a free learning environment.

CONCLUSION

If I follow habit, accept the domination of routine, and do what somebody else says I should do, I will not become the person I may become. I may become. I choose to teach because through teaching I am becoming. I choose to use my freedom for learning and loving, because in so doing I serve myself as I serve others.

"The child can speak for himself," reminds Charles Marcantonio (1968). If not at first, I have patience, and he learns to speak out. And I can listen, and learn, and love.

NOTES TO CHAPTER 14

Nathaniel Gage, now at Stanford, brought together a distinguished group of authors to write *Handbook of Research on Teaching* (1963). Countless interesting studies are reported in this important book, which also contains a number of items which support the techniques recommended in this chapter.

For the secondary teacher, Gaynor Petrequin's *Individualizing Learning Through Modular-Flexible Programming* (1968) offers many worthwhile suggestions.

Paul F. Brandwein, long well known in the teaching of science, has more recently become a noted figure in the teaching of social studies. He wrote a challenging short article, "Notes on Teaching the Social Sciences" (1970). And he served as senior editor to the important new series of social studies texts, *The Social Sciences, Concepts and Values* (1970).

One of the better books on the teaching of reading is *Common Sense in Teaching Reading* by Roma Gans (1963). Gans describes several alternatives and helps teachers appreciate the possibilities in each.

Norma Randolph and William Howe authored a practical guide to student-centered instruction in their *Self-Enhancing Education* (1966). This book is based on years of trial and error learning about what makes for success in combining good teaching with good guidance in the classroom. It is a veritable gold mine for the teacher.

Sheldon Stoff and Herbert Schwartzberg edited a commendable collection of articles on *The Human Encounter* (1969).

A study by Robert L. Spaulding which supports my beliefs is entitled *Achievement, Creativity and Self-Concept Correlates of Teacher-Pupil Transactions in Elementary School Classrooms* (1965). Stanley Coopersmith has done several studies of self-concept and achievement. His book, *The Antecedents of Self-Esteem* (1967), goes a long way to substantiate the values of a self-directed learning program.

John A. Zahorik and Dale L. Brubaker wrote *Toward More Humanistic Instruction* (1972), a practical guide which focuses on informing behavior, soliciting behavior, responding behavior, and reading behavior designed to improve communication about values and feelings. The authors include transcripts of classroom events. They also present the use of gestalt games in the classroom, using contemporary topics such as landlord versus tenant, crossing cultural boundaries, confrontation, and pollution. Lesson plans involve some whole-class and group activities and can be adapted also to individual work.

In recent years, Science Research Associates has published several series of letters. The ones I found most useful were the William Hedges Letters, the Elizabeth Z. Howard Letters, the Joseph Crescimbini Letters, and the Marshall Jameson Letters. The Hedges Letters covered many aspects of individualized instruction.

Audrey D. Sutton, principal of a British primary school, tells of the realities of teacher-pupil interactions at her school. She shows that English teachers cooperate together freely and that the variety of student endeavors is very rich. She acknowledges some of the difficulties encountered in a relatively free learning environment. The book is called *Ordered Freedom* (1970).

Individualized Teaching in Elementary Schools, by Dona K. Stahl and Patricia Anzalone (1970), contains many examples of classroom activities which can be used virtually as presented in the book. My impression is that the authors favor a more teacher-dominated program than I do, but they show awareness of many of the values of freedom and ways in which aspects of freedom can be sought in practice. This is a useful book with many down-to-earth prescriptions.

Who in his right mind can really oppose the idea of accountability? That is like being against motherhood. Every institution must be held accountable, and our schools are no exception. It is possible, however, that the means we choose to achieve accountability may boomerang to destroy or impede the goals we seek so that we end by "losing on the bananas what we made on the oranges". . . . .

When changes to be produced must be made inside the individual where they cannot be directly manipulated, it is the student who knows and the teacher who does not know.

Arthur W. Combs (1972)

Fifteen

KEEPING AND USING RECORDS ON INDIVIDUAL PUPILS

To get the greatest benefits from self-directed learning, I keep records on each pupil and use those records in working with and for that pupil. I start out the year with a manila folder for each pupil. Into it I put anecdotal records, samples of the pupil's work, incidental notes I make on that pupil, notes on my conferences with him and with his parent, and checklists which I use to indicate his successes and his needs in various skills.

Monday morning, in the ninth grade World History class, I observe Joan. Normally, she appears to be a steady plodder, systematically going through her work at a pace slower than most other students. On Monday, though, she works faster, smiles occasionally as she works, and finishes her work before the period ends. What this behavior means, I do not know. By making a brief note of her behavior, I help myself remember, and I preserve for later consideration a record of this moment as I see it: "Joan reads selection in supplementary text. Smiles. Reads. Picks up pencil, writes, smiles, writes." Time required: three minutes for observation, one minute to write note and file it in her folder.

Thursday morning: Joan completes a quiz involving twenty multiple choice questions, one matching exercise, and two essay questions which each require about two or three paragraphs. She goes to the teacher's desk and checks the multiple choice and matching items against the key, marks her two errors, goes back to her desk and looks for the correct answers in the supplemental book, and then turns in her paper. I check her paper and read her essays that evening, make a few marginal notes, and return her paper on Friday. She reads it over, asks me a question to clarify one of my comments, and then turns the paper in. I put it in her folder as a sample of her work that month.

When I teach elementary pupils, I save samples of the pupil's work in various subjects, including basic subjects, supplementary subjects, and creative work such as poems or stories. I make sure that my samples of his work include items done at different times of the day, and also different qualities of his work. In that way I can increase the likelihood that my collection includes something like a representative sampling.

Tuesday morning: In the middle of showing a filmstrip to the World History class, I have a sudden hunch about Joan, so after the strip is over I make a quick note and put it in her file. That evening I may decide my inspiration is pretty silly, but I may not. Hunches are sometimes useful, sometimes not. If I care about myself and about pupils, there is some greater likelihood that my hunches will be worth writing down. In any case, the time required to write such notes seldom exceeds two or three minutes.

Friday morning: Friday is the day when pupils select their own work in the room or in the library, and when I hold individual conferences in the room. I have called two for conferences and two others have asked for them. When I finish the fourth conference, Joan sees I'm free and comes to my desk. We talk for almost five minutes. I commend her for several of her recent jobs and also point out several ways in which she can improve, referring to specific items on specific papers which I pull from her folder. She and I look at these items together. She indicates satisfaction with my comments, smiles, and returns to her seat. I then make a few notes on the conference for future reference. Total time required: 6½ minutes.

When I have a conference with a parent or guardian, I also make at least a brief note of what was said and of any agreements reached. For example, a number of parents wish to see examples of the pupil's work and I often agree to send papers home at least once a week. Other parents wish specific assignments sent home for homework. I encourage parents not to insist on too much work being done at home. A child or young adult needs time and freedom to follow his own pursuits. A loving teacher and a loving parent respect this need and they fulfill their responsibility, in part, by allowing the young person opportunities to do his own thing.

One of the valuable kinds of records I keep is check lists designed to pinpoint skills in which the pupil does well and others in which he needs improvement. Figures 9, 10, and 11 show examples of such check lists.

When I hold a pupil conference, I often—though not always—use a checklist as a shorthand means of conserving a good deal of data for later

Figure 9. Individual Reading Check List

	DATE							SPECIFIC DIFFICULTIES
+ = Good − = Unsatisfactory			Student's name _____					
VOCABULARY								
A. Recognition								
B. Meaning								
C. Dictionary use								
WORD ATTACK								
A. Syllables								
B. Suffixes								
C. Prefixes								
D. Root Words								
E. Accents								
F. Phonetic Skill								
1. Initial Consonants								
2. Consonant Blends								
3. Ending Consonants								
4. Vowels—single								
5. Vowels—combinations								
COMPREHENSION								
A. Main Idea								
B. Details								
C. Imagination								
QUALITY OF ORAL READING								

Figure 10. Thinking Skills Related to Social Sciences, Health and Science Learning

1. **Inquiry and question-asking behavior**

   Skill   *Evidence of Skill*

   Fact questions _____

   Convergent questions _____

   Divergent questions _____

2. **Outreach abilities**

   Skill   *Evidence of Skill*

   Comparing, contrasting _____

   Imagining _____

   Supposing _____

   Anticipating _____

   Relating _____

   Transposing _____

3. **Integrating abilities**

   Skill   *Evidence of Skill*

   Listens to what others say _____

   Shows awareness of what he reads _____

   Uses data and opinions in various ways:

      in asking additional questions _____

      in discussion _____

      in written work _____

   Shows evidence of modifying own
   opinions, beliefs, and behavior as result
   of interaction with people and materials _____

Comments

use. I adapt such a checklist from one used by another teacher, or I prepare one of my own, making changes in it as I figure out ways of improving it.

One advantage of the grid system in the examples above is that I can date all entries and thus get a better idea of the pattern of the individual's work and progress (or retrogression). For example, in reading, a primary student may continue to have difficulty with medial vowels for several weeks. A ninth grade student, by contrast, may be slow in mastering some of the basic research skills, such as using a table of contents, an index, and a card catalog. My notation of such problems will assist me in being current in dealing with each student. Note that each checklist has a space for comments. When I write such comments, I date them, and I comment on some aspect of the student's work or being which is not adequately covered in the other categories on the checklist. For example, a child's morale may be more important than any list of skills, and I try to estimate the state of his morale as I work with him. I never try to fill in a check or a comment in every available space on the check list.

I also notice the specific products of the student: drawings, sculpture, stories, poems. Occasionally I use a camera or a tape recorder to preserve such a product, or single it out for display on a bulletin board—provided he approves. Almost every student will create some special thing every few weeks, especially in a free environment in which he is encouraged to create. If the student keeps a journal, this may add to my view and his view of himself. The loving teacher uses such products to build the student's morale, to improve his self-image, to help him gain needed and wanted recognition, and to round out his picture of the student as a producer/consumer of knowledge. Such products, in many cases, help the teacher serve the student better—as a knowledgeable human resource with many opportunities to help.

So, I maintain a folder with these several kinds of things in it. How do I use the information? First, I read all or part of the contents of each folder from time to time. For example, I may take home three or four folders each night, generally those of students about whom I have some questions, often the folders of students with whom I have scheduled conferences for the next day. I can read Joan's folder tonight and then I am better prepared to confer with her tomorrow. I know some compliments I can justifiably give her, I know two or three or more questions I want to ask her, and I am much better prepared to converse with her sensibly and to answer questions she may have. I'll show her items in her folder to illustrate points as we confer. I can also use the contents of the folder in lesson-planning and in conferring with the parent or with the nurse, counselor, or principal.

There are two additional ways in which I can use the collected information in the folder: in grading, and in articulation. Grading, as I have suggested before, should be a cooperative process in which the student

Figure 11. Self-Concept and Citizenship Notes

Name _____
Nine weeks from _____ to _____

(In the squares, entries can be made based on observation and student performance. Each column can represent one week or one day when evaluation is made.)

I. SELF-CONCEPT					
A. Likes himself					
B. Likes others					
C. Respects others					
D. Respects people					
E. High Morale					
F. Happy					
G. Sad					
H. Angry					
I. Fearful and Hateful					
J. Posture					
K. Satisfied					

Figure 11. Self-Concept and Citizenship Notes (continued)

II. CITIZENSHIP.-CIVIC-RESPONSIBILITY				
A. Honest-Sincere				
B. Dependable				
C. Loyal				
D. Independent				
E. Courageous				
F. Determined				
G. Emotionally Sensitive				
H. Versatile				
I. Thorough				
J. Curious				
K. Self-Critical				

plays an important role. He should suggest his own grades and be able to justify the grades he states. My knowledge of the contents of the folder, plus my grade book, will mean that my participation in this process can be thoroughly grounded. I do not feel I should simply rubber stamp any suggestion the student makes. When I have a folder with samples of his work, I can substantiate my ideas about appropriate grades for this student. As a loving teacher, I seek a knowledgeable partnership with each student, rather than giving him a blank check which I have signed.

Too often we skimp on articulation activities at the end of the year. We may fill in a few blank spaces in the student's cumulative record folder and divide the students into three or four suggested groups for next year's classes. For example, I divide up my third graders into three groups: my recommendation as to how they should be split into next year's fourth grade classes. As a principal, I always arranged for the third grade teachers to meet together, preferably several times, and then to meet jointly with the fourth grade teachers, preferably several times. Each teacher who has kept individual folders on each of his students, as recommended in this chapter, has the capacity to make many valuable contributions to these articulation meetings. He can get down to the basics about each student as a personality and how the student works with others. This may be of enormous help in putting together next year's classes, so that student will get along with student. We cannot create the trouble-free class, but we can use our imaginations in creating classes with good prospects for many successes.

Similarly, junior and senior high teachers should play an active part in recommending class memberships for succeeding semesters or school years. This will, I hope, not be a matter of putting students in so-called ability classes—a cop-out by teachers and counselors which evades meeting individual difficulties head-on. But some individuals work well with others, some seem unable to work with others, and frequently we know that some teachers and students clash—and this seldom can be easily overcome in the fifty-minute period once a day. The judgment of secondary teachers can result in better class assignments in future semesters.

Different teachers have different needs for written records for support of teaching activities. Some of us may become dependent on such records, or we may become so obsessed with writing and collecting them that we have little time left over to utilize what we've collected. Like the miser, we can substitute material things for love. The answer is individual: I keep and use records in my way for my benefit and for the benefit of my students. At the same time, I am an aware, responsive living resource to students and use written records as a supplement to my work.

NOTES TO CHAPTER 15

The following sources will help the teacher develop useful record-keeping devices on individual students: Lazar, Draper and Schwietert, *A*

Practical Guide to Individualized Reading (1960); William Hedges, *The Hedges Letters* (1968); Walcott Beatty, ed., *Improving Educational Assessment* and *An Inventory of Measures of Affective Behavior* (1969); Walter B. Barbe, *Educator's Guide to Personalized Reading Instruction* (1961); Jeannette Veatch, *Reading in the Elementary School* (1966); Paul Plowman, *Behavioral Objectives* (1971).

You will need to remain faithful to your own individuality but at the same time be willing to learn from every possible source.

Robert Biehler (1971)

Sixteen

THE LAST CHAPTER

Teaching is a demanding occupation requiring energy, thought, and imagination. No teacher can perform all the roles that all the various groups demand of us. Each of us must select those tasks which we decide are central to serving our students. In that way, each of us devotes our learning and loving to achieving more humane survival for the human species.

I start with me, just as each child starts with himself. I behave according to my perceptions of the world around me and according to my feelings about myself and my universe. Many children do not receive the physical and emotional love they need as infants and very young children. Both animal and human studies verify the necessity for stroking by parent or parent surrogate, so that the individual will believe in his own identity as he is cherished by significant people in his environment. Because of the deficit in stroking and negative injunctions from parents, many children arrive at school feeling "I'm not OK—You're OK." As a teacher, I can make up for this deficit by stroking the student, by recognizing and affirming his value. Virginia Axline worked with the young boy she called Dibs in play therapy for many months before he could recognize that she accepted him as he was and believed in his capacity to grow. She showed him by word and deed that he didn't have to listen to parental injunctions any longer. He also came to appreciate the fact that his parents loved him. He gradually learned to be more loving toward them and to behave in more lovable ways.

Danny, an only child, spent his third grade year with Ms. Horton and his fourth grade year with Ms. Dane. Danny's parents gave insufficient time and consideration to him—each of them was busy with other pursuits. Danny displayed defiance, sarcasm, destructive behavior, and physical aggression against other students. He sometimes refused to do his work and argued over trifles. Both Ms. Horton and Ms. Dane were patient and caring toward him, although each also exerted pressure on him to conform and to do his school work. Each avoided letting any confrontation with Danny appear to be final or letting him believe that ultimate disaster awaited him for his antisocial behavior. Although no great improvement occurred, Danny managed to stay in school and to achieve above grade level in reading, spelling, and arithmetic. Perhaps if he had experienced self-directed learning for a year or two, Danny might have accepted responsibility for his own behavior and latched on to interesting tasks commensurate with his considerable abilities. The report by Clark Moustakas in *The Authentic Teacher* (1966) does not follow Danny's career beyond his fourth grade year. Virginia Axline had the privilege of seeing Dibs several times in later years and the satisfaction of knowing he developed into a sensitive and effective young man. As I become a significant person in the lives of my students, I increase the likelihood that they and I will make the effort to stay in touch in later years. I stroke the student by accepting him as he is, by believing in his images of his present and future, and by allowing him to select and work on tasks he sees as valid for him. At the same time, I play an active role by conferencing with him and inviting him to include more activities in those he makes his own.

Each of us has what Maslow (1954) calls deficiency motives and growth motives. My physiological need for air is so demanding that I will struggle with all my strength to keep my air supply. Similarly, I make efforts to assure my supply of food and water, my safety, and my "belonging" relationships to others who esteem me. As I become more self-sufficient, I take care of these deficit needs more efficiently and have time left over for growth activities. At the same time my view of others changes. Instead of seeing them as need-gratifiers, I come to see them as unique and potentially interesting peers, and I learn to reach out to them for intimacy and love. As a deficit-motivated teacher, I used to phone a parent to complain about a child's behavior or failure to do his work. As a growth-motivated teacher, I phone a parent to share my enthusiasm about the student's achievement and to strengthen the partnership between us which can lead the parent toward more positive help to the student.

The UN film James Herndon showed, with a black student equally featured with students of other races, provoked hilarity in his classes of black students, because equality was so totally foreign to their experience.

There must be something wrong with that dumb nigger, they said, showing that they had no ability to identify with the positive aspects of the film. The extent of disenchantment with verbal pieties can be so profound as to prevent realistic behavior on one's own behalf. Yet each of us must venture, must risk. Each of us simply has to make the difficult efforts to build bridges to individuals among other groups—Philippino, Japanese-American, Chinese-American, Puerto Rican, Native American, Afro-American, and Chicano—in school and in the community. Some of us, female as well as male, have yet to overcome our prejudices about women being inferior to men. More and more young blacks and black leaders are coming to realize that to aspire to some of the values of white people—good neighborhoods, for example—does not make them "imitation white men."

Loving freedom is not so much freedom *from* people or circumstances, but freedom *to*. I exercise my freedom by reaching out to others, risking in hope of the satisfaction of human relationship. I invite others to reach out to me. Instead of living in fear or in constant yearning, I act *toward* what might be. A hundred years ago, a twelve year old might apprentice himself to a shoemaker or a printer as a way of making it in his world. Today, the same individual faces a bewildering number of choices of how to spend parts of his life. He has freedom to try more things. He learns to use his freedom only through experience. And so the teacher must use his own freedom to give others opportunities to use freedom on a scale appropriate to their contemporary abilities. In this way my freedom expands. Through exercise of freedom, I learn to understand the freedom of others and gradually become a responsible, freedom-using, loving individual. I seek knowing relationships with my world because it is human to seek. I yearn for closure, for completion. When I feel sufficiently secure about my place in the world, I am able to make self-fulfilling prophecies that have to do with creating things (poems, paintings, clothes) and the pleasure of additional enriching friendships with others whose idiosyncrasies I can accept and, progressively, appreciate.

Richard de Charms and his associates (1971) have given elementary students a simple dichotomous way to look at human beings: as relatively helpless "pawns" or as relatively autonomous "origins." They found that students can utilize such a way of thinking to develop greater independence in judgment and behavior. Individuals who come to regard themselves as "origins" behave as self-starters, as creators, as responsible self-evaluators. Similarly, I have known several teachers who used the TA (transactional analysis) idea of Parent–Adult–Child in the classroom with considerable success. Children recognize their own and their fellows' behavior as being Adult, for example, and learn to respond Adult to Adult. They learn to avoid Parental behavior toward each other and to delight in each other's friendly Child aspect. As is always the case, there are tried and true ways to translate theory into classroom practice which will enhance the life of everyone there.

The student becoming an "origin" learns to make wise choices which utilize his scarce resources of time, energy, and talent, to produce what he sees as both valuable in the social sense and self-fulfilling. He tunes in to himself with increasing facility and accuracy. He also can improve his ability to live with uncertainty, to tolerate ambiguity. The dependent individual frantically trying to take care of deficit needs has a heck of a time tuning in to anything but the insistent demands for comfort, safety, and security. The independent individual has more and more time to enjoy himself, his productivity, and his loving relationships. He also can understand his own limitations, although he won't cease trying to go beyond them. He can also recognize the inevitability of uncertainty and of tragedy as a part of everyone's life experience.

In early August, Mr. Widel got the list of students who would be in his class in September. He began making visits to their homes, one or two visits a day in the afternoon and evening. In most cases he phoned before going so that his arrival would not be a complete surprise and so that he went at a time convenient to the family and—as often as possible—when both parents could be present. He usually got a friendly reception. He met many of his future students in their home surroundings and was able to form initial impressions of student–parent relationships. When parents preferred, he met them at school. When school opened in September, he had been to all but two homes and had accumulated a large reservoir of goodwill. The year started well and got better each week. Parent contacts, instead of being fewer because of his pioneering effort, were in fact more frequent and more lasting. He found that report cards and parent conferences tended to be more relaxed experiences and more rewarding, because he had reached out lovingly to the parents.

A junior high or senior high teacher, with 125 to 200 students per day in his classes, cannot see every family before school opens. But he will be able to visit a few families of students in each of his classes. As the year progresses, he can make additional home visits and repeat calls to some homes. Even in today's world, word gets around to other families through the grapevine. This will lead many students and parents to expect good things from the students' contact with this teacher. Once a positive relationship has been established, additional visits can be on the phone. Such partnership with parents goes far beyond being a good public relations exercise. It leads to knowledge which the teacher can use in lesson-planning, in conferencing with individual students, and in his many dealings with other school personnel. Knowing gives increased confidence. In addition, there is a different type of knowing by the student: he knows that this teacher cares about himself as a person and about each student as an individual. He also knows that this teacher can be expected to take appropriate initiative toward solving problems as they arise during the year.

Another way I learn about students is by observing them at school. I pretend I'm a movie camera and record behavior. At the start of the year

I get a manila folder for each student, and my anecdotal observations are kept in the folder along with samples of the student's work and other notes about him. When I have accumulated ten or a dozen anecdotes I read them over to see if I detect any clues about the student's attitudes toward himself, his peers, me, or his school work. I invariably find such clues, perhaps not very distinct at first, but as I make more observations I generally can verify (or amend) a tendency noticed earlier. Then I can decide how to behave in order to help the individual become better aware of himself and of his possibilities. When I know that a student is fearful of failure, I can avoid putting him in situations in which there is a likelihood of failure. At the same time I can help him look at errors, mistakes, and failure in a broader context and to see that everyone makes errors and everyone fails, at times, and that the real measure of a man or a woman is whether he can learn from such experiences and continue his efforts to achieve loving relationships with other people. I can also see that he has instructional materials he can use successfully and opportunities to interact with others in ways that do not stress comparisons in which he may expect to come off badly. I cannot shield him from experience. I cannot make sure that all his experiences will be positive. But I can give thought in my lesson planning to experiences which will have a strong potential for positive outcomes for him. In the same way, I can utilize the interests and talents of the student in additional ways—the artistically inclined student may apply his talents to map-making or drawings for biology which may prove satisfying to him and useful to others.

"A grandmother is a lady who has no children of her own. She likes other people's little girls. A grandfather is a man grand-mother ... Grandmothers don't have to do anything except be there. They're old, so they shouldn't play hard or run." So wrote a seven-year-old (See Wees 1971, p. 86). It's a revealing collection of half-truths, but it's the reality of the perceptions of that child at that time. As teacher, I perceive my class (or classes) in a particular way at any given time. My perceptions, inevitably, are incomplete. Sociometric devices provide me with a considerable range of additional information.

Ms. Jefferson, a dominant English teacher in high school, found that few of her students took initiative, that they worked rather poorly in groups, got noisy whenever she left the room, and failed to cooperate well with a substitute teacher. She realized the need for change and constructed a series of questions to find out student perceptions of her teaching. Many of such sociometric instruments are found in *Diagnosing Classroom Learning Environments* (Fox, Luszki, and Schmuck, 1966). By using feedback from students, Ms. Jefferson found out a lot about how students felt and also got clues which helped her make a new game plan for her class. Her plan included teacher–pupil planning, which showed Ms. Jefferson's loving responsibility toward her pupils as partners in learning. She allowed the students to select the groups in which they thought they could work best, inviting their expression of loving respect toward each other. Students were asked to plan and teach particular lessons to the class or to groups within the class. Ms. Jefferson recognized that we learn best by doing rather than by passively listening. The new system worked much better than the previous one. Both teacher and students also learned a great deal by struggling with elements of the new system which didn't work as smoothly as had been hoped.

While I am finding out about the students and their perceptions and their feelings, I am also planning, with them, a learning environment we can live in. All the essential tasks of teaching—finding out, establishing a learning environment, planning learning activities, and evaluation—are occurring continuously and without any distinct boundaries between them. For example, if I overhear a conversation between two students, it may help me in lesson planning, in improving the arrangement of the room, and in evaluating each of the students I overhear.

A learning environment consists of a large collection of opportunities and invitations. The best way to construct such an environment is to form a working partnership with students to start the activities of learning and loving we initially see, with the understanding we will change the environment as we deem necessary. In concrete terms, this means students will participate in deciding both space and time plans. Do we need a library? Yes! Where do we locate it? Let's put it over here. Do we have enough shelves? No, but I can bring some bricks and boards. Alan has an old rocker he'll bring, Marilyn's mother will lend us a six by nine foot rug, and three of the girls will make overstuffed pillows of bright inexpensive materials.

What do I do today? Well, that can be decided in several ways. "We can have a fixed schedule (arithmetic, social studies, physical education), a flexible schedule, individual schedules made daily by each student, or no set schedule at all." "Wow, that's a mind-blower!" "Let's start out with a fixed schedule in the morning and no schedule for after lunch." "What does that mean to you?" "It means I'd rather you told us what to do and when in the morning, and let us do what we want after lunch." "What do others of you think?" Such down-to-earth discussions lead to agreements, with an implied support for those agreements by the citizens of the class. When the agreements don't work out, the class talks about it and decides on changes. Maybe for a while the whole day must be rigidly scheduled, with students going to activity/interest centers for set spans of time and with set assignments. Perhaps later we learn to use freedom more effectively and can alter or even abandon a schedule. At any rate, we start with ourselves as a group of people with a vast common interest—in learning a few things about ourselves and our world, and hoping to have fun while we do it. No amount of grim-faced systems analysis can beat goodwill and good humor harnessed together. I see it in dozens of classrooms each week. Research findings justify the continuance of such student-oriented classroom programs.

Partnership based on what the teacher is finding out and on the continuing invitingness of life within the classroom leads to positive emotional climates. Each individual begins to see himself and his peers more positively. He sees others as helpers. He forgets his own outmoded pride and asks another for help in science. He's secretly pleased when a girl asks him to help her with a map she's doing.

An anonymous fifteen year old New York ghetto student says, "I think school is alright but teachers are a drag. Schools and I don't agree. Sometimes I hate to get up in the morning. For what? To go to school. Teachers don't understand how we feel. All they no how to do is work work and homework. I think if teaches would take it into consideration that we are Humans, school would be much more fun" (see Joseph, 1969, p. 69).

A suburban or small town student might use different words and he might or might not use better spelling, but his meaning would be basically the same. This student is saying that he believes, truly believes, that school could be fun. Yes, he's willing to learn. Yes, he's willing to work. But he has to see that it has a direct relationship to his here-and-now life. Promises of a good job with General Mills or Ford Motor Company just don't make it with today's students. And why should they? The student lives today for today, even as I do, and he hopes today will have its own share of humor and excitement, as well as its inevitable ambiguous events and the occasional events that turn out badly and even tragically. Each of us, as a teacher, has the opportunity each day to make school a contemporary, meaningful experience for students.

Helen sat quietly at the art center, mixing a little yellow with the brown finger paint. Both hands, squish-squish, large sweeping movements of both arms on the large sheet of paper. No fixed image yet. No hurry. She continued, slowly, almost lazily. After a few minutes she became aware that Archie was intently watching her. Archie, a new student in the class since Thursday, showed some of the uncertainties many students feel when faced with a very different arrangement of learning experiences. The teacher had taken him aside that first day and explained the color-coded pattern: Each group visited each center during the morning with a definite task to perform at each. In the afternoon, students could choose the center(s) in which they would work. Now it was afternoon and Archie, as he had several times before, gravitated to the art center. "I never saw that before—what is it?" he asked. "Finger paint," she replied. "You can mix up any color you like and smear it around on paper til you get a pattern or design you like." Pretty soon Archie sat across the table from Helen, mixing colors and finding out what it was like to be partly immersed in the medium he was using. A few weeks later he was pleased with several of his finger paintings and he found enjoyment in reciprocal relationships with several of his new friends. Archie was on his way.

"Why can't we go on trips?" asked Lumen. "Cause there's no money, that's why," replied Charlotte, "no money for us dumb niggers." This set Mr. Hoskins to thinking. The school district was short of money, and the PTA was barely alive. Yet these kids needed hope and hope would feed on experience. Next evening, he brought it up in the extension class he took: How can I give these kids some chances? At first no one could come up with a suggestion, but then Ms. Talmadge, the instructor, said, "Would you like some college students to lead trips?" "Hey, maybe a college student could take one or two of your eleventh graders at a time to various places," suggested another teacher. Thus began a series of brand new adventures for the juniors in Mr. Hoskins' classes: a series of mini-field trips to the Corps of Engineers field station, a radio station, a ham radio operator, an amateur astronomer, a Fish and Game Commission bird sanctuary, and the consulates of several nations in the nearest major city. Students want to be in on what's happening, and when not able to do so, they like to be close to it. A valuable by-product of taking members of the classes out into the community was that a number of visitors came to the classes to be resource people on many areas of interest to the eleventh graders.

Self-directed learning makes possible a host of combinations among individuals becoming dedicated to learning. When Rosario found out he could choose what he wished to do, he started out with leather craft, later switched to poetry, and over a period of time varied his diet to include all areas of the curriculum. Cathy, a high school senior, focused on the chemistry of nutrition in line with her long-term interest in becoming a public health nurse. John, an advanced placement student, worked with Avery Wilkes, a junior at the local college, and was well on his way to being a journeyman news reporter before graduating from high school. Every day, we see the cumulative results of decades of little faith in students. Surely it's worth trying to see what happens when we make faith operational by allowing students to select their work.

In the same way, self-pacing makes the teacher's loving response operational in the classroom. Students all over the nation, at all levels of education, are proving that self-pacing works in language laboratories, in math courses, in reading with various kits and programs. More students do more and better work when we accept their individual differences in speed of work.

With self-selection and self-pacing, the teacher has time to devote to the vital jobs of teaching—observing, teaching groups, working with individuals, leading the whole class in class meetings, lesson planning, conferencing with individuals, evaluating, and record keeping. In each of these ways the teacher serves as a living resource to students. The teacher thus lovingly accumulates knowledge which he uses to facilitate the forward momentum of students toward goals perceived by students in cooperation with the teacher.

And then there are those moments when, despite much effort, the teacher seems to be up against failure. Norene sat in the eighth grade classroom with a blank expression on her face. Day after day she betrayed no emotion, no interest in what was happening in the world around her. She could not be coaxed into working on an individual or group project. A confirmed sideline sitter. Lara, the student teacher, searched her imagination for a way to reach this withdrawn girl. She came up with a plan and cleared it with the resident teacher and with the vice-principal and principal. On the day arranged for, Lara brought her own two-and-a-half year old son to school and invited Norene to take care of him, not only at the one class they had together, but for the whole day. All of a sudden Norene was an important person with a *people* task to perform. In English class, the teacher drew attention to the little boy's language: How much can he say, how did he learn what he knows? The next period was physical education, and Norene took him to her modern dance class. He sat between her legs and watched intently as the girls danced, and then he got up and danced along with the girls. Wherever Norene took him that day, she became the center of attention, the focus of questions. She got a big load of recognition as a human being in a short time, and she had the opportunity to see herself as an important person, as a valuable being in today's world. She began to find out that her parental injunctions were no longer of use to her. Since that day, she has ventured out into the world, making friends, participating at times in class, rejoining the human race. Lara was the creative student teacher who planned this reaching out to Norene through her son. I work with dozens of such creative student teachers every year.

Ned O'Gorman (1970, pp. 90–91) said to his Harlem "bandits," "We're going on a picnic, all of us." These are black children who "race through the day with the grace and canny order of people who know who they are, who know how to rule. They are expert plotters of their lives: devious, charming, and gentle plotters." They took over a park at Lexington Avenue and 129th Street. Each child was soon drenched in the sand they were generally unused to. One even ate it. A very properly behaved Headstart class walked by "in solemn procession ... looking over their shoulders at the springtime in the playground. Soon they'd be back in their classroom, locked away from the forsythia and the sandpit." Humans, all humans, desire to be a part of real life, to participate in it, rather than always waiting for an "appropriate" time. It's up to us as teachers to participate in the evolving of learning and loving environments which allow children and youth to use their curiosity, their desire, their yearning, in active seeking behavior. That way we are serving as genuine resource people who can join in the enjoyment of a great variety of life experiences. The teacher who adopts SDL has made a redecision about his teaching. In some cases this will be related to a redecision concerning feelings about himself.

In response to a parent's injunction, for example,—"Don't be grown up," a child will "decide" to behave in certain ways that he hopes will insure loving strokes from the parent or parent-substitute all his life. "Whatever form it may take, once the Child has made a Decision, he has forfeited his autonomy. There is a good chance that he will remain stuck in the Injunction and in a script which must support it." Goulding (1972, pp. 105–134) describes a depressed woman of forty-four who had done things to drive people away all her life. She had been told over and over again, both verbally and by nonverbal "messages," that if it hadn't been for her, her mother's life and health would have been very different. The woman evolved a pattern of behaving—a script—which continually reinforced her feelings of worthlessness. If she couldn't easily produce bad feelings about her personal life, she'd fantasize something in the past or future to be depressed about, or, "when all else failed, she would think about the war, the political situation, and become pathologically depressed."

Redecision can occur through a fantasy of the future; in response to the question, "What will you be doing five years from now if you keep on as you are?" The alcoholic, the youth in trouble with the law, the depressed person may be able to recognize the enormity of his predicament and begin to throw it off.

The individual, helped to recall the early childhood feelings, sees the futility of his guilts and his games. He recognizes the fact that his parents, instead of being monsters, were ordinary people trying to get along just as he is—and forgives them for giving him injunctions. Above all, the person feels, deep inside himself, the conviction of rightness about his redecision, and this gives him the drive to begin living his life differently. He's now his own man and glad of it. Such redecisions are made every day. Ned O'Gorman decided to teach in a hostile land—Harlem. Claude Brown gave up a life of crime and went toward a career in law. Anais Nin could have been a moderately successful fiction writer. Instead, she chose to live a varied life as a dancer and writer, as a person who helped others in many ways, and above all as a person who through experience and writing constantly seeks to define and redefine herself. Alan Paton continues to write and speak out against the injustices of his native South Africa. Eleanor Roosevelt refused to yield to her early injunctions and to the restraints imposed by the important people in her adult life, and she became first lady of the world. Albert Schweitzer decided to give up the relative comfort of Europe to serve the great needs of people in Africa.

I decided to teach human beings instead of being hung up on any formal curriculum. So can you.

I have been enjoying the loving and learning involved in writing this book. I have made some new friends through the writing. I have rewritten many pages based on new insights learned along the way. I remain convinced of all the basic beliefs I had when I started. For me, loving and learning are a way of life. I hope they are becoming so for you too.

BIBLIOGRAPHY

BOOKS AND ARTICLES

ACINAPURO, PHILIP J. "*A Comparative Study of the Results of Two Instructional Reading Programs: An Individualized Pattern and Three-Ability Group Pattern.*" Ed. D. Dissertation, Teachers College, Columbia University, New York, 1959.

ALLEN, R. V. and CLARYCE ALLEN. *An Introduction to a Language-Experience Program* (Level I, Language Experiences in Reading, Teacher's Resource Book). Chicago: Encyclopedia Britannica Press, 1966.

ALLPORT, GORDON W. *Becoming.* New Haven, Conn.: Yale University Press, 1955.

––––––. *Pattern and Growth in Personality.* New York: Holt, Rinehart, and Winston, 1961.

ASHTON-WARNER, SYLVIA. *Spearpoint.* New York: Knopf, 1972.

––––––. *Teacher.* New York: Simon and Schuster, 1963.

AXLINE, VIRGINIA. *Dibs: In Search of Self.* New York: Ballantine, 1967.

BARBE, WALTER B. *Educator's Guide to Personalized Reading Instruction.* Englewood Cliffs, N.J.: Prentice-Hall, 1961.

BEATTY, WALCOTT H., ed. *Improving Educational Assessment and an Inventory of Measures of Affective Behavior.* Washington, D.C.: Association for Supervision and Curriculum Development, 1969.

BENNIS, WARREN G., KENNETH D. BENNE, and ROBERT CHIN. *The Planning of Change.* 2d ed. New York: Holt, Rinehart, and Winston, 1970.

BERNE, ERIC. *Transactional Analysis in Psychotherapy.* New York: Grove Press, 1961.

————.*Games People Play.* New York: Grove Press, 1964.

BERSCHEID, ELLEN and ELAINE WALSTER. "Beauty and the Best." *Psychology Today,* March 1972, pp. 42–46, 74.

BETTELHEIM, BRUNO. "Autonomy and Inner Freedom: Skills of Emotional Management," in *Life Skills in School and Society,* ed. Louis J. Rubin, pp. 73–94. Washington, D. C.: Association for Supervision and Curriculum Development, 1969.

BIEHLER, ROBERT F. *Psychology Applied to Teaching.* Boston: Houghton Mifflin, 1971.

BIGGS, EDITH E. and JAMES R. MacLEAN. *Freedom to Learn.* Don Mills, Ont.: Addison-Wesley (Canada) Ltd., 1969.

BILLS, ROBERT E. "Love Me to Love Thee," *TIP (Theory into Practice),* 8 (1969): 79–85. Columbus, Ohio: College of Education, Ohio State University.

BLOOM, BENJAMIN. *Stability and Change in Human Characteristics.* New York: Wiley, 1964.

BORTON, TERRY. *Reach, Touch, and Teach.* New York: McGraw-Hill, 1970.

BOWER, ELI M. and WILLIAM G. HOLLISTER. *Behavioral Science Frontiers in Education.* New York: Wiley, 1967.

BOY, ANGELO V. and GERALD J. PINE. *Expanding the Self—Personal Growth for Teachers.* Dubuque, Ia.: Wm. C. Brown Publishers, 1971.

BRANDWEIN, PAUL. *Notes on Teaching the Social Sciences: Concepts and Values.* New York and San Francisco: Harcourt Brace Jovanovich, 1970.

BRANDWEIN, PAUL F. *et al. Principles and Practices in the Teaching of The Social Sciences: Concepts and Values.* New York and San Francisco: Harcourt Brace Jovanovich, 1970.

BRIDGMAN, P. W. *The Way Things Are.* Cambridge, Mass.: Harvard University Press, 1959.

BROGAN, PEGGY and LORENE K. FOX. *Helping Children Read.* New York: Holt, Rinehart, and Winston, 1961.

BROWN, CLAUDE. *Manchild in the Promised Land.* New York: New American Library, 1965.

BROWN, GEORGE ISAAC. *Human Teaching for Human Learning.* New York: Viking Press, 1971.

BRUNER, JEROME S. *Toward a Theory of Instruction.* New York: Norton, 1969.

BRUNER, JEROME *et al. Man: A Course of Study.* Cambridge, Mass.: Education Development Center, 1967 and following.

BUGENTAL, JAMES F. T. *The Search for Authenticity.* New York: Holt, Rinehart, and Winston, 1965.

BURKHART, ROBERT C. *Spontaneous and Deliberate Ways of Learning.* Scranton, Pa.: International Textbook, 1962.

_____. and HUGH M. NEIL. *Identity and Teacher Learning.* Scranton, Pa.: International Textbook, 1968.

CARVER, RONALD P. "Speed Readers Don't Read; They Skim." *Psychology Today,* August 1972, pp. 22–30.

CHARTERS, W. W., JR. "The Social Background of Teaching," in *Handbook of Research on Teaching,* ed. N. L. Gage. Chicago: Rand McNally, 1963.

CHESLER, MARK and ROBERT FOX. *Role-Playing Methods in the Classroom.* Chicago: Science Research Associates, 1966.

CHRISTIE, T. "Environmental Factors in Creativity." *The Journal of Creative Behavior* 4 (1970): 13–31.

CLARK, MARGARET, ELLA ERWAY, and LEE BELTZER. *The Learning Encounter.* New York: Random House, 1971.

COLES, ROBERT. *The Desegregation of Southern Schools: A Psychiatric Study.* New York: Anti-Defamation League of B'nai Brith, and Atlanta: Southern Regional Council, 1963.

COMBS, ARTHUR W., *Educational Accountability: Beyond Behavioral Objectives,* Washington, D.C.: Association for Supervision and Curriculum Development, 1972.

COMBS, ARTHUR W., DONALD AVILA, and WILLIAM PURKEY. *Helping Relationships—Basic Concepts for the Helping Professions.* Boston: Allyn and Bacon, 1971.

COMBS, ARTHUR W. and DONALD SNYGG. *Individual Behavior, A Perceptual Approach to Behavior.* Rev. ed. New York: Harper and Row, 1959.

COOPERSMITH, STANLEY. *The Antecedents of Self-Esteem.* San Francisco: W. H. Freeman, 1967.

COTE, BERNARD T. and BARBARA GURSKE. *Learning Center Guide.* P.O. Box 8128, San Jose, California 95125: CTM, 1970.

COVINGTON, MARTIN and STANLEY S. BLANK. "Inducing Children to Ask Questions in Solving Problems." *Journal of Educational Research* 59 (1965): 21–27.

CULLUM, ALBERT. *Push Back the Desks.* New York: Citation Press, 1967.

DARROW, HELEN FISHER and VIRGIL M. HOWES. *Approaches to Individualized Reading.* New York: Appleton-Century-Crofts, 1960.

DARROW, HELEN FISHER and R. VAN ALLEN. *Independent Activities for Creative Learning.* No. 21 of Practical Suggestions for Teaching Series, ed. Alice Miel. New York: Teachers College, Columbia University, 1961.

DATTA, SHAKTI. *The Place of Love in Education.* Jullunder-Delhi-Ambala, India: University Publishers, 1960.

DeCHARMS, RICHARD. "From Pawns to Origins: Toward Self-Motivation," in *Psychology and Educational Practice,* ed. Gerald S. Lesser, pp. 380–407. Glenview, Ill.: Scott, Foresman, 1971.

DEMILLE, RICHARD. *Put Your Mother on the Ceiling.* New York: Walker, 1967.

DENNISON, GEORGE. *The Lives of Children.* New York: Random House, 1969.

DINKMEYER, DON. "Child Development Research and the Elementary School Teacher," *Elementary School Journal* 67 (March 1967): 310–316.

DOLL, RONALD C., ed. *Individualizing Instruction.* Washington, D. C.: Association for Supervision and Curriculum Development, 1964.

DREIKURS, RUDOLF, BERNICE BRONIA GRUNWALD, and FLOY PEPPER. *Maintaining Sanity in the Classroom.* New York: Harper and Row, 1971.

EBLE, KENNETH E. *A Perfect Education.* New York: Collier, 1966.

EISELEY, LOREN. *The Firmament of Time.* New York: Atheneum, 1960.

EISELEY, LOREN. *The Immense Journey.* New York: Random House, 1957.

———. *The Invisible Pyramid.* New York: Charles Scribner's Sons, 1970.

ERICKSON, ERIK H. *Childhood and Society.* 2d ed. New York: Norton, 1963.

FADER, DANIEL and ELTON MCNEIL. *Hooked on Books.* Berkeley, California: Berkeley Publishing Corporation, 1968.

FERKISS, VICTOR. *Technological Man—The Myth and the Reality.* New York: Braziller, 1969.

FISHER, ROBERT J. *Learning How to Learn.* New York and San Francisco: Harcourt Brace Jovanovich, 1972.

FLANDERS, NED A. *Analyzing Teaching Behavior.* Reading, Mass.: Addison-Wesley, 1970.

FLEMING, ROBERT S., ed. *Curriculum for Today's Boys and Girls.* Columbus, Ohio: Charles E. Merrill, 1963.

FOLEY, JAMES J. "Teaching and Learning in the Affective Domain," in *Removing Barriers to Humaneness in the High School,* ed. J. Galen Saylor and Joshua L. Smith, pp. 43–50. Washington, D. C.: Association for Supervision and Curriculum Development, 1971.

FOX, ROBERT, MARGARET BARRON LUSZKI, and RICHARD SCHMUCK. *Diagnosing Classroom Learning Environments.* Chicago: Science Research Associates, 1966.

FRANK, LAWRENCE K. "Four Ways to Look at Potentialities," in *New Insights and the Curriculum,* ed. Alexander Frazier, pp. 11–37. Washington, D.C.: Association for Supervision and Curriculum Development, 1963.

FRANKEL, CHARLES. *The Case for Modern Man.* Boston: Beacon Press, 1955.

FRAZIER, ALEXANDER, ed. *The New Elementary School.* Washington, D.C.: Association for Supervision and Curriculum Development, 1968.

———. ed. *New Insights and the Curriculum.* Washington, D.C.: Association for Supervision and Curriculum Development, 1963.

———. *Open Schools for Children.* Washington, D.C.: Association for Supervision and Curriculum Development, 1972.

FREIRE, PAULO. "The Pedagogy of the Oppressed," in *Affirmative Education,* ed. Barry N. Schwartz, pp. 65–73. Englewood Cliffs, N.J.: Prentice-Hall, 1972.

FROMM, ERIC. *The Art of Loving.* New York: Bantam, 1963.

GAGE, N. L., ed. *Handbook of Research on Teaching.* Chicago: Rand McNally, 1963.

GANS, ROMA. *Common Sense in Teaching Reading.* Indianapolis: Bobbs-Merrill, 1963.

GATTEGNO, CALEB. *What We Owe Students: The Subordination of Teaching to Learning.* New York: Outerbridge and Dienstfrey, 1970.

GEORGIADY, NICHOLAS P. and LOUIS G. ROMANO. "Ulcerville, U.S.A.," in *Educational Leadership* 29 (December 1971): 269–272.

GIBLIN, THOMAS, ed. *Popular Media and the Teaching of English.* Pacific Palisades, Calif.: Goodyear, 1972.

GIBSON, JOHN S. *A Program for Elementary School Education,* Vol. II. Medford, Mass.: Lincoln Filene Center for Citizenship and Public Affairs, Tufts University, 1969.

GINOTT, HAIM. *Teacher and Child.* New York: Macmillan, 1972.

GLASSER, WILLIAM. *Schools Without Failure.* New York: Harper and Row, 1965.

GLEASON, GERALD T. *Lakeshore Curriculum Study Council—Individualized Reading.* Milwaukee: University of Wisconsin, May 1970.

_____. ed. *The Theory and Nature of Independent Learning.* Scranton, Pa.: International Textbook, 1967.

GOLDMARK, BERNICE. *Social Studies, A Method of Inquiry.* Belmont, Calif.: Wadsworth, 1968.

GORDON, ALICE K. *Games for Growth.* Palo Alto, Calif.: Science Research Associates, 1970.

GORDON, IRA J. *On Early Learning.* Washington, D.C.: Association for Supervision and Curriculum Development, 1972.

_____. *Studying the Child in School.* New York: Wiley, 1966.

GORMAN, ALFRED H. *Teachers and Learners: The Interactive Process of Education.* Boston: Allyn and Bacon, 1969.

GOULDING, ROBERT. "New Directions in Transactional Analysis: Creating an Environment for Redecision and Change," in *Progress in Group and Family Therapy,* ed. Clifford J. Sager and Helen Singer Kaplan, pp. 105–134. New York: Brunner/Mazel, 1972.

GREER, MARY AND BONNIE RUBINSTEIN. *Will the Real Teacher Please Stand Up?* Pacific Palisades, Calif.: Goodyear, 1972.

GRIER, WILLIAM H. and PRICE M. COBBS. *Black Rage.* New York: Bantam, 1968.

GROFF, PATRICK. "Comparisons of Individualized (IR) and Ability-Grouping (AG) Approaches as to Reading Achievement," in *Elementary English* 40 (March 1963): 258–264.

GROTHE, BARBARA FORD. "Transforming Curiosity into Learning Skills," in *Elementary Curriculum,* ed. Robert E. Chasnoff, pp. 161–164. New York: Pitman, 1964.

GUNTHER, BERNARD. *Sense Relaxation.* New York: Collier, 1968.

HAMILTON, NORMAN K. and J. GALEN SAYLOR, eds. *Humanizing the Second-*

ary Schools. Washington, D.C.: Association for Supervision and Curriculum Development, 1969.

HANSEN, SOREN and JESPER JENSEN. *The Little Red Schoolbook.* New York: Pocket Books, 1971.

HARRIS, THOMAS A. *I'm OK—You're OK.* New York: Harper and Row, 1969.

HASS, GLEN, KIMBALL WILES, JOYCE COOPER and DAN MICHALAK, eds. *Readings in Elementary Teaching.* Boston: Allyn and Bacon, 1971.

HAUGHTON, ROSEMARY. *Love.* Baltimore: Penguin, 1971.

HEDGES, WILLIAM. *The Hedges Letter.* Chicago: Science Research Associates, 1968.

HENRY, JULES. *Culture Against Man.* New York: Vintage, 1965.

HERNDON, JAMES. *How to Survive in Your Native Land.* New York: Simon and Schuster, 1971.

————. *The Way It Spozed To Be.* New York: Bantam, 1969.

HIPPLE, THEODORE W. *Secondary School Teaching.* Pacific Palisades, Calif.: Goodyear, 1970.

HOLT, JOHN. *How Children Fail.* New York: Dell, 1964.

————. *How Children Learn.* New York: Pitman, 1967.

————. *What Do I Do Monday?* New York: Dutton, 1970.

HOWES, VIRGIL M. *Individualization of Instruction.* New York: Macmillan, 1970.

————. *Individualizing Instruction in Reading and Social Studies.* New York: Macmillan, 1970.

————. *Individualizing Instruction in Science and Mathematics.* New York: Macmillan, 1970.

HOWES, VIRGIL, HELEN FISHER, ROBERT E. KEUSCHER, and LOUISE L. TYLER. *Exploring Open Structure.* Encino, Calif.: International Center for Educational Development, 1968.

JACKSON, PHILIP W. *Life in Classrooms.* New York: Holt, Rinehart, and Winston, 1968.

JAMES, MURIEL and DORTHY JONGEWARD. *Born to Win.* Reading, Mass.: Addison-Wesley, 1971.

JERSILD, ARTHUR T. "Behold the Beginner," in *The Real World of the Beginning Teacher,* ed. Don Davies. Washington, D.C.: National Commission on Teacher Education and Professional Standards, National Education Association, 1965.

————. *When Teachers Face Themselves.* New York: Teachers College Press, Columbia University, 1955.

JONES, CHARLES MARTIN. "Editorial." *Psychology Today,* May 1969, p. 4.

JONES, RICHARD M., ed. *Contemporary Educational Psychology.* New York: Harper and Row, 1966.

————. *Fantasy and Feeling in Education.* New York: New York University Press, 1968.

JOSEPH, STEPHEN M., ed. *The Me Nobody Knows.* New York: Avon, 1969.

JOURARD, SIDNEY M. *The Transparent Self.* Princeton, N.J.: Van Nostrand, 1964.

KAGAN, JEROME. "Learning, Attention, and the Issue of Discovery," in *Learning by Discovery*, ed. Lee S. Shulman and Evan R. Keislar, pp. 151–161. Chicago: Rand McNally, 1966.

————. in report at 139th annual meeting of the American Association for the Advancement of Science, as reported by David Perlman in *San Francisco Chronicle*, December 27, 1972.

————. *Understanding Children.* New York: Harcourt Brace Jovanovich, 1971.

KAPLAN, SANDRA A., et al. *Change for Children: Ideas and Activities for Individualizing Learning.* Pacific Palisades, Cal.: Goodyear Publishing Company, 1972.

KELLEY, EARL C. *In Defense of Youth.* Englewood Cliffs, N.J.: Prentice-Hall, 1962.

————. "The Place of Affective Learning," in *Educational Leadership*, 22 (April 1965): 455–457.

KELLY, GEORGE A. *A Theory of Personality.* New York: Norton, 1963.

KNOX, GARY A. *If It Ain't Survival—It's Catastrophe.* Corte Madera, Calif.: Marin Social Studies Project, 1971.

KOHL, HERBERT R. *The Open Classroom.* New York: Random House, 1969.

KRAUSS, RUTH. *A Hole Is to Dig.* New York: Harper and Row, 1952.

LABENNE, WALLACE and BERT GREEN. *Educational Implications of Self-Concept Theory.* Pacific Palisades, Calif.: Goodyear, 1969.

LAING, R. D. *The Divided Self.* Baltimore: Penguin, 1965.

————. *Knots.* New York: Vintage, 1970.

————. *The Politics of Experience.* New York: Ballantine, 1968.

LANSDOWN, BRENDA, PAUL E. BLACKWOOD, and PAUL F. BRANDWEIN. *Teaching Elementary Science.* New York: Harcourt Brace Jovanovich, 1971.

LAZAR, MAY, MARCELLA DRAPER, and LOUISE SCHWIETERT. *A Practical Guide to Individualized Reading.* New York City: Board of Education, Publication No. 40 (October 1960).

LEDERMAN, JANET. *Anger and the Rocking Chair.* New York: McGraw-Hill, 1969.

LEE, DOROTHY. *Freedom and Culture.* Englewood Cliffs, N.J.: Prentice-Hall, 1959.

LEE, DORRIS M. *Diagnostic Teaching.* Washington, D.C.: Department of Elementary-Kindergarten-Nursery Education, National Education Association, 1966.

LEE, DORRIS M. and R. V. ALLEN. *Learning to Read Through Experience.* 2d ed. New York: Appleton-Century-Crofts, 1963.

LEEPER, ROBERT R. and MARY ALBERT O'NEILL, eds. *Hunters Point Redeveloped.* Washington, D.C.: Association for Supervision and Curriculum Development, 1970.

LEIBOW, ELLIOTT. *Tally's Corner.* Boston: Little, Brown, 1967.

LEONARD, GEORGE B. *Education and Ecstasy.* New York: Delacorte, 1968.

LESSER, GERALD S., ed. *Psychology and Educational Practice*. Glenview, Ill.: Scott, Foresman, 1971.

LESSING, DORIS. *The Four-Gated City*. New York: Bantam, 1970.

————. *The Golden Notebook*. New York: Ballantine, 1962.

LEWIN, KURT. *A Dynamic Theory of Personality*. New York: McGraw-Hill, 1935.

LIFTON, ROBERT JAY. *History and Human Survival*. New York: Vintage, 1971.

LIPPITT, RONALD. "The Neglected Learner," in *Teaching Strategies for Elementary School Social Studies*, ed. John U. Michaelis and Everett T. Keach, Jr., pp. 40–48. Itasca, Ill.: Peacock Publishers, 1972.

LIPPITT, RONALD, ROBERT FOX, and LUCILLE SCHAIBLE. *The Teacher's Role in Social Science Investigation*. Chicago: Science Research Associates, 1969.

LITTLE, MALCOLM. *The Autobiography of Malcolm X*. New York: Grove Press, 1965.

LONGWELL, SARAH G. "Progressive Change in Skill Learning," in *Selected Readings on the Learning Process*, ed. Theodore L. Harris and Wilson E. Schwahn, pp. 177–192. New York: Oxford University Press, 1961.

LYON, HAROLD C., JR. *Learning to Feel—Feeling to Learn*. Columbus, Ohio: Charles E. Merrill, 1971.

MANNING, DUANE. *Toward a Humanistic Curriculum*. New York: Harper and Row, 1971.

MARCANTONIO, CHARLES. "Foreword" in *Individuality and Encounter*, Clark Moustakas. Cambridge, Mass.: Doyle Publishing, 1968, p. vi.

MASLOW, ABRAHAM. *Motivation and Personality*. New York: Harper and Row, 1954.

MASSIALAS, BYRON G. and JACK ZEVIN. *Creative Encounters in the Classroom*. New York: Wiley, 1967.

MAY, ROLLO. *Love and Will*. New York: Norton, 1969.

McCORMICK, PAUL and LEONARD CAMPOS. *Introduce Yourself to Transactional Analysis*. Stockton, Calif.: San Joaquin Transactional Analysis Study Group, 1969.

McNASSER, DONALD. "The Frantic Pace in Education." *Journal of Secondary Education* 42 (March 1967):61–62.

MEDLEY, DONALD M. and HAROLD E. MITZEL. "Measuring Classroom Behavior by Systematic Observation," in *Handbook of Research on Teaching*, ed. N. L. Gage, pp. 247–328. Chicago: Rand McNally, 1963.

MIEL, ALICE and PEGGY BROGAN. *More Than Social Studies*. Englewood Cliffs, N.J.: Prentice-Hall, 1957.

MILES, MATTHEW. *Learning to Work in Groups*. New York: Teachers College, Columbia University, 1959.

MILLER, ARTHUR. *Death of a Salesman*. New York: Dramatists Play Service, 1952.

MITCHELL, JULIET. "What Women Know about Love That Men Don't Know about Loving." *Vogue*, August 1, 1972, pp. 96–97.

MONTAGU, ASHLEY. "A Scientist Looks at Love." *Phi Delta Kappan*, 51 (May 1970):463–467.

MOUSTAKAS, CLARK. *The Authentic Teacher.* Cambridge, Mass.: Doyle Publishing, 1966.

———. *Creativity and Conformity.* New York: Van Nostrand Reinhold, 1967.

———. *Teaching as Learning.* New York: Ballantine, 1972.

MUMFORD, LEWIS. *The Pentagon of Power.* New York and San Francisco: Harcourt Brace Jovanovich, 1970.

MURPHY, GARDNER. *Human Potentialities.* New York: Basic Books, 1958.

MURPHY, LOIS *et al. The Widening World of Childhood.* New York: Basic Books, 1962.

NARDINE, FRANK E. "The Development of Competence," in *Psychology and Educational Practice,* ed. Gerald S. Lesser, pp. 336–356. Glenview, Illinois: Scott, Foresman, 1971.

NATALICIO, LUIZ F. S. and CARL F. HEREFORD. *The Teacher as a Person.* Dubuque, Ia.: Wm. C. Brown Publishers, 1971.

NIN, ANAIS. *The Diary of Anais Nin,* ed. Gunther Stuhlmann. New York and San Francisco: Harcourt, Brace Jovanovich; Vol. 1—1966; Vol. 2—1967; Vol. 3—1969; Vol. 4—1971.

NOLEN, WILLIAM A. *The Making of a Surgeon.* New York: Random House, 1970.

O'BANION, TERRY and APRIL O'CONNELL. *The Shared Journey.* Englewood Cliffs, N.J.: Prentice-Hall, 1969.

O'GORMAN, NED. *The Storefront.* New York: Harper and Row, 1970.

OLSON, MARTIN N. "Identifying Quality in School Classrooms: Some Problems and Some Answers." *Metropolitan School Study Council Exchange* (New York). 29 (1971):1–11.

OLSON, WILLARD C. "Seeking, Self-Selection, and Pacing in the Use of Books by Children," *The Packet,* Vol. 7, No. 1. Boston: D. C. Heath, Spring 1952.

OTTO, HERBERT and JOHN MANN. *Ways of Growth.* New York: Viking, 1968.

OVERLY, NORMAN. *The Unstudied Curriculum.* Washington, D.C.: Association for Supervision and Curriculum Development, 1970.

PARKER, BEULAH. *My Language Is Me.* New York: Basic Books, 1962.

PARNES, SIDNEY J. and EUGENE A. BRUNELLE. "Some Recent Books on Creative Intelligence." *The Journal of Creative Behavior,* 1 (January 1967):-105–109.

PEARCE, JUNE and SAUL NEWTON. *The Conditions of Human Growth.* New York: Citadel Press, 1963.

PERKINS, HUGH V. *Human Development and Learning.* Belmont, Calif.: Wadsworth, 1969.

PERLS, FREDERICK S. *Gestalt Therapy Verbatim.* Lafayette, Calif.: Real People Press, 1969.

PETREQUIN, GAYNOR. *Individualizing Learning Through Modular-Flexible Programming.* New York: McGraw-Hill, 1968.

PHILADELPHIA SCHOOL DISTRICT. *Education for Student Concerns.* Philadelphia, Pa.: 1968.

PLOWMAN, PAUL. *Behavioral Objectives.* Chicago: Science Research Associates, 1971.

POSTMAN, NEIL and CHARLES WEINGARTNER. *Teaching as a Subversive Activity.* New York: Delacorte, 1969.

PRATHER, HUGH. *Notes to Myself.* Lafayette, Calif.: Real People Press, 1970.

PRESCOTT, DANIEL A. *The Child in the Educative Process.* New York: McGraw-Hill, 1957.

PRITZKAU, PHILO T. *Dynamics of Curriculum Improvement.* Englewood Cliffs, N.J.: Prentice-Hall, 1959.

————. *On Education for the Authentic.* Scranton, Pa.: International Textbook, 1970.

RANDOLPH, NORMA and WILLIAM HOWE. *Self-Enhancing Education.* Palo Alto, Calif.: Sanford Press, 1966.

ROE, RICHARD L., publ. *Developmental Psychology Today.* Del Mar, Calif.: Communications Research Machines, 1971.

ROGERS, CARL R. *Freedom to Learn.* Columbus, Ohio: Charles E. Merrill, 1969.

————. "The Interpersonal Relationship in the Facilitation of Learning," in *The Human Encounter,* ed. Sheldon Stoff and Herbert Schwartzberg, pp. 418–433. New York: Harper and Row, 1969b.

ROGERS, VINCENT R. *Teaching in the British Primary School.* New York: Macmillan, 1970.

ROSENTHAL, ROBERT and LENORE JACOBSON. *Pygmalion in the Classroom.* New York: Ballantine, 1967.

ROSZAK, THEODORE. *The Making of a Counter Culture.* Garden City, N.Y.: Doubleday, 1969.

RUBIN, LOUIS J. *Life Skills in School and Society.* Washington, D.C.: Association for Supervision and Curriculum Development, 1969.

RYAN, KEVIN and JAMES M. COOPER. *Those Who Can, Teach.* Boston: Houghton Mifflin, 1971.

SCHAEFER, ROBERT J. *The School as a Center of Inquiry.* New York: Harper and Row, 1967.

SCHMUCK, RICHARD, MARK CHESLER, and RONALD LIPPITT. *Problem Solving to Improve Classroom Learning.* Chicago: Science Research Associates, 1966.

SCHMUCK, RICHARD and PATRICIA SCHMUCK. *Group Processes in the Classroom.* Dubuque, Ia.: Wm. C. Brown Publishers, 1971.

SCHUTZ, WILLIAM C. *Joy.* New York: Grove Press, 1967.

SCOBEY, MARY-MARGARET and GRACE GRAHAM, eds. *To Nurture Humaneness.* Washington, D.C.: Association for Supervision and Curriculum Development, 1970.

SEARS, PAULINE. "Self-Concept in the Service of Educational Goals." *California Journal for Instructional Improvement* 7 (May 1964):3–17.

SEARS, PAULINE and EDITH M. DOWLEY. "Research on Teaching in the Nursery School," in *Handbook of Research on Teaching,* ed. N. L. Gage, pp. 814–864. Chicago: Rand McNally, 1963.

SHAFTEL, FANNIE and GEORGE SHAFTEL. *Role-Playing the Problem Story.* New York: National Conference of Christians and Jews, 1952.

SHAPIRO, ALAN, CHARLES McCREA, and VERA BEC. PEOPLE. Chicago: Science Research Associates, 1970.

SHOSTROM, EVERETT L. *Man, the Manipulator.* New York: Bantam, 1968.

SILBERMAN, CHARLES. *Crisis in the Classroom.* New York: Random House, 1970.

SKEEL, DOROTHY J. and OWEN A. HAGEN. *The Process of Curriculum Change.* Pacific Palisades, Calif.: Goodyear, 1971.

SMITH, M. DANIEL. *Theoretical Foundations of Learning and Teaching.* Waltham, Mass.: Xerox College Publishing, 1971.

SOAR, ROBERT S. "Teacher–Pupil Interaction," in *A New Look at Progressive Education,* ed. James R. Squire, pp. 166–204. Washington, D.C.: Association for Supervision and Curriculum Development, 1972.

SOROKIN, PITIRIM A. *The Ways and Power of Love.* Chicago: Henry Regnery, 1967.

SPAULDING, ROBERT L. *Achievement, Creativity, and Self-Concept Correlates of Teacher–Pupil Transactions in Elementary School Classrooms.* Hempstead, N.Y.: Hofstra University, Cooperative Research Project No. 1352, U.S. Office of Health, Education, and Welfare, 1965.

SPOLIN, VIOLA. *Improvisation for the Theater.* Evanston, Ill.: Northwestern University Press, 1963.

SQUIRE, JAMES R., ed. *A New Look at Progressive Education.* Washington, D.C.: Association for Supervision and Curriculum Development, 1972.

STAHL, DONA KOFOD, and PATRICIA ANZALONE. *Individualized Teaching in Elementary Schools.* West Nyack, N.Y.: Parker Publishing, 1970.

STAUFFER, RUSSELL. *The Language-Experience Approach to the Teaching of Reading.* New York: Harper and Row, 1970.

STEINBERG, LEONARD. "Creativity as a Character Trait: An Expanding Concept." *California Journal of Instructional Improvement* 7 (March 1964): 3–9.

STEVENS, JOHN O. *Awareness: Exploring, Experimenting, Experiencing.* Lafayette, Calif.: Real People Press, 1971.

STOFF, SHELDON and HERBERT SCHWARTZBERG. *The Human Encounter.* New York: Harper and Row, 1969.

SUCHMAN, J. RICHARD. *The Elementary School Training Program in Scientific Inquiry.* Evanston, Ill.: College of Education, University of Illinois, 1962.

SUTTON, AUDREY D. *Ordered Freedom.* Encino, Calif.: International Center for Educational Development, 1970.

TANNER, LAUREL and HENRY CLAY LINDGREN. *Classroom Teaching and Learning.* New York: Holt, Rinehart, and Winston, 1971.

TAYLOR, HAROLD. *The World as Teacher.* Garden City, N.Y.: Doubleday, 1970.

———. "The Private World of the Man with a Book," in *The Individual and Education,* ed. Frederick M. Raubinger and Harold G. Rowe, pp. 122–127. New York: Macmillan, 1968.

THATCHER, DAVID. "Teachers Live with Mystery." *Educational Leadership* 28 (April 1971): 739–742.

TORRANCE, E. PAUL and R. E. MYERS. *Creative Learning and Teaching.* New York: Dodd, Mead, 1970.

VALMONT, WILLIAM J. "Creating Questions for Informal Reading Inventories." *The Reading Teacher* 25 (March 1972): 509–512.

VEATCH, JEANNETTE. "Emphasizing Fundamental Principles For Teaching Basic Skills," and "Developing Skills in Various Subject Areas," in *Curriculum for Today's Boys and Girls,* ed. Robert S. Fleming. Columbus, Ohio: Charles E. Merrill Books, 1963.

———. *Reading in the Elementary School.* New York: Ronald Press, 1966.

WAETJEN, WALTER B. and ROBERT R. LEEPER, eds. *Learning and Mental Health in the School.* Washington, D.C.: Association for Supervision and Curriculum Development, 1966.

WALLEN, NORMAN E. and ROBERT M. W. TRAVERS. "Analysis and Investigation of Teaching Methods," in *Handbook of Research on Teaching,* ed. N. L. Gage, pp. 448–505. Chicago: Rand McNally, 1963.

WANN, KENNETH D., MIRIAM SELCHEN DORN, and ELIZABETH ANN LIDDLE. *Fostering Intellectual Development in Young Children.* New York: Teachers College Press, Columbia University, 1962.

WATTS, ALAN W. *Psychotherapy East and West.* New York: Ballantine, 1969.

———. *The Book.* New York: Collier, 1967.

———. *This Is It.* New York: Collier, 1958.

WEES, W. R. *Nobody Can Teach Anyone Anything.* Garden City, N.Y.: Doubleday, 1971.

WEINSTEIN, GERALD and MARIO FANTINI, eds. *Toward Humanistic Education.* New York: Praeger, 1970.

WERTHEIMER, MAX. *Productive Thinking.* New York: Harper, 1945.

WHEELIS, ALLAN. *The Quest for Identity.* New York: Norton, 1958.

WILHELMS, FRED T., ed. *Evaluation as Feedback and Guide.* Washington, D.C.: Association for Supervision and Curriculum Development, 1967.

WOLFSON, BERNICE J. *Moving Toward Personalized Learning and Teaching.* Encino, Calif.: International Center for Educational Development, 1969.

ZAHORIK, JOHN A. and DALE L. BRUBAKER. *Toward More Humanistic Education.* Dubuque, Ia.: Wm. C. Brown Publishers, 1972.

ZELIGS, MEYER. *Friendship and Fratricide.* New York: Viking, 1967.

FILMS AND OTHER MATERIAL

They Can Do It. EDC Film Library, 39 Chapel Street, Newton, Mass.

"Guidance for the Seventies: Kids, Parents, Pressures," a Robert Sande film. The BFA Education Media, 2211 Michigan Avenue, Santa Monica, Calif. 90404.

Synectics, Inc. *Making It Strange.* New York: Harper and Row, 1968.